VoiceXML:
10 Projects to Voice Enable Your Web Site

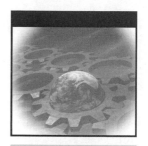

VoiceXML:
10 Projects to Voice Enable Your Web Site

Mark Miller

Gearhead Press™

Wiley Publishing, Inc.

Publisher: Robert Ipsen
Editor: Ben Ryan
Consulting Editor: Donis Marshall
Developmental Editor: Kathryn A. Malm
Managing Editor: Angela Smith
New Media Editor: Brian Snapp
Text Design & Composition: John Wiley Composition Services

Designations used by companies to distinguish their products are often claimed as trademarks. In all instances where John Wiley & Sons, Inc., is aware of a claim, the product names appear in initial capital or ALL CAPITAL LETTERS. Readers, however, should contact the appropriate companies for more complete information regarding trademarks and registration.

This book is printed on acid-free paper. ∞

Published by Wiley Publishing, Inc., New York

Published simultaneously in Canada.

This publication is designed to provide accurate and authoritative information in regard to the subject matter covered. It is sold with the understanding that the publisher is not engaged in professional services. If professional advice or other expert assistance is required, the services of a competent professional person should be sought.

The Gearhead Press trademark is the exclusive property of Gearhead Group Corporation.

Library of Congress Cataloging-in-Publication Data:

ISBN: 0-471-20737-3

Wiley also publishes its books in a variety of electronic formats. Some content that appears in print may not be available in electronic versions. For more information about Wiley products, visit our web site at www.wiley.com.

Printed in the United States of America.

10 9 8 7 6 5 4 3 2 1

A Note from Gearhead Press

Gearhead Press is dedicated to publishing technical books for experienced Information Technology professionals—network engineers, developers, system administrators, and others—who need to update their skills, learn how to use technology more effectively, or simply want a quality reference to the latest technology. Gearhead Press emerged from my experience with professional trainers of engineers and developers: people who truly understand first-hand the needs of working professionals. Gearhead Press authors are the crème de la crème of industry trainers, working at the companies that define the technology revolution. For this reason, Gearhead Press authors are regularly in the trenches with the developers and engineers that have changed the world through innovative products. Drawing from this experience in IT training, our books deliver superior technical content with a unique perspective that is based on real-world experience.

Now, as an imprint of John Wiley & Sons, Inc., Gearhead Press will continue to bring you, the reader, the level of quality that Wiley has delivered consistently for nearly 200 years.

Thank you.

Donis Marshall
Founder, Gearhead Press
Consulting Editor, Wiley Computer Publishing

Gearhead Press Books in Print

(For complete information about current and upcoming titles, go to www.wiley.com/compbooks/)

Books in the Gearhead Press *Point to Point* Series

Migrating to Microsoft Exchange 2000 by Stan Reimer
 ISBN: 0-471-06116-6

Installing and Configuring Web Servers Using Apache by Melanie Hoag
 ISBN: 0-471-07155-2

VoiceXML: 10 Projects to Voice Enable Your Website by Mark Miller
 ISBN: 0-471-20737-3

Books in the Gearhead Press *In the Trenches* Series

Windows 2000 Automated Deployment by Ted Malone and Rolly Perraux
 ISBN: 0-471-06114-X

Robust Linux: Assuring High Availability by Iain Campbell
 ISBN: 0-471-07040-8

Programming Directory Services for Windows 2000 by Donis Marshall
 ISBN: 0-471-15216-1

Programming ADO.NET by Richard Hundhausen and Steven Borg
 ISBN: 0-471-20187-1

Designing .NET Web Services Using ADO.NET and XML by Richard Hundhausen
 and Steven Borg
 ISBN: 0-471-20186-3

Making Win32 Applications Mobile: Porting to Windows CE by Nancy Nicolaisen
 ISBN: 0-471-21618-6

Programming Windows CE Wireless Applications by Barry Shilmover and Derek Ball
 ISBN: 0-471-21469-8

Mastering SQL Server 2002 Security by Mike Young and Curtis Young
 ISBN: 0-471-21970-3

Microsoft.NET Security Programming by Donis Marshall
 ISBN: 0-471-22285-2

Contents

Acknowledgments

When I was first approached by Donis Marshall to write this book, I thought, "No problem. I'll whip it out in a couple of months and be done with it." Anyone who has ever attempted to write a book knows how naïve and uncomprehending that thought was. Over the past ten months, I've needed the support of my friends and family who kept checking in periodically to see if I was "still alive." Yes, I am, and I sincerely thank you for worrying. Can we go to Disneyland now?

The short list for thanks starts with Donis Marshall. Thanks for allowing me to rewrite, change, be late...whatever it took to get the book right.

Bryan Michael at The BeVocal Cafe saw the value of this project right away and didn't hesitate with any type of resources that were necessary to make my job a little easier. The development team at BeVocal was indispensable when I needed quick turnaround confirmation for technical questions. A special thank you to Mukund Bhagavan, Kesava Neeli, and Vavnnet Raja for responding at all hours of the day and night.

Kevin Dowd and Larry Larson provided invaluable technical support when generating the projects for the Brainhat FAQ Engine and the San Francisco Arts Calendar. Thanks also to Richard Weiss for introducing me to VoiceXML and to Tony Caviglia for contributing ideas for the Telephone Dialer project.

Finally, this book would never have been completed without the unwavering support of my wife, Rosemary. Thank you for believing it could be done and making it happen.

Introduction

Playing with a new technology is fun. I have been a teacher in one form or another for over 20 years, but it still gets me excited when I see something that seems so obvious and so simple that it is shocking it hasn't been done before. That's the way I feel about VoiceXML.

VoiceXML makes it possible for anyone who can build a basic Web page to create a voice Web page. The first time I heard about VoiceXML, it took me less than an hour to get my first application up and running. It's just that simple. Simplicity, however, doesn't mean that big things can't be done. If you have called 1-800-555-1212 recently, you have heard a VoiceXML application written by TellMe.com handling the incoming calls through VoiceXML.

Who Should Read This Book

VoiceXML: 10 Projects to Voice Enable Your Website is an outgrowth of my experiments while playing with VoiceXML. One of the problems with many technology books I have seen is that they give you all of the tools, but they don't tell you how to use them. Context is one of the most important parts of learning. I think that people beginning to learn a technology can learn much more from creating and implementing projects than by learning about function sets and where things are on a menu bar.

This book is for beginning voice developers. It assumes no knowledge of VoiceXML or previous experience with the technology. If you are a Web developer or have developed even one Web page, this book is for you. VoiceXML terminology is similar to HTML, but it has a much smaller element set: There are less than 50 elements to learn. The first five projects will bring you up to speed with everything you will need to know when voice enabling your current Web site.

Database managers will find the book interesting if they want to see how to output a database query as a vocal response. Most of the data on the Web is stored in databases, whereas most of the people in the world have access to a telephone. VoiceXML acts as the glue joining the two technologies.

System administrators will be excited to know that VoiceXML can be used to call them on the phone when their systems need help. The application can be set up to call, not beep them, with a system specific message output vocally. With a little more work, simple administration of the system can be handled through the phone call, making it unnecessary to access a computer to make updates.

CGI programmers will have a field day with VoiceXML. Any type of output that is currently generated on a Web site through Perl, ASP, JSP, PHP, or other dynamic content generator can be output as a voice response to be accessed over the telephone.

However, this book isn't for everyone. It is not a reference manual and does not cover advanced techniques of VoiceXML. If you have already developed extensive voice applications or have been a developer on one of the voice portals such as BeVocal, TellMe, or HeyAnita, this probably isn't the book for you. You'd be better off with a detailed examination of the VoiceXML 2.0 specification at the W3C, tearing apart the documentation on the Nuance site for developing complex grammars, or using Bruce Balentine's *How to Build a Speech Recognition Application* style guide. *VoiceXML: Professional Developer's Guide* by Sharma and Kunins has also been getting good reviews as a solid reference manual.

But if you are just getting started with VoiceXML, keep reading.

How This Book Is Organized

This book shows how to build basic VoiceXML applications from existing Web sites through a series of 10 step-by-step projects. Each project begins with a problem statement and a possible solution. The project description follows and includes a brief overview and a list of the components and steps it will take to complete the project. The implementation of the project goes step by step, each phase ending in a hands-on exercise, confirming that the application is working before proceeding to the next stage.

The book is divided into two sections: two chapters of introduction and environment and the 10 projects. Chapter 1 is a general overview of VoiceXML and how it fits into XML technologies. This can be used as an introduction to the technologies or as a brief overview for developers who have previous XML/VoiceXML experience. Chapter 2 looks at the BeVocal Cafe voice portal environment that is used for developing the projects. The tools of the portal are analyzed and basic setup procedures are covered.

Next are the 10 VoiceXML projects. The first five projects take your existing Web site and output it as VoiceXML. Project 1 begins with a basic Hello World application and expands it to a complete VoiceXML application. Projects 2 and 3 add vocal links and contact information. Voice authentication and login processes are covered in Project 4. Project 5 reexamines the first four projects and breaks them into small, reusable templates.

After building the first five projects, you will have a solid understanding of how VoiceXML applications are created. The last five projects are applications built on the foundations of the previous five projects. Projects 6 through 10 can be done in any order; however, from user response, I'd suggest doing Project 6, the telephone dialer project, first because it is pretty impressive when you are trying to explain to your boss or your in-laws how the technology can be used.

Project 6 is a handy project that can be used as a phone book telephone dialer, placing calls through vocal requests. The Report Recorder in Project 7 allows surfers (wave surfers, not Web surfers) to call in reports on beaches from around the world and have the reports generate a wav file that can be heard on a Web site or over the phone. Project 8 uses XML/XSLT technology to create phone quizzes that can be used for games or customer surveys. Project 9 uses the database calendar at the San Francisco Arts Organization to dynamically answer phone requests for entertainment information regarding dates and types of events. The final project, the FAQ engine, is an experimental project for putting a voice interface on an inference engine that can handle questions through natural language processing. The projects are followed by a glossary of terms and acronyms.

Tools You Will Need

The basic projects in this book can be run through one of the online voice portals such as BeVocal, TellMe, or HeyAnita with no additional software. For Projects 6 through 10, you will need the additional software, most of which is freely downloadable and available on the Internet.

What's on the Web Site

An accompanying Web site can be found at http://cafe.bevocal.com/wiley/ 10projects. It contains the latest code for each of the projects, a list of enhancements to the projects that have been suggested by other readers, and links to online resources for further reading.

A special newsgroup has been set up to handle questions, allowing developers to exchange information on how they have expanded the ideas in the book and used them in their own applications. You can log in to the newsgroup at news://cafe.bevocal. 10projects.

My goal on the Web site is to set up a community of developers who would like to extend the projects and add to their usefulness. If you would like to participate, please log in and join us.

Final Thoughts

I hope I have gotten you excited enough to begin your first project with VoiceXML. With this book and access to the Internet, you could have your first project up and running within an hour.

I look forward to seeing you on the Web site and to your participation in the growing community of VoiceXML developers.

PART

One

Introduction

Introduction to VoiceXML

If you have ever designed a Web page, you already have the basic skills needed for developing a VoiceXML application. VoiceXML is a simple, tagged language that is similar to HTML in structure. In fact, it consists of less than 50 elements, making it much smaller than the HTML element set.

HTML gives visitors who come to your site the ability to view content, click links, and move through the pages. VoiceXML will let your visitors do this verbally over the phone. Think of VoiceXML as the HTML of the telephone. It guides users through the content of your site by using a telephone instead of a computer. The VoiceXML application will not be a replacement for your existing Web site, but it will offer your visitors additional access to your site through a highly accessible medium, the standard telephone.

The data on your Web site is the content for dialogs between the user and your Web server. VoiceXML acts as the interpreter between any telephone and your Web site content. Instead of using HTML to access your content visually, VoiceXML creates a verbal interface to the data through a voice gateway, usually housed on a voice portal.

A complete industry called voice portals has sprung into existence within the past two years. Voice portals are service providers who provide space for your voice applications, much as an Internet service provider (ISP) does for HTML Web pages. The voice portal provides the gateway and processing architecture for handling VoiceXML applications that you develop. Portals contain development tools, space allocation, example tutorials, and detailed documentation for the creation of VoiceXML applications. We will be using the services of one of the portals for development of the 10 projects.

A point of confusion among most beginning voice developers is about the telephone itself. VoiceXML allows access to your data through any phone. There is no special hardware attached to your phone, and it is not a secret, James Bond–enabled device.

The second question that usually comes up is, "Well, can I talk to the computer to access the Web site or does it have to be over a telephone?" VoiceXML is a telephone technology and is not normally used for accessing data vocally on a local computer. We will be looking at development environments that can run on your local computer, but these are mainly for VoiceXML testing, not accessing data and Web site content.

To understand how VoiceXML works, we'll first take a brief look at XML and its technologies; then we'll examine how VoiceXML fits in.

XML Overview

XML (eXtensible Markup Language) is a nonproprietary, vendor-neutral way to store and transport data. The XML standard is maintained by the World Wide Web Consortium (W3C), a group that develops common protocols for ensuring interoperability across the Web. The XML technical recommendation can be found at www.w3.org/ TR/REC-xml.

Unlike HTML, the XML language allows the developer to mark up content with definitions of what the data is, not what it should look like. Isolating the data from formatting makes it accessible to any application that understands the XML tag set that is applied to the data. This makes it possible to have one source of data that can be output to multiple formats such as HTML, XML, PDF, and VoiceXML. If the underlying data changes, applications accessing the data will not have to be rewritten to accommodate the new content.

XML is a relatively new technology. It allows developers to create their own tag sets instead of relying on predefined elements such as those in HTML. The most important concept of XML is that the data is marked up with tags that define or describe the data, not what it should look like when it is rendered to output. Instead of using tags to define content as bold or italic, it can describe what the data is, using element names such as authorName or bookTitle. Using tags to describe the data allows the calling application to decide how to format the output without affecting the data. With XML, it is now possible to have one central data source that supplies multiple applications.

Developers were told it was an "HTML killer" when XML first hit the marketplace. Magazine articles insinuated that all Web sites were going to have to be reformatted in XML or left at the side of the road, watching the XML train roar by. As with most hype when a new technology comes out, this turned out to be far from the truth. HTML is alive and well, formatting the content for display in Web browsers on millions of sites, as it will be for many years to come. XML does have its place as a presentation medium when used in conjunction with XSLT, the transformation and formatting language, but it was found to have a better use in the data exchange field.

The most powerful use of XML is in the exchange of data between applications. XML and its derivatives are plain ASCII text. As such, the data is vendor-neutral because most, if not all, major applications can read ASCII. If an industry agrees on a set of XML elements to define the data for that industry, any data that is marked up with those elements will be able to be exchanged between applications. This applies even across platforms. The data can be created in a Unix environment, processed on a Windows box, and stored on a Mac.

XML is an extremely flexible content storage and exchange format. In practice, if your Web site does not exchange or store information with other applications, you are better off staying with the basic HTML that is already on your site. But if you intend to exchange data with companies within your industry, XML is quickly becoming the de facto standard.

XML Architecture

On the simplest level, an XML application is a three-tiered architecture. The first tier is the data layer. The data may be stored in a flat file or in a database. The application layer imports the data and transforms it to the correct output format. This may be done by processing requests from the client and providing dynamic content for formatting or by generating output directly from the application. The display layer can be any mechanism that understands the application's output. Figure 1 shows the structure of a simple XML application.

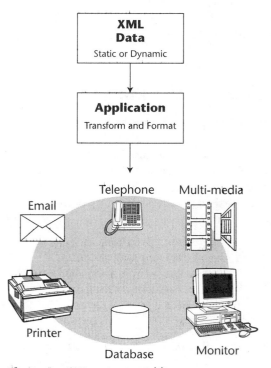

Figure 1 XML systems architecture.

XML is the data layer. It can be stored in various formats such as flat files, relational databases, or even as a stream from another XML application.

An optional component of the system is a DTD, or Document Type Definitions. The DTD holds the definitions of the elements and attributes that can be used when marking up the XML data. The data is compared against the DTD to verify that all elements are defined and the hierarchy of the elements within the data is correct. Most applications begin with a DTD to verify input and test the application during production and then remove it for optimization when the application goes live.

The second tier of the application is the formatting and transformation of the data into a specific output. Because XML is a storage mechanism, not a formatting language, the transformation layer uses a stylesheet to mark up the data for various types of output.

Multiple stylesheets can be used against the same data for outputting to various devices. This is a godsend for documentation managers. In the past, if the same data was to be included in a book, printed through a PDF file, and incorporated into a Web page, three copies of the data would have to be made, one for each of the outputs. It was virtually impossible to keep the three copies in sync. When changes were made to the original data file, the copies of the data would not be updated. With XML, there is only one source of data for all types of output. There are no copies of the data, just the original being accessed by different output type's stylesheets.

The third layer is the output mechanism. The output can be to a computer monitor, a PDA, an Adobe Acrobat PDF file, or a stream to another XML application. The important concept to remember is that the XML data is not changed by the different types of output. The data is stored as XML, formatted and transformed using stylesheets, and then is output to the selected device.

XML versus HTML: Content versus Formatting

As a Web developer, you know that data is incorporated into the HTML page along with the tags that format the data. This is a major problem when the data is needed for other projects. Any application that needs access to the content of your Web page has to figure out a way to strip out the HTML and leave the underlying data. Even when all the tags are stripped out and the data lays bare, there is no way for the calling application to know what the data means. The data and the formatting of the data are combined in such a way that the content of your Web site is virtually useless to other applications.

HTML tags tell us nothing about the content of the data, just what the output should look like when displayed in the browser. In Listing 1, the title, the headline of the page, and the information for each train is surrounded by HTML tags that dictate color, line breaks, and other types of formatting. Any application that wants to access the data will have to figure out a way to strip out the formatting and leave the content.

The HTML example causes two problems. If the Manhattan Transportation Authority (MTA) decided to change the content of the page, the calling application that is trying to

```
1.  <html>
2.    <head>
3.      <title>
4.         Manhattan Transportation Authority:
5.         Subway Update
6.      </title>
7.    </head>
8.    <body text=000000
9.          bgcolor=ffffff
10.          link=0000ff
11.          vlink=000099
12.          alink=aa0000>
13.
14. <div style=text-align:center;
15.              font-weight:bold;
16.              font-size:medium;
17.              margin-bottom:1em>
18.       Manhattan Transportation Authority: Subway Update
19.    </div>
20.    <div>Train 2: On Time</div>
21.    <div>Train 3: On Time</div>
22.
23.    <div style=color:ff0000>
24.         Train 4: Construction at Atlantic Avenue.
25.                  Trains delayed 20 minutes
26.    <div>
27.
28.    </body>
29. </html>
```

Listing 1   Data stored as HTML.

access the data would have to know about the changes and go back to get a new set of data. In addition, if there were changes to the formatting of the MTA page, the calling application would have to be rewritten to strip off the new formatting.

By isolating the data from any formatting, XML does away with these problems. Listing 2 shows the same data stored in XML. The data is surrounded by tags that describe what the data is, not what it should look like. Any application that understands the XML tag set of the MTA can now access the data and output it in any desired format. MTA can change content, add or delete items, and update the schedule without affecting any application that is using the data.

```
1.  <?xml version="1.0"?>
2.  <?xml-stylesheet type="text/xsl" href="intro.xsl"?>
3.
4.  <trains>
5.  <region>
6.  <area>New York City</area>
7.  <management>Manhattan Transportation Authority</management>
8.  <train>
9.      <number>2</number>
10.      <status>
11.          <delay>on time</delay>
12.          <constructionUpdate></constructionUpdate>
13.      </status>
14.    </train>
15.  <train>
16.      <number>3</number>
17.      <status>
18.          <delay>on time</delay>
19.          <constructionUpdate></constructionUpdate>
20.      </status>
21.    </train>
22.  <train>
23.      <number>4</number>
24.      <status>
25.          <delay>20</delay>
26.          <constructionUpdate>
27.              Atlantic Avenue
28.          </constructionUpdate>
29.      </status>
30.    </train>
31.  </region>
32.  </trains>
```

Listing 2   Data stored as XML.

XML Elements

XML data is surrounded by tags called elements. The element names are chosen and
defined by the application developer. Many industry leaders are starting to develop
XML tag sets that will define the data for an entire industry. To exchange information
between companies in an industry, applications within the loop must have access to
the defined tag set and apply it to their data.

The XML element definitions are stored in a DTD document or a schema. In theory,
each industry agrees on the definition of the elements that are most applicable for that
industry and then publishes that definition in a public repository. Anyone who wants

to build an application that is applicable for that industry has access to that DTD/ schema. By adhering to the rules and definitions, an application can now participate in the data exchange of that industry.

Portability, the ability to move data between different operating systems and applications, is one of the most important considerations when a developer chooses to use XML. The data is stored and transported as plain ASCII text, readable on any platform. It can be created on a Unix system and still be accessible to Windows, Macs, and any other platform that can process text.

XML tags by themselves have no special meaning. Each application can use the tag set as it sees fit. That is how different applications can use the same data source to output different formats. For example, when outputting to HTML, the application could give the command, "When you see a management tag, output it as a large headline in blue." A different application using voice as output could access the same data and output the management tag as part of the greeting. If the content within an element is changed, the applications accessing the data would still work properly with no changes to the code.

XML Syntax

XML has a simple set of syntax rules:

- Tags are case sensitive. <Area> and <area> are different elements. By convention, element names should be lowercase.

- The XML document must begin with an XML declaration that states the XML version number. The declaration must be the first character, first position of the document.

- There can only be one root element in XML data. The element is a container for all of the other elements and data in the file.

- Each element must have an opening *and* closing tag. Unlike HTML, where <img>, <br>, and <li> do not have a closing tag, an XML parser will throw an error if the tag is not closed. For shorthand, use a slash to close an element that does not have any content or closing tag: <br/>.

- Elements may nest within each other, but the last open element must be the first one closed. Overlapping elements will cause the XML parser to throw an error. MTA is considered an error, whereas MTA would display properly.

- It is mandatory to quote attribute values. Single or double quotes may be used.

Most major Web browser vendors have created what they consider "smart" browsers. If the HTML code is missing a closing tag or an attribute value is not quoted, the browser will try to display the page anyway. This will not happen with XML. A simple thing like improper nesting of elements will stop the application and supply an error message pointing, it is hoped, to the offending line.

Look at each of the examples in Listing 3. They are perfectly acceptable in HTML, but would throw an error in an XML application.

```
1. This will <bold> not process in XML</BOLD>
2. <img src=mta-logo.gif width=200 height=150>
3. <li>XML vs HTML
4. <i><b>XML</i></b>is stricter than <b><i>HTML</b></i>
```

Listing 3   HTML versus XML syntax.

Line 1 in Listing 3 shows a pretty obvious error: Tags are case sensitive. If the opening tag is lowercase, the closing tag must also be lowercase.

Line 2 contains two errors, one of which most developers who are switching over from HTML to XML might miss. All attribute values must be quoted. In addition, it is mandatory to have a closing tag for every element. Several elements in HTML do not need closing tags: <img>, <li>, <br>, and <p>. In lines 2 and 3 of the example, there must be closing tags for the <img> and <li> elements. XML allows a shorthand notation for combining an opening and closing tag when there is no content between the tags: Putting a forward slash as the last character within the tag <img /> would be considered a correct use within XML.

The errors in line 4 are with the nesting of the tags. XML forces a first opened, last closed syntax.

An XML data set is said to be *well formed* if it adheres to the basic rules of XML syntax construction. The rules may be simple, but they are strictly enforced by XML parsers. To be considered XML compliant, the parser must stop processing the data if an error is found in the syntax of the document. A good parser will actually give you a warning message showing the possible location of the error.

 When creating XML applications, developers must adhere strictly to the syntax rules of the language and the element hierarchical definitions in the DTD, or the application will not run.

DTDs: Defining the XML Elements

An XML application can have an optional set of rules, called a DTD, attached to it. The DTD defines what elements are available to the application, the hierarchical structure of the elements, and what attributes can be carried by each element.

 A document that adheres to the syntax rules of XML is said to be *well formed.* If the document follows the rules established in the DTD, it is said to be *valid.*

A DTD can be defined by the developer of the XML application, usually by analyzing a subset of the data that will be processed. Using Listing 2 as a data example, we can see what elements are used and how they are structured within one another. Listing 4 shows a DTD that describes the MTA data.

```
1. <!ELEMENT trains(region)*>
2.
3. <!ELEMENT region(area, management, train+)
4. <!ELEMENT area          (#PCDATA)>
5. <!ELEMENT management     (#PCDATA)>
6.
7. <!ELEMENT train (number, status)>
8.    <!ELEMENT number       (#PCDATA)>
9.    <!ELEMENT status       (#PCDATA)>
```

Listing 4 Simple DTD.

A DTD holds descriptions of the elements that will be part of the tag set. Each element is defined as a content model, specifying which other elements and what attributes are to be associated with that element. The tag <!ELEMENT> is used to define the content model for each element. The ELEMENT keyword is followed by the name of the element that is to be defined. Parentheses hold the content model for the element, ending with an optional quantifier. Let's see how this is put into action.

Line 1 of Listing 4 defines the top-level element, or root element, as <trains>. According to the syntax rules for XML, there can only be one root-level element. This element will be the container of all other elements in the data. By looking at the data source in Listing 2, we can determine that the only element that is a direct child of the <train> element is <region>, so region is the only element within the content model for <trains>.

Notice the * after the content model. This is a quantifier taken from regular expression language. There are three quantifiers: * means zero or more, + means one or more, and ? defines an element as optional. The * in this case means that a <trains> element may contain zero or more <region> elements.

Because a <trains> element can contain a <region> element, region must be defined. The content model for <region>, shown on line 3, states that a <region> can hold one <area> element, one <management> element, and one or more <train> elements. The commas force the elements to be in the specific order in which they appear within the content model. Each of those three elements must then be defined, as shown on lines 4 through 7.

The content model for <train> must contain one <number> and one <status> element, in that order. Lines 8 and 9 define those two elements.

There are special character references in XML called entities. An entity is like an alias or a shortcut to a larger piece of data. When an element is defined as #PCDATA, those entities are expanded in place within the data. Most of the elements within the DTD will be defined as #PCDATA.

DTDs can be stored internally as part of the data file or externally as a standalone definition set. Most DTDs are externally available to multiple sources of data. The VoiceXML industry has agreed upon the definitions for the VoiceXML element set, in the *VoiceXML 2.0 Working Draft*, and has made it available at www.w3.org/TR/voicexml20. We will be examining different sections of that document during our development of the 10 projects.

Displaying XML with XSLT

XML is a storage and data transfer mechanism and needs to be processed in order to be displayed. Outputting XML data can be done through the formatting and transformation language called XSLT (eXtensible Stylesheet Language Transformations). XSLT can be used to transform data into outputs such as text, HTML, PDF, and even other XML files.

XSLT can transform data on the fly, such as within a Web browser, and it can be used to process the data into files for storage. Figure 2 shows the process flow for taking XML data, processing it with XSLT, and then outputting to various outputs.

XSLT syntax has basic elements that are predefined by the language and functions that transform the data. Listing 5 shows a simple stylesheet that will transform the data shown in Listing 2 into a VoiceXML file that can be accessed over the telephone.

```
1.  <xsl:stylesheet
2.      version="1.0"
3.      xmlns:xsl="http://www.w3.org/1999/XSL/Transform">
4.
5.  <xsl:template match="trains">
6.
7.  <!-- BEGIN VOICEXML OUTPUT -->
8.  <vxml version="2.0">
9.   <form id="greeting">
10.    <block>
11.     You have reached
12.     <xsl:value-of select="region/management" />
13.     in <xsl:value-of select="region/area" />.
14.     Here are the most recent updates to our train time
15.     schedules and delays due to construction:
16.     <break size="medium" />
17.     <xsl:apply-templates select="region/train" />
18.    </block>
19.   </form>
20.  </vxml>
21.  </xsl:template>
22.  <!-- END VOICEXML OUTPUT -->
23.
24.  <!-- INDIVIDUAL TRAIN INFO -->
25.  <xsl:template match="train">
26.     The number <xsl:value-of select="number"/> train
27.     is <xsl:value-of select="status/delay"/>
28.     <xsl:if test="status/delay != 'on time'">
29.     minutes late due to construction at
30.     <xsl:value-of select="status/constructionUpdate"/>
31.     </xsl:if><xsl:text>.</xsl:text>
32.    <break size="small"/>
33.  </xsl:template>
34.
35.  </xsl:stylesheet>
```

Listing 5 Transforming XML into VoiceXML with XSLT.

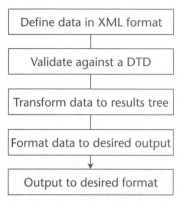

Figure 2   Process flow for transforming and outputting XML as VoiceXML.

The XSLT code in Listing 5 creates VoiceXML output by using templates to format and transform the XML data. Even though you may not be familiar with XSLT, you can see that it is similar in style and syntax to XML with its opening and closing tags, quoted attributes, and hierarchical structure. We will be using stylesheets and XSLT within one of the projects to transform survey data into VoiceXML output.

The transformation by XSLT into VoiceXML could just as easily have been a transformation to text, PDF, or HTML. The power of XSLT is in the transformation of XML data, making it portable across platforms and applications.

VoiceXML

The preceding overview of XML can be directly transferred to the creation of VoiceXML applications. VoiceXML uses the syntax and structure of XML to create a language that makes Web site content available by voice, over the telephone.

VoiceXML Working Draft Specification

The VoiceXML Forum, www.VoiceXML.org, is working with the W3C to create a standardized VoiceXML terminology. Founding members include IBM, AT&T, Lucent, Motorola, and many other companies related to dynamic computer voice generation.

The goal of the VoiceXML Forum is to create a language that gives Web developers the ability to deliver content from their Web site over the telephone by using their existing coding skills. The intention is for the VoiceXML language to act as an interface to the low-level functions of programming and system resource management. The developer learns the tag set of the language, builds an interface, and lets the interface handle the access to the low-level functions.

The W3C has agreed to participate in the development of the VoiceXML 2.0 specification. A specification must go through various stages to be considered a full recommendation by the W3C committee (see Figure 3). A working draft is the first stage on

Step 1: Working Draft

Step 2: Last Call Working Draft

Step 3: Candidate Recommendation

Step 4: Proposed Recommendation

Step 5: Recommendation

Full Description:
http://www.w3.org/Consortium/Process-20010719/tr.html#Recs

Figure 3   W3C stages for specification recommendation.

the way to full recommendation. According to the W3C, the draft should not be used to develop production-level applications. See the warning box for more details.

A working draft document is not a finished proposal and should not be used to create production-level applications. Here's what the W3C has WARNING to say about it: "This is a W3C Working Draft for review by W3C Members and other interested parties. It is a draft document and may be updated, replaced or made obsolete by other documents at any time. It is inappropriate to use W3C Working Drafts as reference material or to cite them as other than 'work in progress.'"

Despite the dire warning on the W3C site, companies are developing applications using the working draft. When you call 1-800-555-1212 to request a phone number, you hear a voice application developed by TellMe.com. The state of Utah has implemented an information hotline whose front end is a VoiceXML application. All of the major voice portals, such as BeVocal, TellMe, and Hey Anita, offer services based upon the working draft. Each of the companies professes to be VoiceXML 2.0 compliant to a major extent. What they will do as the specification changes remains to be seen.

VoiceXML Syntax

The VoiceXML vocabulary is a predefined set of elements using XML syntax. The DTD for VoiceXML is available at www.w3.org/TR/voicexml20. The tag set is relatively small, consisting of about 50 elements with specific rules on where the tags may appear in relation to one another and what attributes each element may carry. We will be developing applications using these specifications, thereby assuring that the applications will be portable across platforms and capable of working with any software that understands, and is in conformance with, the *VoiceXML Working Draft*.

```
1. <?xml version="1.0"?>
2.
3. <vxml version="2.0">
4.    <form id="greeting">
5.       <block>
6.       You have reached Manhattan Transportation Authority
7.       in New York City.
8.       Here are the most recent updates to our train time
9.       schedules and delays due to construction:
10.       <break size="medium" />
11.
12.       The number 2 train
13.       is on time.
14.       <break size="small"/>
15.
16.       The number 3 train
17.       is on time.
18.       <break size="small"/>
19.
20.       The number 4 train
21.       is 20 minutes late
22.       due to construction at Atlantic Avenue.
23.       <break size="small"/>
24.
25.       </block>
26.    </form>
27. </vxml>
```

Listing 6 VoiceXML output from XML data.

VoiceXML is a markup language that uses opening and closing tags to signify events and responses that should be handled by the voice server implementation. When writing a VoiceXML application, the syntax rules for XML apply. Web developers who have a foundation in HTML will find the appearance and style of the language very familiar. Listing 6 shows the output from Listing 2 after it has been transformed into well-formed and valid VoiceXML by the XSLT stylesheet.

Line 1 specifies that this is an XML document. The root element of the document is <vxml>, as shown on line 3. There are only three more elements within the document: <block>, <form>, and <break>. The <form> element is a basic building block for receiving information from the user. The <block> element handles processing of dynamic content, and the <break> element inserts a short pause into the verbal output. We will be looking at the elements in more detail when we start developing applications in the first project.

Processing VoiceXML

A VoiceXML implementation can take voice commands over the phone, translating those spoken commands to text. The Speech-to-Text (STT) engine handles the conversion of spoken language to text. Once the speech has been transformed to text, it is sent to a processing mechanism, which can be any that is available on your Web site. Perl, JSP, ASP, or any other type of processing on the server side can be used to process the request. This gives access to all the resources on the receiving computer, including databases, flat files, and any other types of content that are needed to process the request.

The result of the processing is sent back to the VoiceXML application. The application then translates the results by using a Text-to-Speech (TTS) translator, outputting the response verbally to the caller. In addition, the VoiceXML application can have pre-recorded audio file responses using human voices that are applicable as a response to the request. The application may then ask the user for more information and continue the session or terminate the call.

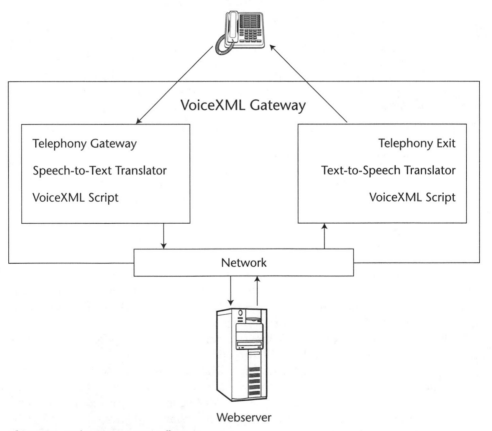

Figure 4   VoiceXML process flow.

One of the most important concepts of the VoiceXML language is that it isolates the user interaction from the processing of a request. As shown in Figure 4, the VoiceXML interpreter handles the interface between the telephone and the processing layer. It does not handle the processing of the request. The VoiceXML front end acts as a filter to the service layer that will actually handle the processing of the request. By creating an interface layer that is independent of any specific processing mechanism, the VoiceXML application is portable across processing platforms.

The user interface consists of a series of dialogs that guide the caller, collecting information for the processing implementation. The interface may be a single document with a set menu or a series of documents that are linked through calls to different Uniform Resource Identifiers (URIs).

Final Thoughts

XML makes it possible to create tag sets for specific industries. The VoiceXML Forum has defined a tag set for developing high-level interfaces for telephone applications. Because of the similarity between HTML and VoiceXML syntax, Web developers will find that it is fairly easy to create voice applications using their existing site content.

In the next chapter, we will set up the work environment so that you can begin creating your own VoiceXML applications.

Setting Up the Working Environment

VoiceXML is an interface layer that acts as an interpreter between the end user and a Web server processing platform. A VoiceXML application accepts speech as input, translates that speech into ASCII text understood by the processing environment, and then formats the results of the processing into verbal output. The VoiceXML application environment can reside locally, maintained and administered by you, or on a remote machine controlled by an Application Service Provider (ASP) that specializes in housing VoiceXML applications.

VoiceXML applications can be static documents with hard-coded data or they can be dynamically generated using CGI, JSP, ASP, or any other type of processing mechanism available on the VoiceXML server or on a remote Web server. This bears repeating. The VoiceXML interface can give access to existing data and processes on your Web server. Instead of accessing the data through a visual Web browser, the data is accessed through a verbal browser.

The VoiceXML interface gives access to existing data and processes on your Web server.

NOTE

Beginning developers will find it easier to use an established vendor to house their applications than to install and deploy a full-blown voice environment with 24-hour, 7-day (24/7) monitoring. Using an ASP still allows access to data on existing Web sites, but it leaves implementation details of the VoiceXML platform to a service provider. In this chapter, we will examine online VoiceXML ASPs and then set up a developer's account with one of the free services.

TIP Setting up an account with an ASP helps new VoiceXML developers concentrate on learning the VoiceXML language and syntax without dealing with the setup or maintenance issues of a VoiceXML implementation.

VoiceXML Portals

A VoiceXML portal acts as a remote gateway to handle the processing of VoiceXML requests. It is comparable to an Internet Service Provider (ISP), providing space for people to build their voice-enabled pages. Creation of scripts, activation of the scripts, and management of the system are handled through a standard Web browser. There is no software to download and install. The ASP provides all the tools and storage space necessary for creating voice applications.

Most VoiceXML ASPs offer free and for-a-fee services to companies that do not want to house production-level applications to run business functions. This can be very economical for companies that cannot afford the $20,000 to $40,000 in-house setup fees or maintain a 24/7 staff to oversee the voice system. We will use a free service to develop our applications.

How It Works

A VoiceXML application housed at a VoiceXML ASP works the same way as a basic Web page. The developer creates a voice page that is stored on a Web server. The voice portal is used as the connection between the data on a Web server and the end user. The Web server may be housed in the same location as the ASP, or it may be accessed remotely through the VoiceXML processing platform. By housing the application on your Web server, your VoiceXML scripts will have access to all of the content and processing mechanisms that are available on that server.

NOTE VoiceXML scripts can be stored on your Web server and accessed through a remote VoiceXML portal, allowing existing content on your Web site to be available to the voice application.

The voice application server is accessed by calling a phone number that is dedicated to processing incoming voice requests. Continuing to use a Web page as an analogy, the phone number is comparable to a Uniform Resource Locator (URL) for accessing a site. Once users connect to the site over the phone, they can surf the content through vocal commands or key input from their telephone.

When surfing the Web, users must have a browser on their local machine to see the Web pages. The browser translates the HTML code from the Web page into viewable content on the user's computer screen. In contrast, the voice browser in a voice application is located within the VoiceXML gateway that answers the phone. This makes it possible for VoiceXML applications to be accessed by any telephone without installing specialized telephone browser software.

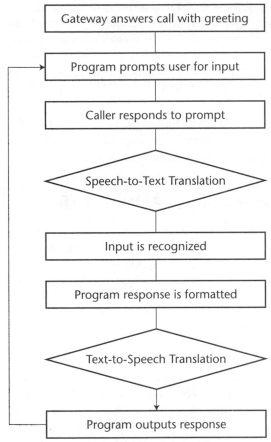

Figure 1   VoiceXML application process flow.

Figure 1 shows the process flow of a typical voice application. The VoiceXML gateway answers the call, outputs a greeting, and then waits for input from the caller. The caller speaks a verbal command that is translated to text by the VoiceXML speech-to-text (STT) translator. The input is sent to the VoiceXML script for processing, returning a response that is reformatted into speech by the text-to-speech (TTS) translator. The dialog continues until the caller hangs up or the script is terminated.

VoiceXML Application Service Providers

There are several application service providers that offer free access to environments that can be used to develop, test, and deploy your VoiceXML applications. The main providers are HeyAnita.com, BeVocal.com, TellMe.com, and VoiceGenie.com. Once you get beyond the press hyperbole and marketing hype, all four companies provide online tools and free space allocation for your VoiceXML projects.

Becoming a developer for any of the portals is free. Fill out the basic contact information and within minutes you can be working on your first application. All interfaces are Web based, through a browser. Try each and select the one that feels the most intuitive and comfortable to you. The examples and code in the 10 projects will use the BeVocal development platform. If you choose to use one of the other vendors, there may be minor differences even though they all profess to be VoiceXML 2.0 compliant.

NOTE   **The 10 projects were developed and tested using the BeVocal development platform. There may be minor differences when running the projects on other voice portals. See your portal's documentation for details.**

Setting Up a Developer Account at the BeVocal Cafe

BeVocal Cafe will be used to develop the projects in this book. I have found that BeVocal is reasonably compliant with the VoiceXML 2.0 specification, provides advanced tools for project development, and has a good support system when problems arise. A toll free number in the United States allows you to place test calls to your applications without incurring any phone charges. There are also numbers available for Europe and other international locations. Check the top of the developer page at cafe.BeVocal.com for the most current numbers.

Create an Account

Create a developer account by going to cafe.bevocal.com and clicking the Signup button at the top left of the page. Click I Agree for the developer's agreement, fill out the registration screen (red asterisk indicates mandatory fields), and click Submit to finish the registration process.

TIP   **When registering for a BeVocal account, give the phone number from which you will be calling when testing your applications. The platform will recognize the number you are calling from and not ask for a developer id to access your account.**

Upon completion of registration, you will be registered as a developer with the BeVocal Cafe. Check your email and you will have received a confirmation letter from BeVocal that will include your username, password, and pin number. Save or print the email as a reminder of your login information. You will need them to confirm your identity when calling in to test your applications.

HANDS ON   **Create a developer's account with BeVocal.**

Tools in the BeVocal Development Environment

BeVocal provides a suite of tools to help the developer create VoiceXML applications. This section will examine the tools that will be used in Part Two, the 10 projects. Log in to your BeVocal account by going to cafe.bevocal.com and entering your user information. On subsequent visits, your username and id will be remembered.

NOTE **The BeVocal platform places a cookie on your machine that remembers your username and password. If you bookmark your developer login page, the login process will be skipped and you will enter directly into the development area on future visits.**

File Management

The first screen in the working environment is the File Management tool shown in Figure 2. This is the central area of your workspace. There are four basic areas within the File Management window: tools menu, local files, remote files, and account info.

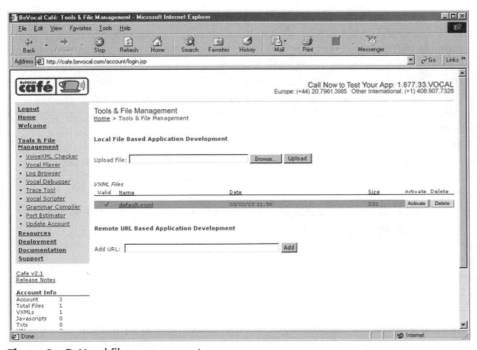

Figure 2   BeVocal file management.

The Tools menu on the top left of the page gives access to the tools of the environment. We will be examining the tools that are used within the 10 projects. Clicking on a tool name will either bring up a Java applet, giving live access to your application data, or it will bring up a new Web window for editing your applications.

Basic information about your account is listed in the bottom left corner of the display. A developer account is allocated 2 MB of space by default. Because VoiceXML is text-based scripting, this allows more than adequate room for creating your applications. If you are developing larger applications that incorporate sound files, like the Star Trek game in Project 8, contact tech support for an increase in your account space allocation.

The Account Info column displays information about the files that have been created or uploaded to your account. Think of it as a mini file manager with added details. When a file is listed as Active, that file is currently available for processing by the BeVocal platform. Only one file can be active at a time. We will learn how to get around this limitation in Project 5. The Account Info column also displays how much space your files are using and how much more space is available in your account.

Only one file at a time can be active within the development environment. You can get around this limitation by creating a file that links to all of your projects and using this file as your entrance page. This will be demonstrated in Project 5.

TIP

The Local File Application Development section lists files that are currently stored in your account. This includes files that were created using the BeVocal environment as well as those that were uploaded from a remote machine. One of these files will be a darker blue than the other rows, marking it as Active. This indicates which application will be run when your account is accessed over the telephone. If no row is dark blue, there is no currently active file. Activate and Delete buttons are available for each file in your account.

Only one application can be active at a time. Clicking the Activate button in a file row will make that file active and deactivate the current application. The Delete button will immediately remove the file from your account with no warning.

A Delete button immediately removes a file from your account with no further warning.

WARNING

There are two methods for adding files to your account. Files can be created in the VoiceXML Checker screen. We will examine this technique in the next section. A second way is to create files on your local computer and upload them to your account. The Upload File form field has a Browse button that is used to access the files on your local hard drive. Once a file has been chosen, click the Upload button and a copy of the file will be moved into your BeVocal account. In either case, you have an allocated space of about 2 MB for file storage.

VoiceXML applications do not have to reside on the BeVocal server. You can store your applications on your own personal Web server just as you would any Web page. The Remote URL Based Application Development interface allows uploading of URLs that can be activated as the initial screen in your application.

 Log in to your account at BeVocal. Click the File Management link on the Tools menu and examine the screen. Verify that default.vxml is available in HANDS ON the VXML file list. This is the file we will be using to verify your development environment is set up properly.

VoiceXML Checker

The VoiceXML Checker, shown in Figure 3, is a tool that determines if your application code adheres to the syntax rules of XML. It can also verify that your application is valid according to the rules of VoiceXML 2.0.

The left side of the screen is identical to the File Management window, showing the Tools menu and the Account Info. The main screen shows a large text area box and four buttons for activating the VoiceXML syntax checker, saving the file to your account, clearing the display box entirely, or setting the text area box back to its default value. The text area box can be used for opening existing scripts or writing new ones from scratch.

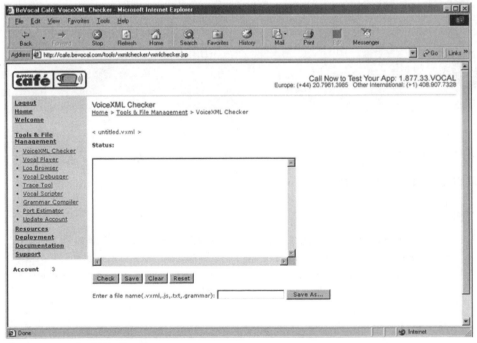

Figure 3 VoiceXML Checker.

Click on the default.vxml filename in the File Management window. This will move you to the VoiceXML Checker page with the default.vxml script inserted into the text area. At the top of the page, a confirmation notice shows that default.vxml is the file displayed. Click the Check button beneath the box holding the VoiceXML code. Look at the status line printed in green over the box. When the status line output is in green, the script is well-formed VoiceXML.

There are two types of syntax checking in the VoiceXML Checker: well formed and valid. A well-formed document is one that follows the syntax rules of XML: attribute values double quoted, opening tags closed, elements nested properly, and so forth. If a call to a document type definition (DTD) is included in the VoiceXML application script, the Checker will also validate the file against the DTD.

Listing 1 shows a call to a DTD on lines 2 through 6. We will be looking at the rest of the code in Project 1. The VoiceXML Checker will examine the code on lines 8 through 16 and make sure it is valid according to the rules established within the DTD.

```
1.  <?xml version="1.0"?>
2.  <!DOCTYPE
3.    vxml
4.    PUBLIC
5.    "-//BeVocal Inc//VoiceXML 2.0//EN"
6.    "http://cafe.bevocal.com/libraries/dtd/vxml2-0-bevocal.dtd">
7.
8.  <vxml version="2.0">
9.    <form id="form">
10.      <block>
11.        <prompt>
12.          Hello World!
13.        </prompt>
14.      </block>
15.    </form>
16.  </vxml>
```

Listing 1   default.vxml script.

Delete the call to the DTD within the default.vxml script. Click the Check button. Red messages indicate an error in the application or are a warning message of a possible problem. Note the error message and scroll down to the bottom of the page to view the specific errors detected.

> There is a warning message stating a <!DOCTYPE> is missing. DTDs are optional when processing a VoiceXML file. The application will still run without one, but it is a good idea to include it during the development process.
>
> Click the File Management choice in the left column menu without saving your changes to the default.vxml script.

VoiceXML scripts can be created from scratch in the Vocal Checker window. Enter the code in the checker window, give the file a name in the Save As form field, and save the file. When you view your list of files in the File Management window, the new file will have been added. This is useful to create batch files, external grammars, and short standalone scripts, which we will examine in later sessions.

TIP

> You can rename a file by using the Save As button of the VoiceXML Checker. Type a name in the text box next to the Save As button and press the button. The original file will not be renamed. A copy of the old file will be given the new name. I use this technique to build up a series of files for a single script, keeping a copy of each stage of the script's development.
>
> Filenames in the BeVocal environment are forced to all lowercase when saving a file.

WARNING

> When using Save As, if there is a file with the specified name already on the server, it will be overwritten without warning.

Log Browser

The Log Browser (see Figure 4) is used to examine the calls that have been placed to your application, giving an analysis of the call flow from the program's point of view. You can search for calls by date range and also include a specific caller's phone number within the search.

The Log Browser has two screens. The opening screen displays a form for choosing a range of dates, a specific caller's phone number, or a basic text search. The four buttons beneath the form are used to control access to the log files. The Submit button brings up a list of files that match the criteria requested in the form, and the Most Recent Log button opens a new window to display a log of the most recent call to your application. Reset returns all of the form fields to their default values.

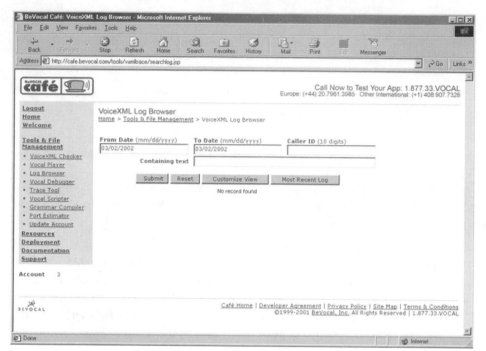

Figure 4   BeVocal Log Browser.

Setting a date range in the form and then clicking the Submit button will bring up a list of calls that were placed to your application during the selected date range, as shown in Figure 5. The default table displays information about each call, including the time the call was placed, the phone number that was dialed, the duration of the call, an error count, and a link to view the log of the call. The output from the Submit button can be configured by clicking on Customize View. The dialog box that appears will contain a list of eight items that can be included in log table.

The second screen of the Log Browser is activated by clicking View Log under the Details column of the Submit output or by choosing the Most Recent Log button. A new window will open, displaying a checklist of events that have been traced and a complete log of the call. The event list is color coded, making it easy to scan the log and view only events of interest. The Apply Default button will reset the form to display all events.

The Log Browser is useful when trying to determine what errors are breaking your application and how the VoiceXML platform is handling processing of your script. As an example, if your base voice application tries to access a Common Gateway Interface (CGI) script that is not available or is returning invalid VoiceXML, the error log will help pinpoint the problem.

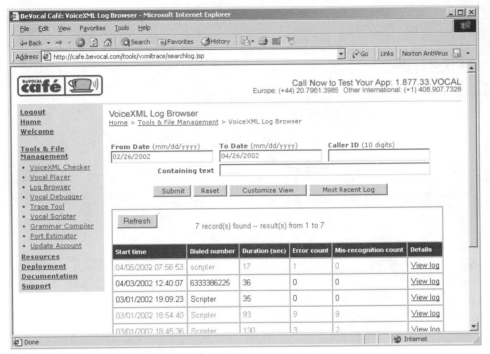

Figure 5 Log Browser date range form.

The Log Browser is also useful while learning how the VoiceXML engine works. The Form Interpretation Algorithm (FIA) is one of the most important concepts that we will discuss throughout the projects. It specifies the precedence of the processing order within an application. The Log Browser gives a detailed account of the processing order and precedence of each of the application's elements.

As a learning tool, the Log Browser display gives a detailed look at the sequence of events that occur during VoiceXML processing.

TIP

You can configure the output of the log by selecting those events you wish to view and then choosing the Apply Filter button. Figure 6 shows log output that displays the platform's verbal output from the program, shown in gray on the screen display, and the Recognition Info that shows the program's analysis of the user's input in orange on the screen display. All other events have been filtered out.

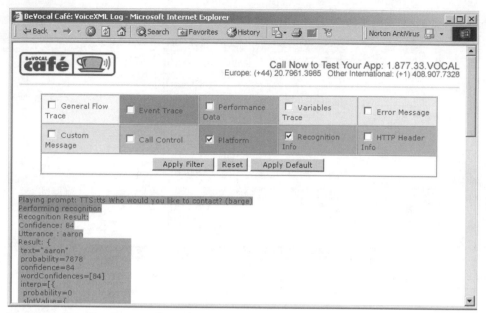

Figure 6 Log Browser configuration.

**Using the Log Browser should be the second level of attack when trying
to debug a script. Debugging starts with the VoiceXML Checker.**

TIP

Vocal Scripter

There are two ways to test your application if it resides on the BeVocal server. The first
is to place a toll-free call to BeVocal (1-877-332-8625 within the United States). It is fun
to hear your first application, but it becomes cumbersome if you don't have an extra
phone line. It takes a lot of time to check your script every time a change is made.

BeVocal provides the Vocal Scripter (see Figure 7) as part of the developer's tool kit.
The Vocal Scripter allows you to interact with your application without having to
make a phone call. The Scripter is a Java Applet that accepts text instead of voice as
input to the VoiceXML interpreter.

**Keep the VoiceXML Checker and the Vocal Scripter open in two different
windows, allowing changes in the VoiceXML Checker to be viewed
immediately as output in the Vocal Scripter.**

TIP

The Vocal Scripter has two modes for processing input: interactive mode, which is
the default, and batch mode. The interactive mode acts as a text-based keyboard entry.
Output from the VoiceXML script is displayed in the main window of the applet. User
input is typed into the text box at the bottom of the page and the input is processed by

Figure 7   BeVocal Vocal Scripter.

the VoiceXML platform, whose output is displayed in the main window. The Record mode logs the input sequence from the user and stores it in memory until Save to Disk is selected. To temporarily stop the logging process, use the Stop button. Clear Buffer clears the log's memory and begins recording from scratch.

Batch mode is for processing a set of input statements that have been saved in a file. This allows multiple line input without having to enter each line by hand. Batch Mode is good for checking responses to a predefined scenario when testing changes to an application. Make changes to a script through the Vocal Checker window and then test the changes with a batch file in the Vocal Scripter window.

Use batch mode to process a predefined sequence of input statements while changing the processing script in the VoiceXML Checker window.

TIP

There are three methods for creating a batch file. Using the Save to Disk button after recording user input will save the user input to the file specified in the Record User Input form field. The Voice Checker interface can also be used to create the batch file from scratch, saving it with the .txt file extension. For large batch files, you can create the file on your local machine and upload it to the voice server through the file management interface.

To activate a batch file for processing, click the Batch Mode radio button after placing a call to the VoiceXML script with the Dial button. A confirmation notice will appear in the display window, and the script will automatically process input that was stored in the selected file.

Click the Dial button to activate the Vocal Scripter. A Dialing in Progress notice will be displayed in the applet window. When a connection has been established with the voice server, the verbal output from the script will be prefaced with an OUTPUT —> symbol. The script will pause, waiting for user input at appropriate points. Type a response in the User Input field at the bottom of the applet, using the Enter key when finished. The application processing will continue until the script terminates or the user chooses the Hang Up button. All applications will automatically time out after 1 hour.

 A no-input event is created when a user does not respond to a request from the voice server. The Vocal Scripter does not have a button for handling this event. It will sit and wait until the application times out. Pressing the Enter key on your keyboard when there is no text in the input field will activate a no-input event.

Activating an Application

BeVocal provides two ways for the public to access your test applications. You can demo an application for private use by selected clients, or you can showcase your work, making it available through the marketing area of the BeVocal Web site.

To demo an application, choose the Deployment option in the menu of any BeVocal Cafe Web page within your developer area. You will see a list of the possible ways to deploy your application. Choose Demo from the left-hand menu. The Deployment screen, as shown in Figure 8, will show a list of all VoiceXML files available in your account. Choose a file to deploy by clicking on it.

Step 2 of the deployment will ask for a demo id number. This will be used to identify your demo when users are placing a call to your application. I usually check the "automatically generate an id" box when deploying an application. This assures me that the id is unique and I won't have to keep guessing to find one. Enter a short statement describing your application in the description box. The description will appear on the BeVocal demo page when other developers are looking to see what kind of applications you are working on.

If you would like to showcase your application in the BeVocal marketing area, select the "I want to showcase my application" box at the bottom of the page, as shown in Figure 9. Clicking the Deploy button will bring up a page of legalese from the BeVocal lawyers. Confirm you have read the Legal Agreement by selecting the I Agree button.

 You must enter a short description to demo an application. If you are just testing the environment, put a short phrase or the word *test* in the description box.

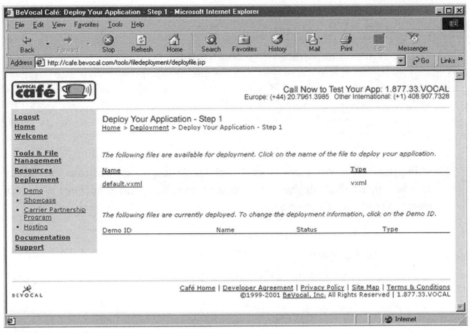

Figure 8   Deployment screen, step 1.

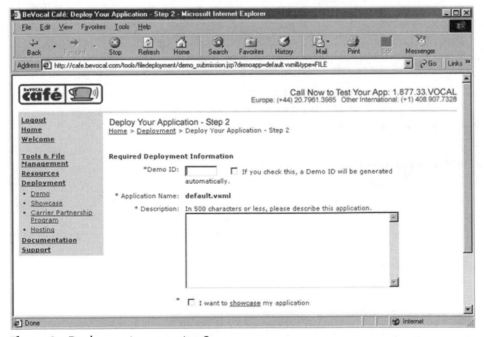

Figure 9   Deployment screen, step 2.

Step 3 of the deployment procedure displays a confirmation notice stating that your application has been activated as a demo. To check the demo, call 1-800-4BeVocal and say "BeVocal Cafe." Speaking your demo id will activate your VoiceXML application.

To disable your application in the demo area, click the Demo button in the left-hand menu. Scroll down to the bottom of the page to view the applications that are currently deployed in your account. Click the id number of the application you would like to disable, bringing up a screen that will display a Disable radio button at the bottom of the page. Choose Disable and click Submit to remove your application from the active demo area.

 Using the demo area enables you to make prototype applications available to your clients without them having to access your private account with your developer id and pin number.

TIP

Documentation and Support

Like all of the major voice portal vendors, BeVocal has extensive documentation and examples for VoiceXML. Most documentation is available in downloadable PDF format and can also be viewed on the Web. The VoiceXML Reference and Grammar Reference come in handy when trying to pound out a solution. As your projects get more advanced, you will also want to use the Speech Objects Reference for examples of using prebuilt modules to accept spoken dates, locations, and number formats. We will use some of the speech objects within the projects and will learn when and how to use them.

BeVocal Cafe also has six newsgroups that are available to all developers. I've found the moderators to be extremely responsive as well as knowledgeable because they are developers who are building and maintaining the BeVocal environment. Most activity is on the cafe.bevocal.grammars and cafe.bevocal.vxml groups. Direct response from the support staff is available at cafesupport@bevocal.com.

 Click the Documentation button at the top of any BeVocal Cafe page. Choose the Speech Objects Reference from the left-hand menu to get an overview of speech objects and how they can be used.

HANDS ON

Miscellaneous Tools

Other tools in the BeVocal arsenal are the Vocal Player, Vocal Debugger, Trace Tool, and Grammar Compiler. As your applications get larger and more complex, you will want to take advantage of the more extensive capabilities of these tools.

The Vocal Debugger and Trace Tool allow you to follow a script as it is running. The Vocal Player can replay calls to your application, making it useful for following a dialog or checking assumptions about grammar usage. Grammars are essential to all interactive VoiceXML applications and will be a substantial part of each of the 10 projects. The Grammar Compiler precompiles a large grammar set, optimizing your program when it contains large grammars.

Testing Your Environment

After looking over the BeVocal developer environment, verify that your account is set up and working properly. Click Vocal Scripter in the left-hand column of any of the development windows. A new window will pop open. Wait a few seconds while the Java application loads. Click the Dial button and verify that your script runs by checking the output in the right-hand window. You will see verification that Dialing is in progress, followed soon after by a Connection established message. The script will run, outputting "Hello World." At this point, the session ends because there are no more events to process.

Congratulations! Your working environment with BeVocal is set up properly and you are ready to start coding your first project.

In addition to testing the Hello World application through the Vocal Scripter, place a call to your account through the BeVocal line at 877-338-6225.

HANDS ON

Final Thoughts

The easiest way to get started with VoiceXML application development is by using one of the free online services. We will be using the BeVocal Cafe as our development environment for the projects in this book. Other free voice portal services are available through HeyAnita, TellMe, VoiceGenie, and various other online companies. They offer an assortment of development tools and extensions to the VoiceXML platform that are comparable to the BeVocal environment. Choose the environment that feels most appropriate to you and set up an account.

After testing your developer's environment, you will be ready to start coding your first VoiceXML application. The first five projects create templates for the components of most Web sites: content, links, contact information, and secure login. We'll start with creating a basic VoiceXML page.

PART

Two

The Projects

Building Basic Pages
with VoiceXML

Beginning to use VoiceXML to build voice applications as an extension to your Web site is as simple as learning how to build your first Web page with HTML. VoiceXML has a predefined set of markup elements that can be applied to your online content for output. This first project will be used as a template for subsequent projects. It contains the basic building blocks that can be used as an underlying structure for expansion to production-level applications.

THE PROBLEM

Most Web developers don't have experience with voice applications. They need a step-by-step solution to get an initial project up and running.

THE SOLUTION

Create a basic template that can be used for developing larger applications. Building the template includes creating, debugging, and deploying the template.

Project Description

This project starts with the construction of a simple *Hello, World* application to verify that the VoiceXML development system is working properly. From that point, the template is expanded in four segments, building a basic application that will accept user input, make a choice based upon that input, and output the appropriate response. Along the way, the Form Interpretation Alogorithm (FIA) will be discussed as the basic process controller behind VoiceXML. The project is completely self-contained with no reference to outside data sources other than the DTD used for validation of the application.

To complete this project you will:

1. Create a *Hello, World* application.
2. Verify that the application is working.
3. Add multiple dialogs to the template.
4. Accept user input with yes/no grammar.
5. Set up error checking.
6. Insert meta data for the project description.

You Will Need

✔ **A connection to the Internet**

✔ **A developer account with a voice portal such as BeVocal, TellMe, HeyAnita, or VoiceGenie**

✔ **Example scripts from cafe.bevocal.com/wiley/10projects**

✔ **The VoiceXML 2.0 Working Draft from www.w3.org/TR/voice20**

✔ **The Speech Synthesized Markup Language Specification from www.w3.org/TR/speech-synthesis**

VoiceXML Elements Used in This Project

ELEMENT NAME	DESCRIPTION
<block>	A container of (noninteractive) executable code
<else>	Used in <if> elements
<field>	Declares an input field in a form
<filled>	An action executed when fields are filled
<form>	A dialog for presenting information and collecting data
<goto>	Go to another dialog in the same or different document

VoiceXML Elements Used in This Project   *(Continued)*

ELEMENT NAME	DESCRIPTION
<grammar>	Specifies a speech recognition or DTMF grammar
<help>	Catches a help event
<if>	Simple conditional logic
<noinput>	Catches a noinput event
<nomatch>	Catches a nomatch event
<prompt>	Queues speech synthesis and audio output to the user
<vxml>	Top-level element in each VoiceXML document

Source: *VoiceXML 2.0 Working Draft*, section 1.4

Call Flow

Figure 1.1 shows the call flow that will be used for the final application. The user places a call to the application, hears a greeting, and then is given some basic information. A yes or no response is elicited from the user; the VoiceXML output is based on the user's response. Error checking verifies that the user has input a recognizable response before the application continues and concludes processing.

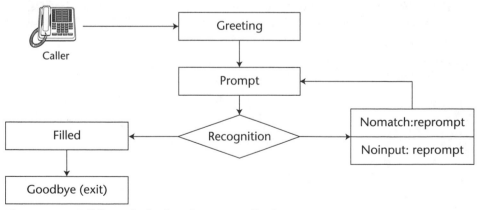

Figure 1.1   Call flow of a basic VoiceXML application.

Create a *Hello, World* Application

A simple *Hello, World* application verifies that your environment is set up and working properly. By getting the words *Hello, World* as output from the system, you will confirm that the syntax of your application is correct, your development environment is working properly, and you are ready to develop a more complex application.

 Reading through the application is instructive, but it is not enough. If you have not set up your working environment, stop now and register for a developer account with one of the voice portals. The projects in this book were developed on the BeVocal platform.

Follow along through each step of the development process and code the application as it is presented. Making mistakes is part of the process. Get your application running properly in its simple stages, and the rest will fall into place much more smoothly.

The VoiceXML template application in Listing 1.1 begins with an XML declaration on line 1. Line 3 establishes the root element, <vxml>, for the document. The root element is used to encompass all other elements within the application. No elements can reside outside of the root element.

A *version* attribute is required within the <vxml> element. It specifies the version of VoiceXML used for processing the document. The most current version of VoiceXML is 2.0, a major update from VoiceXML 1.0. The most significant change in the specification is that VoiceXML 2.0 is synchronized with the Speech Synthesis Markup Language (SSML). The World Wide Web Consortium (W3C) has mandated that any platform professing to be VoiceXML compliant must adhere to the SSML specification. If there is a conflict between the definitions in VoiceXML 2.0 and SSML, SSML definitions are to take precedence.

```
1. <?xml version="1.0"?>
2.
3. <vxml version="2.0">
4.  <form>
5.   <block>
6.    <prompt>Hello, World!</prompt>
7.   </block>
8.  </form>
9. </vxml>
```

Listing 1.1   Hello World application.

Over 20 elements have been modified from the VoiceXML 1.0 specification to synchronize with the SSML. Additionally, there are dozens of clarifications and miscellaneous notes within the new spec. See Appendix J of the *VoiceXML 2.0 Working Draft* for a comprehensive list of changes.

 Appendix J of the *VoiceXML 2.0 Working Draft* has a comprehensive summary of deprecated elements, modified elements, and clarifications NOTE of the specification.

<form> Elements

<form> elements are the building blocks of a VoiceXML application. In a simplistic sense, VoiceXML forms are like HTML forms, collecting information from the user through input fields and then sending the input to the voice interpreter or a Web server to be processed.

A <form> can hold four types of elements: <field> for collecting user input, <var> for variables limited to the scope of the form, <catch> event handlers for processing specific events, and processing logic within the <filled> element. We will be examining each of these field-level items as our project expands.

<form> elements can carry two attributes. The *id* attribute is a unique name for the form, making it possible to access the form from within the current document or from an external document. A *scope* attribute within a <form> element defines the scope of the form's grammar. Grammars, rules that define what the user may speak as input, can have a scope at the complete document level or within that form's dialog only. The default is for the current dialog to be scoped locally.

The <form> element on line 4 of Listing 1.1 specifies the beginning of a dialog within the application. Think of a dialog as a conversation between the user and the application. An application may contain multiple dialogs, each contained within its own form. The order of processing of the dialogs is controlled by the FIA, which we will be looking at later in this project.

The *Hello, World* application has a single <form> element that contains a <prompt> element nested within a <block> element. Because no user input is requested, there is no grammar defined within the form.

<block> Elements

A <block> element on line 5 holds executable content. <block> elements can hold any other elements that need processing, such as assigning variables, playing audio files, moving to other dialogs, and handling errors. We will make extensive use of <block> as our projects develop.

<block> elements can carry three attributes: *name*, *expr*, and *cond*. The *name* attribute of a block is a unique identifier that is used to access the block during the FIA. The *expr* and *cond* attributes are part of the FIA form processing and will be discussed when we take a look at the FIA.

<prompt> Elements

The <block> contains a <prompt> element that will be output by the Text-to-Speech (TTS) interpreter. A <prompt> acts as a controlling mechanism for the output of computer-generated speech, prerecorded prompts, and audio files. The most useful attributes of the <prompt> element are *bargein*, *cond*, *count*, and *timeout*.

When a TTS engine is outputting prompts, it is sometimes more user friendly to let callers interrupt the output than to force them to listen to the complete reading or recording. Setting the *bargein* attribute to true allows the user input to be received immediately and causes the TTS engine to stop its output, returning control to the VoiceXML interpreter for further processing.

A *cond* attribute can be used to test for a specific condition, determining whether or not the <prompt> should be played. The default *cond* is true.

The VoiceXML interpreter keeps track of the number of times a <prompt> has been repeated. The default value of *count* is 1. It is incremented each time the prompt is played through. The *count* attribute is useful for checking how many times the <prompt> has been activated. By setting *count* within a <prompt>, a different output can be activated if the user is repeatedly returned to the prompt because of lack of input or inability to match the recognized grammar.

As an example of using *count*, look at the following code fragment:

```
<block>
  <prompt count="1">What is your phone number?</prompt>
  <prompt count="3">
    I need your phone number in order to proceed.
  </prompt>
</block>
```

The first prompt requests the user's phone number. The default error checking of the VoiceXML interpreter will wait for a specified amount of time for user response, increment the count attribute by 1, and read the prompt again if the user has not responded. If the user does not respond again, *count* is incremented to 3, and the second prompt is activated.

The *timeout* attribute holds a value of a time in seconds for activating a no-input error message. The format is a number in seconds followed by an s: 5s. The length of the default *timeout* is platform specific.

Section 4, System Output, of the *VoiceXML 2.0 Working Draft* is one of the most extensive sections in the document. It deals with how prompts are handled, available attributes, prompt selection, and input collection.

TIP

Strictly speaking, <prompt> elements are not mandatory when outputting TTS from within a block. Any literal text within a <block> element will be output by the VoiceXML processor. However, not using <prompt> elements limits the ability to supply attributes that will allow the end user to give input before the end of the prompt or for the developer to define a condition that would alter the output from the prompt.

TIP Many times errors will occur because the definitions of elements within the W3C specification restrict which elements may nest within other elements. By far, trying to nest elements incorrectly within other elements is the most common mistake when beginning VoiceXML development.

HANDS ON Create the *Hello World* template in your voice portal account.

Verify that the Application Is Working

Verify the output of the basic template by making a phone call to your application. If the words *Hello, World* are output, you are ready to move on to the next section. If the phrase is not heard, examine the error messages output by the development environment and make changes accordingly.

Figure 1.2 shows the output of the application when displayed within the Vocal Scripter at BeVocal. (See Chapter 2 for instructions on using the Vocal Scripter.) The Vocal Scripter can be used as a quick check for application process flow instead of using the telephone each time a new section is added to the template.

Figure 1.2 Screen shot of Vocal Scripter.

WARNING

Make sure your application is working properly at each step. Sometimes a simple missed quotation mark or improperly nested tag will keep you scratching your head for hours. It is part of the learning process. Find out where the simple errors are now, and you will know where to look for them when your applications stumble in the future.

Add Multiple Dialogs to the Template

A <form> within a VoiceXML application is a standalone dialog that can be accessed by using its unique name, or id. The application can have an unlimited number of forms, making it possible to create dialogs that move back and forth in a natural-sounding discourse with the user. Listing 1.2 is a simple application with forms for greeting the user, outputting content, and exiting the application.

```
1.  <?xml version="1.0"?>
2.
3.  <!DOCTYPE vxml
4.     PUBLIC
5.     "-//BeVocal Inc//VoiceXML 2.0//EN"
6.     "http://cafe.bevocal.com/libraries/dtd/vxml2-0-bevocal.dtd">
7.
8.  <vxml version="2.0">
9.
10.    <form id="greeting">
11.      <block>
12.        Welcome to Mars Colony 7.
13.        <goto next="#main-content"/>
14.      </block>
15.    </form>
16.
17.    <form id="maincontent">
18.      <block>
19.          Your first day on our colony will be full of surprises.
20.          Please don't hesitate to contact us if you get lost.
21.          <goto next="#goodbye"/>
22.      </block>
23.    </form>
24.
25.    <form id="goodbye">
26.      <block>
27.        <prompt>
```

Listing 1.2 Multiple dialogs.

```
28.          Enjoy your stay. Goodbye.
29.        </prompt>
30.      </block>
31.    </form>
32.
33. </vxml>
```

Listing 1.2 Multiple dialogs. *(continued)*

VoiceXML is a markup language that has a predefined set of elements, attributes, and rules on how each element may be used in an application. Placing a call to a DTD at the top of the application forces validation of the structure of the document against the rules established within the DTD.

DOCTYPE

The DOCTYPE instruction specifies what the root element will be and gives information about the creation of the DTD, who maintains it, and where it is located. Once the VoiceXML application has been debugged, there is no longer a need for a call to the DTD; it will only slow down the processing of your application.

Lines 3 through 6 of Listing 1.2 force validation of the application against the VoiceXML DTD.

TIP

Always use a call to the DTD when building a VoiceXML application. It will catch syntax errors and help with debugging along the way. When the application is completed, remove the call to the DTD to optimize your script.

A <form> element is used on lines 10 through 15 to create the opening dialog. The form is given the attribute *id*, which can be used to access this dialog from anywhere else in the application. The <block> element contains literal output for the TTS interpreter and ends with a <goto> element to control the process flow of the application.

<goto> Elements

The <goto> element is used to transition to other dialogs. It can be applied in three ways. It can move to another form item in the same dialog, jump to a completely new dialog within the current document, or transfer processing to another document entirely.

The *nextitem* attribute is used to send processing to another item within the same dialog. This overrides the FIA mechanism that automatically accesses the next form item in the dialog. The *next* attribute uses the name of another dialog within the same document as its value, preceded by a number (#) sign. This sign is called a fragment identifier. It is used to move directly to a specific location in the document.

If a form ends without a transition from a <goto> element, that is a signal for the application to terminate.

An application is automatically terminated when a form ends without a transition to another dialog.

An absolute or relative reference to an external VoiceXML document can also be the value of the *next* attribute. The reference may include a fragment identifier for accessing a specific dialog within the new document. By default, the first form within the document will be accessed unless there is a fragment identifier at the end of the Universal Resource Identifier (URI).

Many programmers are adamantly opposed to using goto statements. However, the VoiceXML language uses the <goto> element extensively for transitioning between dialogs. We will look at possible alternatives in future projects when examining the <submit> and <subdialog> elements.

Two other forms make up the balance of Listing 1.2. Taking a high-level overview, there are three forms: one for a greeting, one for holding content, and one for a graceful exit from the script. Most of the activity within the application will be developed within the *maincontent* form, using the *greeting* and *goodbye* forms as framing mechanisms for entering and exiting the script.

Using your existing *Hello World* template, create a VoiceXML application that has three forms: a greeting, a body, and an exit or goodbye. Verify that your forms are working before proceeding to the next section.

Be careful when creating ids and names for forms and fields. The name, or identifier as it is technically called, must begin with an ASCII letter or underscore. The name may then contain any sequence of ASCII letters, underscores, digits, or dollar signs. If the id or name does not adhere to the rules that have been established by the ECMA specification, a syntax check will not throw an error, but the application will not run. An extremely vague error message pointing to a line that contains a name or an id is usually a naming-convention problem.

Accept User Input with <field> and Yes/No Grammar

The *maincontent* form can be expanded to accept user input with the <field> element. Listing 1.3 shows that there can be multiple field level items in a single form.

```
1.  <form id="maincontent">
2.
3.     <block>
4.       Your first day on our colony will be full of surprises.
5.       Please don't hesitate to contact us if you get lost.
6.     </block>
7.
8.     <field name="accesscode">
9.
10.      <prompt>
11.        Do you have a community transporter access code?
12.      </prompt>
13.
14.      <grammar>
15.        <![CDATA[
16.          [yes no]
17.        ]]>
18.      </grammar>
19.
20.      <filled>
21.        <if cond="accesscode == 'yes'">
22.          <goto next="#goodbye"/>
23.        <else/>
24.            Your access code is the word "guest".
25.            <goto next="#goodbye"/>
26.        </if>
27.      </filled>
28.
29.    </field>
30.
31.  </form>
```

Listing 1.3   Accepting user input.

A <field> element acts like the HTML <input> element for creating a field within a form. The field accepts user input and stores it in a variable, using the field's name as the variable name. The fields are processed in document order unless <goto> is used to move to a specific item or form. Attributes for a <field> element include *name*, *cond*, *type*, and *modal*. We have previously seen *name* and *cond* attributes, but *type* and *modal* are new.

type and *modal* Attributes

VoiceXML has a set of built-in grammars that can be used to retrieve user input for common items such as a date, phone number, and currency. By using the *type* attribute and specifying a data type as its value, the developer does not have to include a grammar for that field. Built-in types include:

boolean	Tests for true or false
date	Accepts spoken date input as a date or a term, such as *tomorrow*
digits	Integers 0 through 9
currency	Is relative to the current locale
number	Accepts spoken input
phone	Accepts spoken phone numbers
time	Accepts input phrases for time and outputs time relative to the locale

The *modal* attribute within a <field> element mutes all global grammars from being accessed. The default is false, making global links and variables accessible within the dialog. Setting the value to true will temporarily disable all grammars except for those in the current field.

The opening <block> element in Listing 1.3, lines 3 through 6, is exactly the same as that in the basic application template previously developed. It presents the user with a short introduction to the form.

More on <field> Elements

The <field> element starting on line 8 of Listing 1.3 has a *name* attribute with the value of *accesscode*. It contains a verbal prompt for the user. A verbal prompt acts the way a literal text label does in HTML forms, giving a clue to the user about what is expected as input.

In order for a field to accept spoken input from the user, a grammar must be defined. The <grammar> element on lines 14 through 18 contains a set of utterances that the user may speak as acceptable input. We have set up a very restricted grammar, only accepting *yes* or *no* as a response. Any other response will be handled by the default error handling of the VoiceXML application.

The use of square brackets around the words *yes* and *no* identify the two words as individual items or tokens. As grammars become more complex, they will use other types of regular expression quantifiers to build various optional or mandatory utterances. These will be examined in future projects.

Placing the grammar within a CDATA section allows the developer to use special characters such as <, >, and & within the grammar. A CDATA section outputs its contents as literal text, without being parsed by the VoiceXML interpreter. As your grammars get more complex, it will become mandatory to encompass them within CDATA sections. In the simple case of the yes/no grammar, it is not necessary to use the CDATA section, but it is a good habit to develop.

The <filled> element on lines 20 through 27 is used to process any input that was recognized as acceptable grammar. In the application being developed, if the user says "yes" or "no," the field called *accesscode* will be assigned that value. The <filled> element can then perform some kind of action or processing based upon the user input.

<if> Elements

The <if> condition on lines 21 through 26 checks the value that is stored in the *accesscode* field and process accordingly. The *cond* attribute holds a test to see if a statement is true or false. If the *accesscode* field contains yes, which will be perceived as a true condition, go directly to the goodbye dialog. The <else/> tag hands any other condition that falls through the initial test. Because there were only two possibilities in the grammar, yes or no, the no condition is handled by giving users a temporary access code and then sending them to the goodbye dialog.

When testing a condition, the double equal sign (==) is used as comparison. A single equal sign (=) is used as an assignment operator, not a comparison. Another potential pothole when checking a condition is the single quotes inside a set of double quotes. The field name is not quoted, but the literal value that is being checked must be single quoted or it will be perceived as a variable or field name. A simple rule is if it is a field name or variable, do not use the single quotes within the double quotes.

Continue developing your template by inserting a field to accept user input within the *maincontent* form. Verify that your application works properly before proceeding to the next section.

Set Up Error Handling

Basic error handling, such as when the user makes an utterance that is not recognized by the grammar or the user does not supply any input at all when prompted, is the responsibility of the VoiceXML platform. The VoiceXML developer can override the platform error messages by including context-specific messages in the application.

Listing 1.4 adds explicit error handling to the previous script with <noinput> and <nomatch> elements. In addition, a series of help messages are inserted that use the *count* attribute for controlling access to the items.

```
1.  <?xml version="1.0"?>
2.
3.  <!DOCTYPE vxml
4.  PUBLIC
5.  "-//BeVocal Inc//VoiceXML 2.0//EN"
6.  "http://cafe.bevocal.com/libraries/dtd/vxml2-0-bevocal.dtd">
7.
8.  <vxml version="2.0">
9.
10.  <form id="greeting">
11.    <block>
12.      Welcome to Mars Colony 7.
13.      <goto next="#maincontent"/>
14.    </block>
15.  </form>
16.
17.  <form id="maincontent">
18.
19.    <block>
20.    Your first day on our colony will be full of
21.    surprises. Please don't hesitate to contact
22.    us if you get lost.
23.    </block>
24.
25.    <field name="accesscode">
26.
27.      <nomatch count="1">
28.        I'm sorry I don't speak Klingon.
29.        Please just say "yes" or "no".
30.      </nomatch>
31.      <nomatch count="2">
32.        There seems to be a problem with my translator.
33.        Try one more time.
34.        <reprompt/>
35.      </nomatch>
36.      <nomatch count="3">
37.        Please go to the nearest manned transporter to
38.        receive instructions on using the transporter.
39.        <goto next="#goodbye"/>
40.      </nomatch>
```

Listing 1.4 Error handling.

```
41.
42.    <noinput count="1">
43.      I didn't hear anything.
44.      <reprompt/>
45.    </noinput>
46.    <noinput count="2">
47.      To access the community transporter, you must have
48.      a transporter code.
49.      <reprompt/>
50.    </noinput>
51.    <noinput count="3">
52.      Sorry, I'm not a mind reader. Please go to the
53.      nearest manned transporter for help.
54.      <goto next="#goodbye"/>
55.    </noinput>
56.
57.    <help count="1">
58.      To move around the colony you will need a code
59.      to access the transporter beam.
60.      <reprompt/>
61.    </help>
62.    <help count="2">
63.      When you were booked to arrive at the colony,
64.      you were issued a transporter code. If you
65.      have lost your code, speak the word "guest"
66.      at any transporter and a new one will be issued.
67.      <goto next="#goodbye"/>
68.    </help>
69.
70.    <prompt>
71.      Do you have a community transporter access code?
72.    </prompt>
73.
74.    <grammar>
75.      <![CDATA[
76.        [yes no]
77.      ]]>
78.    </grammar>
79.
80.    <filled>
81.      <if cond="accesscode == 'yes'">
82.        <goto next="#goodbye"/>
83.      <else/>
84.        Your access code is the word "guest".
85.        <goto next="#goodbye"/>
86.      </if>
87.    </filled>
```

Listing 1.4 Error handling. *(continues)*

```
88.  </field>
89.  </form>
90.
91.  <form id="goodbye">
92.  <block>
93.    <prompt>
94.       Enjoy your stay. Goodbye.
95.    </prompt>
96.  </block>
97.  </form>
98.
99.  </vxml>
```

Listing 1.4   Error handling. *(continued)*

The <field> element named *accesscode* starting on line 25 contains a prompt for a user to input a yes or no response. Lines 27 through 68 handle the response if the user says something other than yes or no.

<nomatch> and <noinput> Elements

If the developer has not provided an explicit nomatch event, the platform must handle the event with a message such as "I'm sorry, I didn't understand." Default handlers for <help>, <nomatch>, and <noinput> events are mandated by the VoiceXML 2.0 specification. Within the specification, see section 5.2.5 for a comprehensive list of default handlers.

NOTE   **The VoiceXML 2.0 specification mandates that specific events such as <help>, <nomatch>, and <noinput> have default values set by the platform. The developer may override the platform responses by invoking explicit handlers for the events. See section 5.2.5 of the VoiceXML 2.0 specification for more details.**

The <nomatch> and <noinput> elements on lines 27 through 55 override the platform-supplied error messages.

The *count* attribute in each of the <nomatch> and <noinput> elements keeps track of the number of times the user has responded inappropriately to a prompt. There is no assigned limit to the number of <nomatch> or <noinput> elements that may be contained within a field, but a good user interface will offer some kind of exit after a limited number of errors. The exit could be a message stating that something is not working properly, sending users to the *goodbye* form or dynamically transferring them to a live receptionist, as we will see in Project 3.

The <reprompt/> element on line 34 sends processing to the original prompt that is trying to elicit a response from the user. Notice that <reprompt/> is not used in the first <nomatch>. It is assumed that the user still remembers the prompt but just hasn't responded correctly. The third <nomatch> element outputs a detailed help message to the user and then exits the application through the *goodbye* form.

Users who reach a third <nomatch> or <noinput> situation are usually lost within the application, do not know the correct utterances to the prompt, or need help. Provide some kind of mechanism that will move them to a different part of the application or connect them with an operator for personal assistance.

TIP

Lines 42 through 55 handle processing with the <noinput> element when the user does not provide any input. Just as with the <nomatch> element, the platform will provide defaults if error handling is not specified. The *count* attribute keeps track of the number of times there is no input from the user.

Even if you do not supply any <nomatch> or <noinput> elements, the VoiceXML platform will output simple error messages. This is mandated by the VoiceXML specification. In most cases, however, it is more appropriate to supply context-sensitive messages for a more user-friendly speech interface.

NOTE

The <help> elements on lines 57 through 68 provide context-sensitive help messages when the user speaks the word "help." If help messages are not provided by the developer, the platform will supply a message by default, but it is usually something as useless as "There is no help message available." Once again, the *count* attribute and the <reprompt/> element can be used to create context-sensitive help messages.

Let the user know that help messages are available by mentioning it at the entrance to your application. "Welcome to Mars Colony 7. You may say 'Help' at any time if you are having difficulty."

TIP

Put error handling into your application with the <nomatch>, <noinput>, and <help> elements. Place a call to your application and verify the responses when the various events happen.

HANDS ON

<help>, <noinput>, and <nomatch> messages should get longer and more explicit as the count attribute gets higher. The user needs more instructions in order to proceed and does not understand what has been requested.

TIP

Form Interpretation Algorithm

The underlying processing sequence within any VoiceXML application is controlled by the FIA, which determines when each form item will be visited by checking the guard condition of the field-level items. In this section, we will examine how form items are selected for processing, how guard conditions are set, and the order in which processing occurs.

 This section is a brief overview of the concepts of the FIA. Extensive explanations and examples are in sections 2.1.6 and Appendix C of the VoiceXML 2.0 Working Draft.

Basic Concepts of FIA

As we have seen while developing the Basic Pages project, forms are used to create dialogs and interaction between the VoiceXML application and the user. The FIA defines the sequence for processing events once a form has been accessed. The interpretation is done in three stages: select, collect, and process. A field-level item is selected for processing, user information is collected for that item, and the input is processed. The FIA continues until all items within the form have been processed, or processing transitions to another dialog.

Selection Phase

During the selection phase, the FIA accesses field-level items within a form in document order: first seen, first processed. See Table 1.1 for a list of field-level items. Each form item has a guard condition associated with it that determines whether or not the item should be visited during processing. By default, a field-level item's guard condition is set to false, forcing the item to be visited. The FIA checks the guard condition of an item and moves to the collection phase for that item if the guard condition is false. When the guard condition is true, the item is skipped.

Table 1.1   Field-Level Items

FIELD-LEVEL ITEM	DEFINITION
<field>	Declares an input field in a form
<object>	Interact with a custom extension
<record>	Records an audio sample
<subdialog>	Invokes another dialog as a subdialog of the current one
<transfer>	Transfers the caller to another destination

Collection Phase

The collection phase is used to accept input from the user and check the input against the grammars active for that item. Upon entrance to the field item, the FIA will queue and play all prompts and then wait for user input. The guard condition of the item is set to true when an utterance is recognized. The user input is stored in the field's name variable and can be accessed during the processing phase.

Processing Phase

The processing phase takes the input from the collection phase and processes it according to its context. When a user utterance is recognized as part of the collection phase, the FIA will set the guard condition of that item to true, making it inaccessible for selection. The actions within the <filled> element are executed and processing continues by selecting the next available form item.

Error handlers are activated if there is a problem with the user input. The FIA will respond with the defined condition within the handler, which could be to exit the application, replay the prompt, or transition to another item as defined by the developer.

Ending the FIA

The selection-collection-process sequence continues until all guard conditions within the form have been set to true. Transitions to other dialogs or documents are handled with a <goto> or <submit> element. If a transition to another dialog is not found, the processing ends and the application is terminated.

 Processing does not automatically fall through from <form> to <form>. An explicit <goto> or <submit> must be used to transition to another form or document once all of the guard conditions within the form have been set to WARNING true. If there is not a transition from the form, the application will terminate.

Analyzing the FIA Sequence

To get a clearer picture of how the FIA moves through an application, we will run the script from Listing 1.4 and use the output from the Vocal Scripter and Log Browser at BeVocal to see the behind-the-scenes processing. Listing 1.5 shows the output from the Vocal Scripter when the script is run.

The first line of output in Listing 1.5 comes from the *greeting* form. Lines 2 through 5 are generated from the first <block> within *maincontent*.

Line 6 is a prompt, requesting a response from the user. The user input does not match anything within the grammar for that field, so the output on lines 9 and 10 come from the <nomatch> element, which has a count of 1. The user then responds with "no," which is an acceptable response, generating an access code word. The *goodbye* form outputs a message and the application terminates.

```
1.   OUTPUT --> Welcome to Mars Colony 7.
2.   OUTPUT --> Your first day on our colony will be
3.            full of surprises.
4.   OUTPUT --> Please don't hesitate to contact us
5.            if you get lost.
6.   OUTPUT --> Do you have a community transporter
7.            access code?
8.   USER --> what?
9.   OUTPUT --> I'm sorry I don't speak Klingon.
10.          Please just say "yes" or "no".
11. USER --> no
12. OUTPUT --> Your access code is the word "guest".
13. OUTPUT --> Enjoy your stay. Goodbye.
```

Listing 1.5   Vocal Scripter output.

Listing 1.6 is a partial output from the Log Browser. It will allow us to follow the FIA as it selects, collects, and processes the form field values.

NOTE   **Most of the major portals have some kind of logging system so that developers can view the output after an application is run. Check the documentation on your platform for more information.**

```
1. Entering FIA for: form
2.   Attributes: scope='dialog'id='greeting';
3. FIA: Initialization Phase:
4. Initializing item block3174 at : 11
5. FIA: Select Phase
6. Guard condition for block block3174 is true
7. FIA: Item Selected: block block3174
8.
9. Setting block form item variable block3174 to true.
10.
11. Execute Content for <block> at line 11
12. GOTO : next attribute is: #maincontent
13. Finished Executing Content
14. Playing all queued prompts
15. Playing prompt: TTS: Welcome to Mars Colony 7.(bargein)
16.
17. Entering FIA for: form
```

Listing 1.6   Log Browser output.

```
18.   Attributes: scope='dialog'id='maincontent';
19. FIA: Initialization Phase:
20. Initializing item block3178 at : 19
21. Initializing item accesscode at : 24
22.
23. FIA: Select Phase
24. Guard condition for block block3178 is true
25. FIA: Item Selected: block block3178
26.
27. Setting block form item variable block3178 to true.
28.
29. Execute Content for <block> at line 19
30. Finished Executing Content
31. FIA: Process Phase
32. FIA: Select Phase
33. Guard condition for block block3178 is false
34. Guard condition for field accesscode is true
35. FIA: Item Selected: field accesscode
36. Calculating queued prompts.
37. Current counter is : 1
38. Adding prompt : prompt3203 to queued prompt list
39. Executing field item accesscode at : 24
40.
41. Playing prompt: TTS: Your first day on our colony
42.   will be full of surprises. Please don't hesitate
43.   to contact us if you get lost. (barge)
44. Playing prompt: TTS: Do you have a community transporter
45.   access code? (barge)
46.
47. Performing recognition
48. THROW nomatch: Platform error:{
49.   results=[{
50.    interp=[]
51.    text="what?"
52.    probability=1
53.    confidence=100
54.   }]
55.   type="REJECTED"
56.   textRecresult=""
57.   numFrames=5
58. }
59.
60. FIA: Process Phase
61. Searching for handler for nomatch; count = 1
62. Execute Content for <nomatch> at line 26
63. Finished Executing Content
64.
```

Listing 1.6 Log Browser output. *(continues)*

```
65. FIA: Select Phase
66. Guard condition for block block3178 is false
67. Guard condition for field accesscode is true
68.
69. FIA: Item Selected: field accesscode
70. Executing field item accesscode at : 24
71. Playing prompt: TTS: I'm sorry I don't speak Klingon.
72.    Please just say "yes" or "no". (barge)
```

Listing 1.6   Log Browser output. *(continued)*

Keep a copy of Listing 1.4 handy so that you can compare the script to what is being seen by the FIA.

When a VoiceXML application is accessed, the FIA accesses the first form in the application by default. Lines 1 and 2 of Listing 1.6 confirm that the FIA has accessed a form whose *id* is *greeting* and whose grammar *scope* is set to *dialog*. Looking at the script in Listing 1.4, you will find that the scope for the form's grammar has not been set, so the default value of scope is set by the platform.

The Initialization Phase referred to on line 3 sets the count values in all applicable fields to 1 and initializes all field-level variables to undefined or an *expr* value supplied by the developer. When a variable is set to undefined, it makes that field item accessible during the selection phase. The developer may set a default value for a field item that would make the FIA skip over the item during processing. We will see uses for this when we look at the <clear> element in another project.

In addition to a variable name, each field-level item also contains a guard condition that is set to true by default. The guard condition must be true in order for an item to be accessible to the FIA. The developer may insert a conditional statement within the *expr* attribute to force the FIA to evaluate whether the item should be accessed.

Line 11 of Listing 1.4 has a <block> element that is initialized to begin the FIA processing of the greeting form. The guard condition for the block is checked on line 6 of Listing 1.6 to verify it is true, allowing the FIA to proceed to the next phase of selection. The block item itself is then selected, the variable value of the block is set to true on line 9, and the content of the block is executed. Access to the <goto> element is confirmed on line 12, setting up the transfer of processing to the *maincontent* form.

Because there is no collection phase in a <block> element, the processing phase begins. Line 14 of Listing 1.6 confirms that all prompts are queued and ready to play. Line 15 confirms that a TTS prompt is being output. Once the processing has been completed, the FIA begins again within the *maincontent* form, having been explicitly sent there from the <goto> element on line 12.

The *maincontent* form is initialized on lines 19 through 21. The select phase then checks the guard condition for <block> and finds it to be true, allowing the FIA to select the block to queue for processing and setting the guard condition to false. The select phase begins again at line 32, skipping over the <block> item and selecting the *accesscode* field item. The FIA checks the *count* attribute and, finding it to be 1, adds it to the queued prompts list. The prompts are played starting on line 41 during the processing phase and then the FIA waits for user input.

Users may interrupt a prompt depending upon its *barge* condition. If the condition is set to true, as it is by default, experienced users will not have to wait for the prompt to be completed before speaking their input. A barge condition might be set to false if the developer wants to force the user to listen to a complete prompt, for example, when an advertiser is involved.

Lines 47 through 58 check to see if the user input is recognized. A *nomatch* error is thrown because the input of "what?" does not match the available grammar. The *probability* and *confidence* levels are used by the FIA to determine the likelihood that the utterance is a part of the grammar.

The processing phase checks to see if the developer has provided an error handler for *nomatch* items with a count of 1. In this case, it finds one on line 27 of the script. If no explicit handler is found, the platform will output a generic *nomatch* error message. The *nomatch* prompt is played on lines 71 and 72, allowing the user another chance at responding.

The FIA will continue through the form until all field items have been set to true and their corresponding guard conditions are true. If there is no transition to another form or document from a form, the application will terminate, as demonstrated in the good-bye form of Listing 1.4.

 Call your application or run it through the Vocal Scripter. View the output in the Log Browser, tracking the FIA as it moves through each form and field item.

HANDS ON

Insert Meta Data for the Project Description

Meta data is information about the VoiceXML application that is used to identify the application to other programs. The information is not heard or viewed by the user of the application, but it is useful for storing author information, search engine terms, and other application-specific items. Listing 1.7 shows the basic meta data elements that are recommended by the W3C.

```
1.  <vxml version="2.0">
2.
3.    <meta name="author"        content="Eliza, Counsel to the Universe"/>
4.    <meta name="copyright"    content="Mars Colony 7: 2041"/>
5.    <meta name="description"
6.       content="Welcome to Mars Colony 7, the solar system's premier
7.       jumping off point for the rest of the universe."/>
8.    <meta name="keywords"     content="Mars, colony, space vacations"/>
9.    <meta name="maintainer"
         content="DynamicData@colony7.mars.solarsystem"/>
10.   <meta name="robots"          content="robot-rules.txt"/>
11.
```

Listing 1.7 Meta data. *(continues)*

```
12. <form id="greeting">
13.    <block>
14.       Welcome to Mars Colony 7.
15.       <goto next="#maincontent"/>
16.    </block>
17.  </form>
18. ...
19. </vxml>
```

Listing 1.7   Meta data. *(continued)*

Each <meta> element carries a *name* attribute followed by a *content* attribute. Lines 3 through 10 display each of the <meta> elements recommended as a minimum by the VoiceXML specification. The author, copyright, and maintainer <meta> elements contain information about the creation of the application. The description and keyword <meta> elements are used by search engines to know how to index your site and make it available to users who might be searching for the type of content contained on your site. The robot <meta> element points to a location on your system that describes to the search robots which documents should or should not be accessed when creating a search index for your site.

It is not mandatory to include <meta> elements within your application, but it is useful for providing application-to-application information. The W3C specification suggests that author, copyright, description, keywords, maintainer, and robots meta elements are used as a minimum set of information for each application.

NOTE

Include the basic <meta> elements within your application and verify that the program works exactly as before.

HANDS ON

Final Thoughts

We have come a long way since beginning this project. You now have a template that can be used for developing more-complex applications. By using this template, your future applications can handle user input errors, include application-to-application information through <meta> elements, process multiple dialogs within a single VoiceXML document, and build fields and grammars for accepting user input.

The listings for this project can be downloaded from the BeVocal Web site at cafe.bevocal.com/wiley/10projects. They are saved as text files, useful as templates for creating your own VoiceXML scripts.

In the next project, we will expand the basic VoiceXML application by developing links to other pages.

Creating Links

One of the reasons the World Wide Web continues to grow is because it gives programmers the ability to create links to a wide array of resources. A "mom and pop" online bookstore can sell any book in print by linking to Amazon, Barnes and Noble, or Books-A-Million. VoiceXML has several ways to create links. In this project, we'll investigate the tricks and traps associated with vocal linking by creating an information resource for the Mars 7 Colony Visitor's Bureau.

THE PROBLEM

A VoiceXML application that has any kind of complexity will use multiple data sources and content resources for its output. How can the application access the data sources through one central document?

THE SOLUTION

Create complex application flow using the various linking mechanisms available in VoiceXML to access a variety of data sources, internally and externally.

Project Description

This project demonstrates the linking mechanisms available in VoiceXML. A client calls the Information Center on Mars Colony 7. The automated telephone assistant greets the user and then offers information on a list of subjects. The user chooses a subject from the main menu. For ease of script maintenance, the data for each of the subjects is stored in a separate document and is accessed by links from the main document. The information on the subject selected is gathered from the external documents and output to the user.

To complete this project, you will:

1. Create a Welcome template.

2. Use <goto> to control call flow.

3. Build conditional processing in fields.

4. Create global links.

5. Develop a <menu> of items.

6. Link menus as hierarchies.

7. Consolidate responses with <subdialog>.

8. Handle requests dynamically with <submit>.

You Will Need

✔ **A connection to the Internet**

✔ **A developer's account with a voice portal**

✔ **Example scripts from cafe.bevocal.com/wiley/10projects**

✔ **A Web server capable of CGI processing**

✔ **Perl script for handling dynamic processing**

VoiceXML Elements Used in This Project

ELEMENT NAME	DESCRIPTION
<block>	A container of (noninteractive) executable code
<choice>	Defines a menu item
<else>	Used in <if> elements
<elseif>	Used in <if> elements
<enumerate>	Shorthand for enumerating the choices in a menu

VoiceXML Elements Used in This Project *(Continued)*

ELEMENT NAME	DESCRIPTION
<field>	Declares an input field in a form
<filled>	An action executed when fields are filled
<form>	A dialog for presenting information and collecting data
<goto>	Go to another dialog in the same or different document
<grammar>	Specifies a speech recognition or DTMF grammar
<if>	Simple conditional logic
<link>	Specifies a transition common to all dialogs in the link's scope
<menu>	A dialog for choosing amongst alternative destinations
<noinput>	Catches a noinput event
<nomatch>	Catches a nomatch event
<prompt>	Queues speech synthesis and audio output to the user
<return>	Return from a subdialog
<subdialog>	Invoke another dialog as a subdialog of the current one
<submit>	Submits values to a document server
<vxml>	Top-level element in each VoiceXML document

Source: *VoiceXML 2.0 Working Draft*, section 1.4

Call Flow

Figure 2.1 diagrams the call flow for the final application. The client is greeted by the vocal assistant and is asked about their previous visits to the colony. The client responds and is given either information related to their response or is walked through a dialog to gather more specific information. When processing is finished, the program exits.

Create a Placeholder Template

Four elements within VoiceXML handle transitioning to other dialogs: <choice>, <goto> <link>, <subdialog>, and <submit>; each controls the transition in a different way. We will start this project with a review of the <goto> element described in Project 1 and then investigate the three other elements as alternative ways to move around the application.

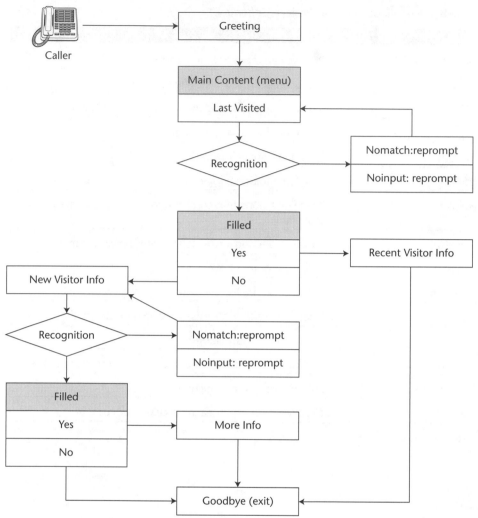

Figure 2.1   Call flow of expanded VoiceXML application.

Review of <goto>

Project 2 begins by extracting sections of Project 1 to create a placeholder template. The template defines the major dialog areas within the script. Listing 2.1 shows three <form> elements that are used to create the greeting, hold content, and exit the script, respectively.

```
1. <?xml version="1.0"?>
2.
3. <!DOCTYPE vxml
4.   PUBLIC
5.   "-//BeVocal Inc//VoiceXML 2.0//EN"
6.   "http://cafe.bevocal.com/libraries/dtd/vxml2-0-bevocal.dtd">
7.
8. <vxml version="2.0">
9.
10. <form id="greeting">
11.   <block>
12.     Welcome to Mars Colony 7.
13.     <goto next="#maincontent"/>
14.   </block>
15. </form>
16.
17. <form id="maincontent">
18.   <block>
19.     I am your personal vocal attendant.
20.     <goto next="#goodbye"/>
21.   </block>
22. </form>
23.
24. <form id="goodbye">
25.   <block>
26.     <prompt>
27.       Enjoy your stay. Goodbye.
28.     </prompt>
29.   </block>
30. </form>
31.
32. </vxml>
```

Listing 2.1 Placeholder template.

The *greeting* and *maincontent* forms transition to new dialogs with the <goto> element. Use of <goto> was covered in Project 1. To quickly review, <goto> is used to transition from one dialog to another, either within the same document or to an external document. If a form does not contain an explicit transition to another dialog, the application is terminated.

HANDS ON

Use your developer account at BeVocal to create the VoiceXML script shown in Listing 2.1. Verify that the script is working properly before proceeding.

Conditional Processing

In addition to transferring processing to other dialogs within an application, <goto> elements can also control the flow of processing within a single form. Listing 2.2 shows simple conditional processing within a form that uses <goto> for transitioning to various field level items.

```
1.  <form id="maincontent">
2.    <block>
3.      I am your personal vocal attendant.
4.    </block>
5.
6.    <field name="lastVisit">
7.      <grammar>
8.        <![CDATA[
9.          [ yes no ]
10.        ]]>
11.      </grammar>
12.
13.      <prompt>
14.        Have you visited the colony within
15.        the past 6 months?
16.      </prompt>
17.
18.      <filled>
19.        <if cond="lastVisit == 'yes'">
20.          <goto nextitem="visitedYes"/>
21.        <else/>
22.          <goto nextitem="visitedNo"/>
23.        </if>
24.      </filled>
25.    </field>
26.
27.    <block name="visitedYes">
28.      Welcome back.
29.      <goto next="#goodbye"/>
30.    </block>
31.
32.    <block name="visitedNo">
33.      Please contact visitor services if you need anything.
34.      <goto next="#goodbye"/>
35.    </block>
36.
37.  </form>
```

Listing 2.2   Field-level transitions.

Listing 2.2 expands the *maincontent* form to include an introductory block, a field-level grammar, a prompt for user input, a conditional check to see where processing should transition, and two blocks to accept the <goto> transition.

The *lastvisit* <field> contains a simple grammar definition on lines 7 through 11. The <prompt> on lines 13 through 16 elicits a response from users regarding their previous visit to the colony. If the user utterance is recognized as acceptable grammar, the <filled> element is accessed and the <if> statement beginning on line 19 is processed.

The CDATA section surrounding the acceptable utterances is not mandatory in this instance, but it is a good habit to develop for future construction of more complex grammars.

The input stored in *lastvisit* is checked against the string *yes* on line 19, and if found true, processing transitions to the field item named *visitedYes*.

This is different from what we saw in Project 1. Here a <goto> element transitions to another field item with the *nextitem* attribute, as opposed to the *next* attribute, which moves to another form or document. The default sequence for processing form items is document order, each item being selected by FIA in sequence until the last item is accessed or processing is transferred to another dialog. The *nextitem* attribute forces the FIA to access a specific field item within the current form, overriding the default access sequence.

The <else> clause in the <if> condition on line 21 handles a *no* (negative) response from the user and sends processing to the *visitedNo* block within the same form.

At this stage of the project's development, the *visitedYes* <block> and the *visitedNo* <block> contain simple TTS output and then transfer processing to the *goodbye* form, exiting the script. The two blocks are mainly placeholders to be used for inserting more complex processing as the application is developed.

When starting out, it is easy to get the *next* and *nextitem* syntax mixed up. Think of *nextitem* as a local identifier that stays within is designated area. The *next* attribute has a much broader scope and is used to move to other forms or other documents.

Change the existing script for this project to include the new *maincontent* form. Check the syntax of the application with the VoiceXML Checker and then run the application. Verify that processing is completed through the three main sections and that the conditional statement works before proceeding to the next section.

More Conditional Processing

Conditional processing within a VoiceXML document can be much more than just checking the input against a grammar. A condition can test the results of a computation, force multiple conditions to be true, or select one of a number of possible conditions. Standard math operators such as +, -, *, !=, and == are available for testing a condition. Listing 2.3 shows examples of conditional processing using the operators.

```
1. <if cond="visitedYes"> : variable visitedYes must contain a value.
2. <if cond="planet == 3"> : variable planet must contain 3 as its value.
3. <if cond="total > 1000"> : variable total must be greater than 1000.
4. <if cond="total &lt; 1000> : variable total must be less than 1000.
5. <if cond="number-of-visits != 0"> :  value of number-of-visits does
   not equal 0.
6. <if cond="home =='terra' || home =='earth'"> : value of home must be
   terra or earth.
7. <if cond="planet == 'mars' &amp;&amp; month == 'june'"> :  value of
   planet must be mars and value of month must be june.
8. <if cond="verify-indentity(name,ssn)"> : verify return value from
   verify-indentity() function is true.
```

Listing 2.3   Examples of conditional operators.

Example 7 contains an example of an XML entity in place of literal ampersand symbols. There are three special characters in XML that must be escaped as entities when used within parsed text: <, <=, and &. Each of these must be replaced with its entity equivalent in order to satisfy the VoiceXML parser.

 Conditional syntax must adhere to the ECMAScript standard as set by the ECMA at www.ecma.ch/ecma1/STAND/ECMA-262.htm.

NOTE

Expanding the VoiceXML Script

<field> elements are more versatile than <block> elements because they can be used to hold grammars and prompts for extracting information from the client. The two ending <block> elements in Listing 2.2 can be changed to hold more prompts and conditional processing by replacing the <block> elements with <field> elements, as shown in Listing 2.4.

```
1.  <field name="visitedYes">
2.    <grammar>
3.     <![CDATA[
4.       [ yes no ]
5.     ]]>
6.    </grammar>
7.
8.    <prompt>
9.      Welcome back. There have been some additions to
10.   the colony in the past few weeks. Would you like
11.   to hear about them?
12.   </prompt>
13.
14.   <filled>
15.    <if cond="visitedYes=='yes'">
16.      There is free, hot pizza available on level seven.
17.      Space gliding is no longer available on the golf
18.      course in parsec 391.
19.      The Black Sun tavern is confined to use by those
20.      110 years old and above.
21.      <goto next="#goodbye"/>
22.    <else/>
23.      <goto next="#goodbye"/>
24.    </if>
25.   </filled>
26.  </field>
27.
28.  <field name="visitedNo" type="boolean">
29.    <prompt>
30.    The colony has Visitor Booths for
31.    newcomers. Would you like to hear about them?
32.    </prompt>
33.
34.    <filled>
35.    <if cond="visitedNo=='yes'">
36.      Visitor booths are located every 10 parsecs
37.      within each quadrant. Stand in front of a
38.      visitor booth and say "Hello, Hal" to access
39.      the latest events and activities within that
40.      quadrant.
41.      <goto next="#goodbye"/>
42.    <else/>
43.      <goto next="#goodbye"/>
44.    </if>
45.   </filled>
46.  </field>
```

Listing 2.4   Expanding the VoiceXML script.

Listing 2.4 has changed the <block> elements to <field> elements, keeping the same name. This allows the field items to be used as extended prompts and additional conditional processing. A question is asked, a response is elicited, and processing proceeds depending upon the response. Throughout, <goto> is used to pass processing on to the appropriate section.

The *visitedYes* field begins with a simple yes/no grammar definition on lines 2 through 6. A <prompt> welcoming the user back is output, confirming to users that their previous response was understood and the dialog can continue. The <prompt> requests additional input from users, asking if they would like to hear about recent additions to the colony. If the user says *yes*, a list of recent changes to the colony is spoken and then processing jumps to the *goodbye* form for a graceful exit from the application.

 Nesting an <if> element within a <filled> element is a good way to handle responses to yes/no input.

TIP

The *visitedNo* field starting on line 28 has a *type* attribute of *boolean*, activating a built-in grammar provided by the VoiceXML platform. The *boolean type* checks for a positive or negative response. If the user utters a positive response, the <if> condition outputs information about visitor booths and then passes processing to the *goodbye* form, whereas a negative response jumps directly to the *goodbye* form. Project 1 has extensive coverage of the *type* attribute and its applicable values.

 Using the *type* attribute within a field is like having a set of predefined modules that handle basic grammar creation.

TIP

 Change the appropriate <block> elements to <field> elements in your application, adding prompts and conditional processing. Use the *type* attribute within the <field> elements to take advantage of predefined boolean grammar. Upload your application and verify that it is functioning properly before proceeding.

HANDS ON

Accessing External Resources

Not only can the <goto> element be used to transfer processing within a single document, but it can also transfer to external resources. The <goto> elements all point to items within the document in the current script. To make the application more robust, they can point to a URI instead, allowing content to be stored as external resources. Isolating content to external resources makes it possible to build an application that does not have to be reprogrammed every time the content changes.

Application Root Document

A VoiceXML application can contain many documents and resources linked together by an application root document. One document within the application is designated by the developer to be the application root document. It contains all global variables, links, grammars, properties, and catch events for the application.

Other documents that make up the application are considered leaves of the application root. In order for a document to be considered part of an application, the *application* attribute within the <vxml> element must be set to the application root document name. However, the application root document itself will not carry the *application* attribute. There is no limit to the number of leaves within an application.

The application root document is always loaded when an application is running. This creates two possible scenarios: Either the root document is processing by itself or one of the leaf documents is processing while the application root document is still loaded.

In this project, links.vxml will be designated as the application root document. Listing 2.5 shows the first external document of the links.vxml application.

```
1.  <?xml version="1.0"?>
2.
3.  <!DOCTYPE vxml
4.  PUBLIC
5.  "-//BeVocal Inc//VoiceXML 2.0//EN"
6.  "http://cafe.bevocal.com/libraries/dtd/vxml2_0_bevocal.dtd">
7.
8.  <vxml version="2.0" application="links.vxml">
9.
10. <form id="greeting">
11.    <block>
12.       You are now in the Previous Visitor Info Center.
13.    </block>
14.
15. <field name="timeframe">
16.
17. <grammar>
18.   <![CDATA[
19.     [ week month continue ]
20.   ]]>
21. </grammar>
22.
23. <prompt>
24.   If you were here within the last week, say "Week".
25.   If you were here within the last month, say "Month".
26.   Otherwise, say "Continue".
```

Listing 2.5 First external resource. *(continues)*

```
27. </prompt>
28.
29. <filled>
30. <if cond="timeframe=='continue'">
31.   It has been over a month since your last visit.
32.   <goto next="links-changes.vxml#continue"/>
33. <elseif cond="timeframe=='month'"/>
34.   Several things have changed since your visit last month.
35.   <goto next="links-changes.vxml#month"/>
36. <else/>
37.   Welcome back. It is good to see you again so soon.
38.   Nothing has changed in the past week.
39.   <goto next="links.vxml#goodbye"/>
40. </if>
41. </filled>
42.
43. </field>
44. </form>
45.
46. </vxml>
```

Listing 2.5   First external resource. *(continued)*

The beginning of Listing 2.5 looks the same as other VoiceXML applications we have created except for the *application* attribute within the <vxml> element on line 8. The links.vxml document created in the first phase of this project is designated as the application root document.

The *greeting* form beginning on line 10 contains a confirmation to users that they have entered a new area in the application. Because there are no visual clues for users within a VoiceXML application, verbal confirmation is necessary for users to keep a mental image of their location within the dialog.

Use verbal prompts when transitioning to a new area in the application to help users feel a sense of structure.

TIP

The *timeframe* field on line 15 starts with definitions of the grammar expected as input from the user. The grammar terms are surrounded with square brackets, making each word an individual token. The <prompt> starting on line 23 requests information on the last time the user visited the colony.

Each line within the prompt ends with a word from the grammar, letting the user know what values will be acceptable as input. A good user interface will give explicit instructions on what words will be recognized as appropriate utterances for a field.

TIP

When asking for information from the user, always include an appropriate response from the defined grammar as part of the prompt. It is extremely difficult to process open-ended questions when the user does not know what is expected as input.

The <filled> element on line 29 sets up a conditional statement to process the user input. The value stored in the *timeframe* variable is checked for the word *continue*. If the condition is found to be true, a short <prompt> is output on line 31 and processing transitions to the links-changes.vxml document.

Because each of the fields within an application document contains a unique *name* attribute, the fields can be accessed directly when making a call to the document. Notice the use of the number sign on line 32 to specify a certain location, a fragment identifier, within the called document. A fragment identifier may also be used without reference to a URI, transferring processing to another form within the current document.

NOTE

You can access a specific location within a document by using a fragment identifier.

If the test condition on line 30 is false, processing falls through to the <elseif> condition on line 33. The *timeframe* variable is checked against *month,* and if true, sends processing to the *month* fragment identifier in the links-changes.vxml document.

The final <if> condition is checked with the <else/> element on line 36. If the user has visited the colony within the past week, acknowledgment is given on line 37, with processing moving back to the root document on line 39. The fragment identifier at the end of the URI specifies that access should be made directly into the *goodbye* form when making the transition.

WARNING

Root document variables and grammars are always available when an application is running. However, the form names are not considered variables and cannot be accessed without a direct call to the document.

HANDS ON

Create the links-previousvisitor-info.vxml script and upload it to the same directory as the links.vxml script.

Another External Data Source

Listing 2.6 makes a call to links-changes.vxml. The links-changes.vxml file will hold the various changes within the colony based upon a specific timeframe. The form names within the document are used as fragment identifiers when accessing the document.

```
1.  <?xml version="1.0"?>
2.  <!DOCTYPE vxml
3.   PUBLIC
4.   "-//BeVocal Inc//VoiceXML 2.0//EN"
5.   "http://cafe.bevocal.com/libraries/dtd/vxml2-0-bevocal.dtd">
6.
7.  <vxml version="2.0" application="links.vxml">
8.
9.  <form id="continue">
10. <block>
11. Within the past six months the following changes
12. have taken place in the colony.
13. The holodeck is now open 36 hours per day, closed
14. from 36 hours to 40 hours, solar time.
15. The golf course can be used for solar gliding,
16. provided you have a reservation.
17. Shuttle crafts to the lunar hotsprings may be paged
18. by saying the words "lunar springs" at any visitor
19. vid-phone.
20. <goto next="links.vxml#goodbye"/>
21. </block>
22. </form>
23.
24. <form id="month">
25.   <block>
26.    Within the last month the following change
27.    has taken place in the colony.
28.    The golf course can be used for solar gliding,
29.    provided you have a reservation.
30.    <goto next="links.vxml#goodbye"/>
31.   </block>
32. </form>
33.
34. </vxml>
```

Listing 2.6   Another external resource.

Listing 2.6 contains two forms, *continue* and *month*. Line 7 sets the application root document to links.vxml. The form ids are used by the calling application to access specific locations within the document. The <goto> elements on lines 20 and 30 link back to the links.vxml document, using fragment identifiers to transfer processing to the *goodbye* form instead of accessing the file from the first form dialog.

Create the links-changes.vxml document and store it with the rest of the pages in your application.

HANDS ON

Setting Up the *maincontent* Form

To finish this phase of development, the *maincontent* form of the root document must be changed in order to access the external documents.

The *lastVisit* field in Listing 2.7 holds a simple prompt with a call on line 20 to the external file links-previousvisitor-info.vxml, which holds the previous visitor information. The field *visitedYes* has been deleted because it has been replaced by the external file.

```
1.  <form id="maincontent">
2.      <block>
3.          I am your personal vocal attendant.
4.      </block>
5.
6.      <field name="lastVisit">
7.        <grammar>
8.          <![CDATA[
9.            [ yes no ]
10.           ]]>
11.       </grammar>
12.
13.       <prompt>
14.         Have you visited the colony within
15.         the past 6 months?
16.       </prompt>
17.
18.       <filled>
19.         <if cond="lastVisit=='yes'">
20.           <goto next="links-previousvisitor-info.vxml"/>
21.         <else/>
22.           <goto nextitem="visitedNo"/>
23.         </if>
24.       </filled>
25.     </field>
26.
27.     <field name="visitedNo">
28.       <grammar>
29.         <![CDATA[
30.           [ yes no ]
31.           ]]>
32.       </grammar>
33.
34.       <prompt>
35.         The colony has Visitor Booths for
36.         newcomers. Would you like to hear about them?
37.       </prompt>
```

Listing 2.7 The maincontent form. *(continues)*

```
38.
39.        <filled>
40.          <if cond="visitedNo=='yes'">
41.            Visitor booths are located every 10 parsecs
42.            within each quadrant. Stand in front of a
43.            visitor booth and say "Hello, Hal" to access
44.            the latest events and activities within that
45.            quadrant.
46.            <goto next="#goodbye"/>
47.          <else/>
48.            <goto next="#goodbye"/>
49.          </if>
50.        </filled>
51.      </field>
52.
53.    </form>
```

Listing 2.7 The maincontent form. *(continued)*

There are now three files in the application: links.vxml, the application root document; links-previousvisitor-info.vxml, which holds the conditional processing for previous visitors; and links-changes.vxml for holding the actual information that will be output to the user.

Alter the *maincontent* form in the links.vxml document to contain a call to the links-previousvisitor-info.vxml file when users confirm that they have previously visited the colony. Delete the *visitedYes* field from the original application.

Test the application to verify that all leaf documents within the application can be reached. Use the Log Browser for tracing the FIA activity through the application.

<link> Elements

A <link> element in VoiceXML is the counterpart to an <a> tag in HTML. The link can contain a *next* or *expr* attribute that holds a URI for transitioning. The *next* attribute functions just as the *href* attribute does in the HTML anchor tag, whereas the *expr* attribute dynamically generates the URI using ECMAScript syntax. Either *next* or *expr* can be defined within a single <link> element, but not both.

Each <link> has a grammar attached to it. The grammar of a <link> is scoped within the context of its parent element. A <link> element that is a child of <vxml> will be accessible anywhere within the application, including leaf documents in a multiple document application. Links within <form> or <field> elements are scoped to be active within the context of that element.

In our current application, we will insert a global <link> that will reload the application root document whenever the user says "start over," and we will override the default *help* handler with an application-specific message.

Reloading a Document

Because the application root document is always active when an application is processing, global links, variables, and grammars can be defined at the top of the application and accessed from any document that is part of the application. This is useful for creating phrases that will transfer the user to a specific section of the application without having to go through a forced sequence of events.

From a developer's standpoint, a global <link> can be used to restart a program dynamically instead of terminating a phone call and redialing to reactivate the application. This is extremely useful when testing various dialog scenarios in a voice application.

In Listing 2.8, a global link is created on line 2 by using the <link> element with a *next* attribute of *links.vxml*. The grammar contains the phrase *start over*, which will activate the link from anywhere within the application. When the link is activated, the *links.vxml* document reloads, resetting all variables and fields to their default values.

NOTE

Reloading a document with a global link clears all variables and sets all values within the application back to default.

TIP

Put a *start over* link at the top of all of your applications as a child of the <vxml> element. It will save time when testing dialog scenarios.

```
1.  <vxml version="2.0">
2.  <link next="links.vxml">
3.    <grammar>
4.      <![CDATA[
5.        [(start over)]
6.      ]]>
7.    </grammar>
8.  </link>
9.  . . .
10. </vxml>
```

Listing 2.8   Start over link.

The grammar defined on line 5 of Listing 2.8 uses parentheses to force a complete phrase to be spoken as a sequence instead of as individual words when activating the link.

Use parentheses within grammar definitions to force complete phrases to be spoken.

Insert a link at the top of the links.vxml file that will reload the document when the user says "start over." Test the link by activating it from different dialogs within your application, confirming that it is available within all documents of the application.

Testing Scenarios

It is often desirable to have a complete run-through of your application and then start it over immediately to try a different scenario. It is possible to add a hidden link within the goodbye form that is accessible to the developer for testing purposes.

The original *goodbye* form in Listing 2.1 contains a <block> with a single <prompt> for outputting an exit message to the user. Listing 2.9 adds two event handlers to the form: *nomatch* and *noinput*. They both serve the same purpose. The only grammars that are currently active in the form are the default event handlers of the application and the *start over* link at the top of the document. If the user does anything other than say "start over," a *nomatch* or *noinput* event will be thrown and the application will exit.

Insert *nomatch* and *noinput* event handlers within the *goodbye* form. Test your changes by calling your application and running through multiple scenarios, using the hidden prompt within the *goodbye* form to reload the document.

```
1. <form id="goodbye">
2.   <field>
3.     <prompt>
4.       Enjoy your stay. Goodbye.
5.     </prompt>
6.     <nomatch><exit/></nomatch>
7.     <noinput><exit/></noinput>
8.   </field>
9. </form>
```

Listing 2.9 Creating hidden link activation.

Catching Events

A <link> element can be used to catch events that are normally handled by the VoiceXML platform, such as when the user says "help" or a *nomatch* error is thrown. The platform is obligated to catch *help*, *noinput*, *nomatch*, *exit*, and *error* events.

Using the *event* attribute within a <link> throws a new event instead of transitioning to a new dialog or document. When the event is thrown, it is handled at the location from which it has been called and does not automatically proceed to a transition. This is useful for creating global messages without interrupting the flow of the application.

When an event is thrown, it is handled at the location from which it has been called and does not proceed to a new document

NOTE

The <link> element on line 4 of Listing 2.10 defines *help* as the type of event to catch. Lines 5 through 14 define a grammar that will activate the help event.

```
1.  <vxml version="2.0">
2.
3.  <!-- GLOBAL HELP LINK -->
4.     <link event="help">
5.        <grammar root="helpVocab">
6.           <rule id="helpVocab">
7.              <one-of>
8.                 <item>help</item>
9.                 <item>help me</item>
10.                <item>i'm lost</item>
11.                <item>where am i</item>
12.              </one-of>
13.           </rule>
14.        </grammar>
15.     </link>
16.
17. <!-- GLOBAL HELP OUTPUT -->
18.    <help>
19.       <prompt>
20.          You have reached the Mars Colony 7
21.          tourist info center. I can help you
22.          find your way around the Mars 7 Colony.
23.       </prompt>
24.       <reprompt/>
25.    </help>
26. ....
27. </vxml>
```

Listing 2.10 Handling events with a link.

The <grammar> element on line 5 carries a *root* attribute, pointing to a rule that will be used as the root-level grammar for this dialog. The *helpVocab* rule definition begins on line 6. Each of the items within a rule is considered an individual phrase that can trigger the event. This is a simple way of creating a list of grammar items. When the help grammar is recognized as valid user input, the global help message on lines 20 through 22 is output. The <reprompt/> element on line 24 forces a repeat of the <prompt> from the dialog that threw the event.

Events handled by links are processed within the location from which they are called. In Listing 2.10, if the user asks for the help link while in the links-previousvisitor-info.vxml document, processing will pause within that document. The help link will output the text within the <prompt> starting on line 18 and processing will continue from the previous visitors information document in the location from which the event was called.

The <rule>, <one-of>, and <item> elements within the <grammar> element of Listing 2.10 are not defined in the VoiceXML specification. The W3C Speech Recognition Grammar Format at www.w3.org/TR/speech-grammar, sections 2 and 3, defines those elements. It is the intention of the VoiceXML working group to synchronize with those definitions.

Insert a *start over* link at the top of your application. Test your application, verifying that the *help* and *start over* links work properly. By using the *start over* link, you can test your application multiple times with a single call.

Creating Menus

Sometimes it is convenient to give the caller a list of choices and then transition to a specific dialog based upon that choice. The <menu> element can be used to output a list of choices within a <prompt> with a vocabulary that is more flexible than that typically contained within a <grammar> element.

The <menu> element in Listing 2.11 is at the same level as a <form> element within the VoiceXML document structure.

In place of field-level items, a <menu> contains one anonymous field that holds a single <prompt>. Grammar is dynamically generated with the <enumerate/> element to access the vocabulary stored within the <choice> elements. We will look at <enumerate> and <choice> a little farther down.

The *accept* attribute of a <menu> element specifies whether the dynamically generated grammar must be spoken exactly or if a section of the phrase will be recognized as valid input. If the *accept* attribute is set to *exact*, the user must speak the complete phrase in order for the input to be recognized. When the value is set to *approximate*, the interpreter will accept a subset of a <choice> phrase. As an example, the user could say "group activities," "group," or "activities" as recognizable grammar from the <choice> element on line 10. The *accept* attribute can be overridden at the <choice> level, as we will see.

```
1.   <menu id="guidechoices"
2.           accept="approximate"
3.           dtmf="true">
4.     <prompt>
5.        I am your personal vocal attendant.
6.        What subject are you interested in?
7.          <enumerate/>.
8.     </prompt>
9.       <choice next="#activities">
10.       group activities
11.   </choice>
12.   <choice next="#restaurants">
13.       popular restaurants
14.   </choice>
15.   <choice next="#changes">
16.       changes to the colony
17.   </choice>
18.   <nomatch>
19.      You must choose from: <enumerate/>
20.   </nomatch>
21. </menu>
```

Listing 2.11   Creating a menu.

Keypad input from the telephone can be accepted as input from a menu by setting the *dtmf* (dial tone multifrequency) attribute of <menu> to true. A *dtmf* number will be allocated starting at 1 to each <choice> element, up to 9. The sequence will automatically be generated based upon the document order of the <choice> elements. In our application, *activities* will receive 1, *restaurants* 2, and *changes* 3.

A *scope* attribute can be set to limit the grammar recognition to the current dialog only or to make it available throughout the execution of the document. The default value of the *scope* attribute within a menu is *dialog*. Scoping the dialog to document level within an application root document can be useful when building a menu that would be accessible to a multidocument application.

<enumerate> Elements

The <enumerate> element selects the content of the <choice> elements and outputs it in document order. The <prompt> starting on line 4 outputs a question and is followed by the <enumerate> element for listing the choices available. Line 19 uses <enumerate/> within the <nomatch> block to again reiterate the choices if a user has not spoken a recognizable phrase from the list of choices. <enumerate> does not carry any attributes.

<choice> Elements

A <choice> element contains the content that will be output by the <enumerate> element and the attributes for controlling acceptable input from the user. Although there is no restriction on the number of <choice> elements within a menu, it is difficult for a user to keep track of multiple choices when there is no visual reenforcement. A good user interface will limit the choices to a maximum of five.

Keep menu lists to a maximum of five items. The user has no clues other than the vocal prompt to keep track of choices.

TIP

A <choice> element can carry multiple attributes, including *dtmf*, *accept*, *next*, *event*, and *expr*. Using the *dtmf* attribute is a way to allocate a specific single digit to represent a choice. The user may input the digit from the telephone keypad in lieu of speaking a phrase from the grammar. When *dtmf* is set within a <choice> element, it will override the value that is set at the menu level.

The *accept* attribute of a <choice> element can have a value of *exact* or *approximate*, overriding what has been set in the <menu> element.

We have seen *next*, *event*, and *expr* in other contexts, and they work the same way here. *next* is a specific URI that will transfer processing to a new dialog, *expr* can dynamically generate the URI for the transition, and *event* will throw an event handler instead of forcing a transition.

Create a menu with an id of *guidechoices* and use it as the default form upon entrance to the links.vxml application. Rename the *maincontent* form to *changes*, which will be accessed from one of the <choice> elements in the menu.

HANDS ON

Because there is no longer a *maincontent* form, the <goto> element in the greeting form needs to point to the *guidechoices* <menu> element. You will also need to include placeholder forms to handle activities and restaurants.

Compare your updated links.vxml document to Listing 2.12. Place a call to your application and verify that all links and menus are working properly.

```
1.  <?xml version="1.0"?>
2.
3.  <!DOCTYPE vxml
4.    PUBLIC
5.  "-//BeVocal Inc//VoiceXML 2.0//EN"
6.  "http://cafe.bevocal.com/libraries/dtd/vxml2-0-bevocal.dtd">
7.
```

Listing 2.12   Updated links.vxml.

```
8.  <vxml version="2.0">
9.
10. <!-- START OVER -->
11. <link next="links.vxml">
12.   <grammar>
13.   <![CDATA[
14.   [(start over)]
15.   ]]>
16.   </grammar>
17. </link>
18.
19. <!-- GLOBAL HELP LINK -->
20.   <link event="help">
21.     <grammar root="helpVocab">
22.       <rule id="helpVocab">
23.         <one of>
24.           <item>help</item>
25.           <item>help me</item>
26.           <item>i'm lost</item>
27.           <item>where am i</item>
28.         </one-of>
29.       </rule>
30.     </grammar>
31.   </link>
32.
33. <!-- GLOBAL HELP OUTPUT -->
34.   <help>
35.     <prompt>
36.       You have reached the Mars Colony 7 tourist info center.
37.       I can help you find your way around the Mars 7 Colony.
38.     </prompt>
39.     <reprompt/>
40.   </help>
41.
42. <!-- GREETING -->
43. <form id="greeting">
44.   <block>
45.     Welcome to Mars Colony 7.
46.     <goto next="#guidechoices"/>
47.   </block>
48. </form>
49.
50. <!-- MENU -->
51. <menu id="guidechoices"
52.       accept="approximate"
53.       dtmf="true">
54.   <prompt>
```

Listing 2.12 Updated links.vxml. *(continues)*

```
55.        I am your personal vocal attendant.
56.        What subject are you interested in?
57.        <enumerate/>.
58.    </prompt>
59.    <choice next="#activities">
60.      group activities
61.    </choice>
62.    <choice next="#restaurants">
63.      popular restaurants
64.    </choice>
65.    <choice next="#changes">
66.      changes to the colony
67.    </choice>
68.    <nomatch>
69.      You must choose from: <enumerate/>
70.    </nomatch>
71. </menu>
72.
73. <!-- ACTIVITIES FORM: PLACEHOLDER -->
74. <form id="activities">
75.   <block>
76.     Info about activities.
77.     <goto next="#goodbye"/>
78.   </block>
79. </form>
80.
81. <!-- RESTAURANTS FORM: PLACEHOLDER -->
82. <form id="restaurants">
83.   <block>
84.     Info about restaurants.
85.     <goto next="#goodbye"/>
86.   </block>
87. </form>
88.
89. <!-- CHANGES FORM -->
90. <form id="changes">
91.   <field name="lastVisit">
92.     <grammar>
93.       <![CDATA[
94.         [ yes no ]
95.       ]]>
96.     </grammar>
97.
98.     <prompt>
99.       Have you visited the colony within
100.       the past 6 months?
101.     </prompt>
102.
```

Listing 2.12 Updated links.vxml.

```
103.     <filled>
104.     <if cond="lastVisit=='yes'">
105.     <goto next="links-previousvisitor-info.vxml"/>
106.     <else/>
107.     <goto nextitem="visitedNo"/>
108.     </if>
109.     </filled>
110.   </field>
111.
112.   <field name="visitedNo">
113.     <grammar>
114.       <![CDATA[
115.         [ yes no ]
116.       ]]>
117.     </grammar>
118.
119.     <prompt>
120.       The colony has Visitor Booths for
121.       newcomers. Would you like to hear about them?
122.     </prompt>
123.
124.     <filled>
125.       <if cond="visitedNo=='yes'">
126.         Visitor booths are located every 10 parsecs
127.         within each quadrant. Stand in front of a
128.         visitor booth and say "Hello, Hal" to access
129.         the latest events and activities within that
130.         quadrant.
131.         <goto next="#goodbye"/>
132.       <else/>
133.         <goto next="#goodbye"/>
134.       </if>
135.     </filled>
136.   </field>
137. </form>
138.
139. <!-- GOODBYE FORM -->
140. <form id="goodbye">
141.   <field>
142.     <prompt>
143.       Enjoy your stay. Goodbye.
144.     </prompt>
145.     <nomatch><exit/></nomatch>
146.     <noinput><exit/></noinput>
147.   </field>
148. </form>
149.
150. </vxml>
```

Listing 2.12   Updated links.vxml. *(continued)*

Link Menus as Hierarchies

Menus can link with other menus to create a hierarchy of structure. The main menu in the current application presents choices that jump directly to the content of each choice. An alternative is to create a set of submenus that will give users more choices and then send them to the selected resource.

The <menu> on lines 1 through 11 of Listing 2.13 is the same menu that is already available in the application. Instead of pointing to a form called *activities*, line 7 points to another <menu> that starts on line 13.

```
1.  <menu id="guidechoices" accept="approximate">
2.     <prompt>
3.        I am your personal vocal attendant.
4.        What would you like to hear about?
5.          <enumerate/>.
6.       </prompt>
7.        <choice next="#activities">group activities</choice>
8.        <choice next="#restaurants">popular restaurants</choice>
9.        <choice next="#changes">changes to the colony</choice>
10.     <nomatch>You must choose from: <enumerate/></nomatch>
11.  </menu>
12.
13.    <menu id="activities" accept="approximate" dtmf="true">
14.      <prompt>
15.        <enumerate>
16.          For information about <value expr="_prompt"/>,
17.          press <value expr="_dtmf"/>.
18.        </enumerate>
19.      </prompt>
20.        <choice next="#gliding">solar gliding</choice>
21.        <choice next="#golflunar"
22.              accept="exact">lunar golf</choice>
23.        <choice next="#golfweightless"
24.              accept="exact">weightless golf</choice>
25.        <choice next="#hottub">hot tub ski lift</choice>
26.        <nomatch>
27.          That activity is not available.
28.          Choose from: <enumerate/>
29.        </nomatch>
30.    </menu>
31.  <!-- PLACEHOLDER FOR SOLAR GLIDING -->
32.  <form id="gliding">
33.    <block>
34.      Info about solar gliding.
35.      <goto next="#goodbye"/>
36.    </block>
```

Listing 2.13 Submenus.

```
37.  </form>
38.
39.  <!-- PLACEHOLDER FOR LUNAR GOLF -->
40.  <form id="golflunar">
41.    <block>
42.      Info about lunar golf.
43.      <goto next="#goodbye"/>
44.    </block>
45.  </form>
46.
47.  <!-- PLACEHOLDER FOR WEIGHTLESS GOLF-->
48.  <form id="golfweightless">
49.    <block>
50.      Info about weightless golf.
51.      <goto next="#goodbye"/>
52.    </block>
53.  </form>
54.
55.  <!-- PLACEHOLDER FOR HOT TUB -->
56.  <form id="hot tub">
57.    <block>
58.      Info about the hot tub ski lift.
59.      <goto next="#goodbye"/>
60.    </block>
61.  </form>
```

Listing 2.13   Submenus. *(continued)*

The <menu> on line 13 offers the user a subset of activities that point to the appropriate resources. A new technique is introduced on lines 16 and 17 using _prompt and _dtmf as values of an expression. The _prompt variable works with the <enumerate/> element to act as a for-each loop, outputting each of the grammar phrases defined in the <choice> elements. The same is true for the _dtmf variable. This allows creation of sentences that give the user a choice of using vocal responses or the telephone keypad as input. It is assumed that each of the *next* values of the <choice> element is pointing to a form that has been defined within the document and is accessed through the fragment identifier (#).

The <nomatch> element on lines 26 through 29 give a warning message if the input is not recognized and then repeats the list of choices.

TIP

Instead of giving the user a long list of items to choose from, break the list into subgroups and build hierarchies of menus to access the choices.

Update your application by changing the *activities* form to a menu called activities. Create a placeholder form for each of the activities that gives a brief description of the activity and then sends processing to the goodbye form.

Creating Pauses

When you listened to your application, you heard the list of choices spoken as one long phrase. The <break> element can be used to put pauses in the output to make it more comprehensible and user friendly, as shown in Listing 2.14.

The <break> element can be set to a platform-specified duration using small, medium, or large as a value for the *size* attribute. If you desire more control, a specific duration of milliseconds can be set using the *time* attribute to set the pauses.

Check the platform documentation to determine what values are set as default for small, medium, and large.

Create pauses with your menu choices, testing the different sizes and durations to see which is most appropriate for your application.

```
1.  <choice next="#activities">
2.      group activities
3.      <break size="small"/>
4.  </choice>
5.
6.  <choice next="#restaurants">
7.    popular restaurants
8.    <break time="500msec"/>
9.  </choice>
10.
11. <choice next="#changes">
12.   changes to the colony
13. </choice>
```

Listing 2.14   Creating pauses in TTS output.

Modularize Processing with Subdialogs

Code that handles multiple instances of the same process is usually referred to as a subroutine or function in most programming languages. The VoiceXML term for this is subdialog. The subdialog is used for handling repetitive processing when several forms or items need the same type of processing. In our application, when a user chooses to hear about activities or restaurants, we will need to collect the same type of information in both cases. A subdialog will be used to gather that information.

Listing 2.15 assumes the user has selected to hear more information about the ski lift and hot tubs. Lines 2 through 4 are a verbal confirmation to the user that the request for information has been understood. Line 5 is the call to a subdialog, and lines 6 through 12 are a <block> that handles the return values from the subdialog. We will return to an examination of this section after looking at the subdialog.

```
1.  <form id="hottub">
2.      <block>
3.          The hot tub ski lift is our most popular activity.
4.      </block>
5.      <subdialog name="result" src="#personalinfo">
6.        <filled>
7.          You are from <value expr="result.planet"/>.
8.          Your gender is <value expr="result.gender"/>.
9.          There are <value expr="result.quantity"/>
10.       in your party.
11.        <goto next="#goodbye"/>
12.       </filled>
13.     </subdialog>
14.  </form>
15.
16.    <form id="restaurants">
17.      <block>
18.        There are 7438 restuarants in your current parsec.
19.      </block>
20.      <subdialog name="result" src="#personalinfo">
21.        <filled>
22.          You are from <value expr="result.planet"/>.
23.          Your gender is <value expr="result.gender"/>.
24.          There are <value expr="result.quantity"/>
25.          in your party.
26.          <goto next="#goodbye"/>
```

Listing 2.15 Subdialogs. *(continues)*

```
27.        </filled>
28.      </subdialog>
29.    </form>
30.
31.    <form id="personalinfo">
32.      <block>
33.        I need some information from you so that I can
34.        provide the most appropriate recommendation.
35.      </block>
36.      <field name="planet">
37.        What planet are you from?
38.        <grammar>
39.          <![CDATA[
40.            [ mercury venus earth mars jupiter
41.              saturn uranus neptune pluto]
42.          ]]>
43.        </grammar>
44.      </field>
45.      <field name="gender">
46.        What is your gender?
47.        <grammar>
48.          <![CDATA[
49.            [ male female android]
50.          ]]>
51.        </grammar>
52.      </field>
53.      <field name="quantity" type="number">
54.        How many in your party?
55.        <filled>
56.          <return namelist="planet gender quantity"/>
57.        </filled>
58.      </field>
59.    </form>
```

Listing 2.15   Subdialogs. *(continued)*

<subdialog>

Subdialogs allow the VoiceXML developer to build reusable blocks of code that can be saved as a predefined library of functions or as a simple subroutine within an application. The <subdialog> element is used to access the subdialog, sending it variables and waiting for return values from the routine.

NOTE **The <subdialog> element is not the subdialog; it is the call to the subdialog. The subdialog itself is pointed to by the *src* attribute of the <subdialog> element.**

The subdialog is called from the <subdialog> element through the *src* attribute. The value of the attribute is a URI that uses a fragment identifier to access the subdialog. A *name* attribute within the <subdialog> element is used for referencing the return values sent back from the subdialog. Listing 2.15, line 5, shows a <subdialog> element named *result* placing a call to the *personalinfo* subdialog. The subdialog looks like a regular <form> block except for the <return> element on line 56, which we will discuss a little later.

The call to the subdialog in this application is very simple, sending processing to the subdialog and then accepting the return values. Calls to subdialogs can also pass parameters to the subdialog through <param> elements. This will be examined in future projects.

The form at lines 31 through 59 of Listing 2.15 is the subdialog that will collect information from users and make it accessible to the calling routines. The form starts with a <block> prompt, explaining to users why the information is being requested. Fields are used to prompt users for their planet, gender, and number in their party. The names of these fields will be used to access user input when processing is returned to the calling routine.

The third <field> element, on line 53, contains a *type* attribute, which is used to force a data type of *number* from the user. Error checking is handled by the platform unless the developer handles errors explicitly.

<return> Elements

The <filled> element starting on line 55 contains a <return> element that is used to send the user input back to the calling routine. The <return> is used to end a subdialog or short-circuit the rest of the subdialog if it is used before the subdialog is completed. This is useful for handling test conditions and returning the results to the calling routine.

The *namelist* attribute within a <return> element is a space-delimited list of the field names that have been processed. By default, if there is no *namelist* attribute, no variables are returned.

Using Returned Values

Lines 7 through 9 of Listing 2.15 demonstrate how to access the named variables that have been returned from the subdialog. The <subdialog> element has a name of *result* and is used to store the return values from the subdialog. Access the results of individual fields by preceding the field name with the subdialog name followed by a dot. In the code sample, to access the input for planet, you would use *result.planet*. The

<value> elements on lines 7, 8, and 9 use the *expr* attribute to output the results. Line 11 finishes the processing with a call to the *goodbye* form.

Lines 16 through 29 handle processing of the restaurant form. Line 20 makes a call to the same subdialog that the hot tub form used. This shows the power of using sub-dialogs. No matter how many times the application needs to collect user information, one routine can be used for the processing.

Adding a subdialog to your script that will request information from the user. Name the subdialog *personalinfo*. Update the hot tub and restaurants forms with a call to the *personalinfo* subdialog. Run through multiple sets of input to verify that the subdialog is working properly.

HANDS ON

If you are using the BeVocal development environment, create a batch file that holds multiple sets of input. The batch file will be processed without you having to enter any input from the keyboard.

TIP

Handle Requests Dynamically with <submit>

The final type of link in the project is generated with the <submit> element. <submit> is similar to a <goto> element, but in addition to jumping to a new section for process-ing, it can pass variables to a script. This is useful when doing CGI-type processing to generate dynamic content from previous user input. To send data to a script, the URI of the script must be inserted as a *src* attribute of the <submit> element.

In Listing 2.16, the call to the subdialog on line 3 retrieves information from users and stores it in the *result* variable for later access. A prompt assures users they are in the correct location by outputting a message regarding restaurants.

```
1.  <form id="restaurants">
2.    <block>
3.      <subdialog name="result" src="#personalinfo"/>
4.      <prompt>
5.        There are 7,438 restaurants in your current parsec.
6.      </prompt>
7.      <submit
8.        next="http://www.your-server.com/links-submit.cgi"
9.        namelist="result.planet result.gender result.quantity"
10.       method="post"
11.       fetchtimeout="10s"/>
12.   </block>
13. </form>
```

Listing 2.16   The <submit> element.

The <submit> element beginning on line 7 carries four attributes that specify what data should be sent and how it should be submitted. We have discussed *next* (the URI where the data should be sent), *expr* (a dynamically generated URI), and *namelist* (names of the variables to send), but the *fetchtimeout* and *method* attributes are new.

fetchtimeout determines how long the interpreter should wait before issuing a time-out if the script cannot be accessed. A *fetchaudio* attribute is also available, pointing to a URI that plays a sound file while the resource is being fetched.

The *method* attribute can be a value of *post* or *get*. These are the same values used by any CGI script using the HTTP protocol on your current Web site. In general, *post* is the most useful because of its ability to send large amounts of data.

Use Listing 2.16 as a template to make changes to the restaurant form in your application. The next section will create a script called links-submit.cgi, which will handle the processing of the user input.
HANDS ON

Processing User Input with a Script

To complete the next step, you will need an account with an Internet service provider that allows CGI processing with Perl. JSP, ASP, and Cold Fusion will work as well; just change the script accordingly.
WARNING

To dynamically process a request from a <submit> element, the data must be sent to a Web server for processing. Listing 2.17 is a Perl script that accepts the data from the <submit> element, processes the input, and then sends processing back to the *goodbye* form in the links.vxml document.

```
1. #! /usr/bin/perl5 -w
2.
3. use CGI qw(:standard);
4. use CGI::Carp qw(fatalsToBrowser);
5. use strict;
6. $|++;
7.
8. print header;
9.
10. my $planet = param('result.planet');
11. my $gender = param('result.gender');
12. my $quantity = param('result.quantity');
13.
14. print <<VXML;
15. <?xml version="1.0"?>
16.
17. <vxml version="2.0">
```

Listing 2.17 Perl script for processing a submit request. *(continues)*

```
18.    <form>
19.      <block>
20.          You are from $planet.
21.          Your gender is $gender.
22.          There are $quantity in your party.
23.          We recommend that you eat at home.
24.          <goto next="links.vxml#goodbye"/>
25.      </block>
26.    </form>
27. </vxml>
28.
29. VXML
```

Listing 2.17   Perl script for processing a submit request. *(continued)*

The first line of the Perl script in Listing 2.17 specifies the location of the Perl inter-preter on the processing machine. The -w switch turns on warning messages. Line 3 imports the Perl CGI module that will handle the bulk of the CGI processing. Lines 4 and 5 do error checking. For optimization, they should be commented out when the script is debugged and running properly. Line 6 turns off buffering so that output is sent immediately from the server.

The header method from the CGI module is used on line 8 to print the correct header to standard out, which, in this case, is the voice browser. Lines 10 through 12 use the param method from the CGI module to assign values to the three variables that have been passed from the <submit> element.

The code in lines 15 through 27 is contained within a Perl *print here* statement. Line 14 specifies that the end of the print statement will be the literal characters VXML on a single line by itself. Anything before that will be output as if each line had its own print statement.

Everything from here should look familiar by now: the XML declaration and the <vxml> root element containing a <block> of literal text. What might not be familiar is the use of the variables within the output. The variables that were assigned values at the top of the script can be embedded directly in the print statement. When the script processes, those variables will be expanded, leaving their values as the output.

The <submit> element that called this script does not function like the <subdialog> element; it is like the submit button on an HTML form. Once the data is submitted, the script is in control of the processing, making the calling document no longer available. The script controls all processing from that point and does not return to the calling rou-tine as a <subdialog> or subroutine would. To return to the calling application, the URI of the application has to be explicitly stated as a *next* attribute within a <goto> element.

WARNING **Most voice portal developer accounts do not make a complete URL address available for returning to the calling application. As a work-around, place a copy of your links.vxml project script into the same directory as the Perl script on your Web server. Use it to verify that everything is working properly. When the call to the script is made, it will use the copies of the VoiceXML scripts to continue processing.**

HANDS ON **Install the Perl script on your Web server. Copy your links.vxml, links-changes.vxml, and links-previousvistor-info.vxml scripts into the same folder. Run the project through multiple scenarios, preferably using batch processing.**

Final Thoughts

VoiceXML linking is much more powerful than HTML because of the many ways in which links can control the process flow of an application. This project examined five ways to create links within a VoiceXML application: <goto>, <menu>, <link>, <sub-dialog>, and <submit>.

The use of hierarchical menus is one of the best ways to make your voice applications user friendly. The template developed in this project can be easily transformed into a help desk, office FAQ, or information kiosk. It can also be used as an entrance to a site of multiple voice applications: Build a menu pointing to each application and let the user choose which one to hear.

The listings for this project can be downloaded from the BeVocal Web site at cafe.bevocal.com/wiley/10projects. They are saved as text files, useful as templates for creating your own VoiceXML scripts.

The next project will continue to use links as we develop a generic contact application that will give your clients various ways to contact your company.

Contact Us

Most Web sites have a Contact Us section, which displays various ways a user can contact the company or Web staff. I've always been intrigued with the possibility of using a robot like Hal from the movie *2001* for handling this type of mundane chore. Not only would it be able to give you basic responses to your contact requests, but it could also help do simple tasks like taking messages or transferring calls to a person. This project can be used to lay the groundwork for developing a semi-intelligent answering system that handles the time-consuming chores of your front office staff.

THE PROBLEM

Using a live receptionist to answer basic questions about your company or to take phone messages is a waste of personnel time and company resources.

THE SOLUTION

Access to basic contact information about your company through verbal output of an address can be handled with an automated system. The user has the choice of requesting company information, leaving voicemail, or speaking with a live receptionist.

Project Description

The Contact Us project creates an automated system for answering basic telephone inquiries about your company. The user calls your company and is greeted upon entrance by the VoiceXML application. A short menu describes the type of information services available: company address, request to leave voicemail, or ask to speak to a receptionist. If the request is for a mailing address or business location, a prerecorded location message is output. The user may also choose to record a voice message that will be stored on the company Web server for later retrieval. As a final choice, the user may request to speak to a receptionist.

To complete this project you will:

1. Create a skeleton template.
2. Use variables for global values.
3. Repeat content and control application flow.
4. Record and save a message.
5. Transfer a call.

You Will Need

✔ **BeVocal developer account**

✔ **Access to a Web server with CGI capabilities**

✔ **Perl 5 installed on the Web server**

✔ **Perl script for processing a recording**

✔ **Download files: cafe.bevocal.com/wiley/10projects**

VoiceXML Elements Used in This Project

ELEMENT NAME	DESCRIPTION
<block>	A container of (noninteractive) executable code
<break>	Inserts a pause in the TTS output
<choice>	Defines a menu item
<else>	Used in <if> elements
<elseif>	Used in <if> elements
<field>	Declares an input field in a form
<filled>	An action executed when fields are filled

VoiceXML Elements Used in This Project   *(Continued)*

ELEMENT NAME	DESCRIPTION
<form>	A dialog for presenting information and collecting data
<goto>	Go to another dialog in the same or different document
<grammar>	Specifies a speech recognition or DTMF grammar
<if>	Simple conditional logic
<link>	Specifies a transition common to all dialogs in the link's scope
<menu>	A dialog for choosing among alternative destinations
<nomatch>	Catches a nomatch event
<prompt>	Queues speech synthesis and audio output to the user
<record>	Records an audio sample
<transfer>	Transfers the caller to another destination
<var>	Declares a variable
<vxml>	Top-level element in each VoiceXML document

Source: *VoiceXML 2.0 Working Draft*, section 1.4

Call Flow

Figure 3.1 shows the call flow for the Contact Us application. When a call is received, the main menu of three choices is presented to the user. The user may choose to hear the company address, leave a voice message, or speak with a live receptionist. The company address is a verbal output, hard-coded into the application. The voicemail routine accepts a verbal message from the user and then stores it on a Web server for access by the company staff. The live receptionist is reached through the call transfer routine. Exiting the application is through the typical *goodbye* form.

Repeating Content and Controlling Application Flow

We will build the Contact Us project in sections, adding components until we have a complete application. The first component is the address field, as shown in Listing 3.1. It is a long prompt that ends with a conditional statement asking if the user would like to hear a repeat of the information.

```
 1.  <?xml version="1.0"?>
 2.
 3.  <vxml version="2.0">
 4.  <var name="companyName" expr="'Mars Colony 7'"/>
 5.  <form id="address">
 6.      <field name="snailMail" type="boolean">
 7.
 8.        <prompt>
 9.          <value expr="companyName"/>
10.           is located on the fourth planet of
11.           the local solar system <break size="small"/>
12.           third quadrant <break size="small"/>
13.           northern section <break size="small"/>
14.         parsec 7891<break size="small"/>
15.         The main intersection is 12th Street and Vine.
16.         Would you like me to repeat the address?
17.      </prompt>
18.
19.        <filled>
20.          <if cond="snailMail">
21.             <clear/>
22.          </if>
23.        </filled>
24.      </field>
25.    </form>
26.  </vxml>
```

Listing 3.1 Repeating blocks of information.

Listing 3.1 begins with an XML declaration and sets the root element of the document to <vxml>. As with most programming languages, VoiceXML allows storage of global values in a variable. A global variable holding the company name is initialized on line 4 within the <var> element.

<var> Elements

A variable is useful when a string value is used several times in the same application. In this instance, the company name will be repeated three or four times within various forms throughout the application. This makes it simple to change the output of the name wherever it appears in the application by changing the value stored in the variable.

A <var> element can carry two attributes: *name* and *expr*. The value of the *name* attribute is used to access the content of the variable, which is stored in the *expr* attribute. Literal content and dynamically generated content can be stored within the variable. Literal content, such as the name of the company, must be single quoted within double quotes. This indicates to the VoiceXML interpreter that the value of the variable is not to be interpolated but should be output as literal text.

The *expr* attribute can also hold a script expression that will generate its content dynamically, such as using a field value to check a condition. If a variable is initialized with no content, the value is set to undefined.

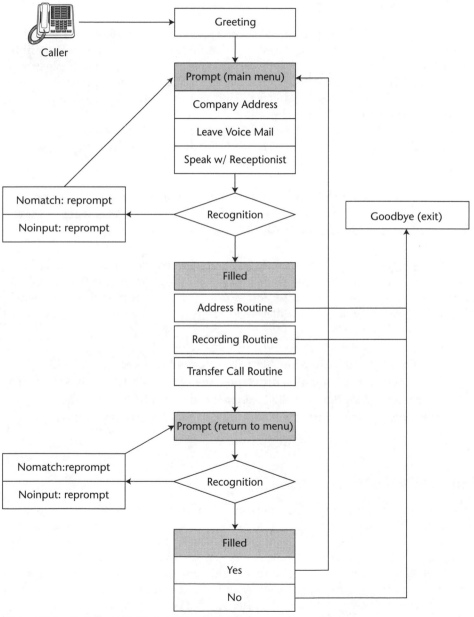

Figure 3.1 Call flow of Contact Us application.

When creating values for a string variable, the value must be single quoted within double quotes, whereupon it will not be interpolated by the
WARNING VoiceXML interpreter. A value within double quotes will be interpreted as a unique form, variable, or field name, not as a simple string.

Predefined Grammars

VoiceXML provides built-in, predefined grammars for several data types. The built-in grammar is accessed through the <field> type attribute and is used to limit user input to a specific data type. The *type* attribute can hold various values such as boolean, currency, digits, phone, and other types supplied by the VoiceXML interpreter. The types are defined by the *VoiceXML 2.0 Working Draft*, section 2.3.1.1, and are implemented relatively consistently across platforms.

A <form> holding a single <field>, snailMail, starts on line 5 of Listing 3.1. The boolean built-in type will handle user input as a true or false response, making it unnecessary to create a grammar for this field.

Use a boolean type when responses to a prompt are a simple yes or no. The VoiceXML interpreter is able to handle boolean types of responses as input,
TIP making it unnecessary to create a grammar for the field.

If a built-in type does not have a desired behavior, the developer must create an explicit grammar for that item. As an example, the developer might want the word *sure* to be considered a positive response from a user. The boolean type does not include *sure* as part of its vocabulary, so it will have to be created as a specific, field-level grammar by the developer.

Use the *type* attribute within a <field> element to access predefined grammars for fundamental data types. See section 2.3.1.1 of the *VoiceXML*
TIP *2.0 Working Draft* for detailed explanations of available types. The list includes boolean, date, digits, currency, number, phone, and time types.

Pauses in Output

Lines 8 through 17 in Listing 3.1 create a <prompt> that outputs the company name followed by the company's address information. The <value> element on line 9 carries an *expr* attribute that accesses the *companyName* variable. Note that the value of the *expr* is in double quotes so that the variable *companyName* can be interpolated.

The <break> element is used to control the time span, or pauses, between spoken lines. This is useful when a long series of lines is being output, such as lines 9 through 16, giving the user a chance to mentally process what is being said.

The <break/> element can carry one of two attributes: *time* or *size*. The *size* attribute uses a relative time description such as none, small, medium, or large, the duration of which depends on the platform. A *time* attribute specifies an exact duration for the output to pause. It may be expressed in seconds (1.5 s, 3 s, and so on) or in milliseconds for more fine-grained control (225 ms, 150 ms, and so on). The default of <break/> is set to the platform defined *medium*.

Use the <break> element to create pauses in output when the user may be taking notes.

TIP

The user utterance is checked against the built-in boolean grammar to see if the utterance is recognized as a positive or negative response. When the response is recognized, it is stored in the *snailMail* variable for access within the <filled> element. The boolean type will throw an error if the user input is not understood, re-prompting for a second utterance.

Built-in grammar types contain default error checking that will handle unrecognized utterances, prompting the user for more input.

NOTE

The <filled> block beginning on line 19 controls processing of the user input. The logic is a little subtle here. Line 20 checks the condition of the *snailMail* field, which is holding the user input. If the condition is true, the user has uttered a positive response. Usually, when a positive response is received from a user, processing continues to the next item. In this case however, a *yes* response, which will be considered positive, indicates that the user desires to hear the prompt again. The <clear/> element on line 21 resets all field values within the current form to empty, sending the processing back to the top of the form to output the address prompt and receive new input from the user. We will examine the FIA at the end of this project to get a better understanding of how the <clear/> element functions.

A negative response from the user will pass processing out of the form, terminating the application.

Begin a new VoiceXML application. Create a prompt for your application that outputs your company's address. Use the <var> element to include your company's name as a global variable at the top of the script. If you have several lines of output, use the <break/> element to include short pauses between lines.

HANDS ON

Recording a Message

The automated receptionist can offer the caller the possibility of recording a voice message or hearing the company address. We'll expand the script in Listing 3.1 to include a set of menu choices and then build the recording script for the voice message.

Menu Choices

The menu in Listing 3.2 shows an alternative to the type of menu developed in Project 2. Instead of having <enumerate/> read through a list of choices, a detailed <prompt> is output.

```
1.  <?xml version="1.0"?>
2.
3.  <vxml version="2.0">
4.  <var name="companyName" expr="'Mars Colony 7'"/>
5.
6.  <!-- MAIN MENU -->
7.  <menu id="mainmenu">
8.    <prompt>
9.      To hear the address of Mars Colony 7, say "Address".
10.      To leave a voice message, say "Voice".
11.   </prompt>
12.
13.   <choice next="#address">
14.     <grammar>[ (address ?please) ]</grammar>
15.     Address
16.   </choice>
17.   <choice next="#voice">
18.     <grammar>[ (voice ?message) voicemail ]</grammar>
19.     Transfer
20.   </choice>
21.   <nomatch>
22.     Your choices are <enumerate/>
23.     Try again.
24.   </nomatch>
25.  </menu>
26.
27.  <!-- SNAIL MAIL -->
28.  <form id="address">
29.      <field name="snailMail" type="boolean">
30.
31.       <prompt>
32.         <value expr="companyName"/>
33.         is located on the fourth planet of
34.         the local solar system <break size="small"/>
35.         third quadrant <break size="small"/>
36.         northern section <break size="small"/>
37.       parsec 7891<break size="small"/>
38.       The main intersection is 12th Street and Vine.
39.       Would you like me to repeat the address?
40.      </prompt>
41.
```

Listing 3.2   Menu choices.

```
42.    <filled>
43.       <if cond="snailMail">
44.          <clear/>
45.       </if>
46.    </filled>
47.   </field>
48. </form>
49.
50. <!-- VOICE MESSAGE -->
51. <form id="voice">
52.    <block>
53.       Process a voice message.
54.    </block>
55. </form>
56.
57. </vxml>
```

Listing 3.2 Menu choices. *(continued)*

The advantage of the new technique is in the ability to control verbal output of the initial <prompt> while at the same time having an extended grammar. If the user does not answer with an exact utterance as directed in the menu output, the explicit <grammar> defined on lines 14 and 18 will still be able to recognize the input. The <grammar> on line 14 allows the user to speak an optional *please* after requesting the company address, and line 18 offers multiple ways of asking to leave a voice message.

Another advantage of this type of menu construction is that the <prompt> on lines 8 through 11 is much more natural sounding than a simple list of available options. However, <enumerate/> is still used within the <nomatch> on line 22 because it is assumed that the user has already heard the first <prompt> of full instructions and just needs to hear the list of available options. The bare words on lines 15 and 19 are used as the list items for <enumerate/>.

Lines 51 through 55 are placeholders for checking the process flow when testing this phase of the application.

Add a menu to the application that gives access to the company address and offers to record a message. Use a placeholder to process the voice HANDS ON message. Check your application through the Vocal Scripter.

Recording a Message

When a user chooses to leave a voice message, the message is stored as a wav file on a Web server and is accessed through a Web page or a second VoiceXML application. The Web page can be accessed through a visual Web browser, displaying a listing of available recorded messages.

```
1.  <form id="voice">
2.  <record name="voiceMessage"
3.         beep="true"
4.         maxtime="10s"
5.         finalsilence="1.5s"
6.         type="audio/wav">
7.    <prompt>
8.      You will have 10 seconds to record a message.
9.      Please speak after the tone.
10.   </prompt>
11. </record>
12.
13. <!-- OFFER TO RECORD AGAIN -->
14. <field name="processMessage" type="boolean">
15.   <prompt>
16.     Here is your message <value expr="voiceMessage"/>
17.     Is this the message you would like to send to
18.     <value expr="companyName"/>
19.   </prompt>
20.
21.   <filled>
22.     <if cond="processMessage">
23.       Please wait while your message is being saved.
24.     <else/>
25.       <clear/>
26.     </if>
27.   </filled>
28. </field>
29.
30. <subdialog name="saveMessage"
31.           src="recording.cgi"
32.           method="post"
33.           enctype="multipart/form-data"
34.           namelist="voiceMessage">
35.     <filled>
36.       <audio>Your message has been sent</audio>
37.     </filled>
38. </subdialog>
39. </form>
```

(handwritten annotation: "audio" above line 16)

Listing 3.3 Recording a message.

Listing 3.3 begins with a form that is given a unique id of *voice* on line 1. Lines 2 through 11 use the <record> element. <record> is a field-level element that records input from the user, making the recording available through access of the *name* attribute. The recording is stored in memory and is accessed directly as the value of the *name* attribute or sent to a Web server for processing and storage.

<record> Element Attributes

The attributes on lines 3 through 6 set the properties for the <record> element. *beep* specifies whether there should be a sound played when it is time for the user to speak. The beep sound is implementation specific.

On some VoiceXML development environments that offer online script checking, setting the beep attribute to true will cause an error, terminating
WARNING **the script. Setting the beep value to false allows use of the platform's dynamic checker.**

The *maxtime* attribute limits the user to a specific length of message in seconds. For demonstration purposes and to allow the developer to test the application without overloading the system, the value has been set to 10 seconds. This value should be changed to a more appropriate length, such as 30 seconds, when the application goes into production.

finalsilence has a value that determines when the user has finished speaking a message. One and a half seconds is the industry default. *type* specifies what type of binary data will be sent to the server.

For a complete list of <record> element attributes and their default values, see section 2.3.6 of the *VoiceXML 2.0 Working Draft.*
NOTE

The <prompt> on lines 8 and 9 lets the user know what is expected as input.

A good user interface will let users know exactly what is expected of them. Let callers know how much time they have for recording a message and
TIP **when they should start speaking and then give them an aural indication that the recording process has begun.**

Confirming the Recording

Letting a user confirm or rerecord a message is a courtesy that is not extended on most voicemail systems. We use it here to make the application more user friendly, especially in the absence of a live receptionist. Users may rerecord their message as many times as they like before confirming that it is to be saved.

The <field> item on lines 14 through 28 of Listing 3.3 is used to play back a user's message to confirm that it is what they wanted to record. The field *type* on line 14 is set to boolean, letting the platform handle yes/no responses to the <prompt> that starts on line 15. Inserted within the <prompt> is a <value> element whose expression is the field name variable that holds the message that was recorded. The output from the <value> element is the actual recording of the speaker's input that is being held in memory. The recording will not be committed to storage until it has been processed by a Web server.

Line 18 contains a call to the *companyName* variable, outputting the company name that is stored in the global variable defined at the top of the script.

The <filled> condition on lines 21 through 27 holds an <if> statement, checking the user's response. The condition attribute on line 22 checks the value stored in the *processMessage* field. If the condition is true, a confirmation message is output and processing falls though to the *saveMessage* subdialog. When the response is false, or negative, the <clear/> element on line 25 clears all values in the current form and starts processing over from the top of the current form. Default error checking within the boolean type will handle any other input, reprompting the user for a valid response.

Processing with <subdialog>

The field-level items we have used so far transfer processing in a linear fashion. Default processing falls through to the next field-level item when the previous field within the active dialog has been filled. The <subdialog> element allows more control over processing by permitting access to routines that are outside of the current form, dialog, or document. A <subdialog> acts like a call to subroutine. Once the subroutine has finished, processing returns to the point of the originating call. Subdialogs are convenient for creating modules or routines that can be used by multiple applications.

Subdialogs can also reside locally within the document itself. If a routine is used multiple times within the lifetime of the application, creating a subdialog does away with redundant coding and the possibility of coding errors when replicating a process.

The <subdialog> element is not the subdialog itself; it is the call to the subdialog.

NOTE

Attributes of <subdialog>

The <subdialog> block beginning on line 30 of Listing 3.3 contains a call to the script, recording.cgi, which will process the user input and store it as a wave file. The attributes of the <subdialog> element define how the data should be sent to the processing script.

The value of the *src* attribute within the <subdialog> element on line 31 is the location of the processing script that will save the recording. The script may reside on any Web server that has dynamic processing capabilities and is accessible to the VoiceXML application. The scripting language for processing the recording can be Perl, Java, ASP, Python, or any other language available on the server. The current project shows an example of saving the recording using a Perl script, as documented in the next section.

Most VoiceXML portals do not allow dynamic processing of scripts on their development platform. Developers must have access to their own Web server for processing and saving of recorded messages.

NOTE

The *method* attribute specifies how the data should be sent to the Web server. HTTP protocol handles the exchange of information between the VoiceXML browser and the Web server that will save the recording. The post method specifies that the URL named within the *src* attribute is a processing script and that the data being sent with the request is to be processed by the script.

The *enctype* attribute of type multipart/form-data is used to pass large amounts of data to the Web server as a single chunk. According to the *VoiceXML 2.0 Working Draft*, section 5.3.8, "It is probably inappropriate to attempt to URL-encode large quantities of data" by using any other method.

A list of variables can be passed to the server through the *namelist* attribute. The variables may be <field> names or explicitly declared variables. By default, all variables in the current dialog are sent unless otherwise specified. In our application, *voiceMessage* is the only variable being sent as data. This contains the encoded voice input from the user and makes it available for processing by the Web server script.

Most demonstrations of the <record> element use the <submit> element to send processing to the script. However, <submit> is very restrictive because it does not return processing to the calling application. Using <subdialog> allows you to modularize your code into generic chunks that can be used by multiple applications.

Section 2.3.4 of the *VoiceXML Working Draft* is a detailed discussion of the <subdialog> element and its attributes.

NOTE

Once the message has been saved on the Web server, processing returns to line 36, giving users a verbal confirmation that their message has been saved. At this phase of the project, we have not created the processing script on the Web server. That will be handled in the next section.

Insert a <record> element into the *voice* form. Add a field that allows users to listen to what they have recorded. End the form with a subdialog that passes the recording to a script. (The script will be covered in the next section.)

HANDS ON

Saving a Recording

The VoiceXML interpreter does not handle processing of the recorded input. It passes the data to a script on a Web server for dynamic processing. The code in Listing 3.4 shows how CGI processing with Perl would handle saving the data as a wav file and then return processing to the calling application. The same type of processing could be done with PHP, JSP, ASP, or any other type of dynamic processing available on your server.

```
1.  #!/usr/bin/perl5
2.
3.  use CGI qw(:standard);
4.  $|++;
5.
6.  my $pathToRecordings='http://www.yourserver.com/recordings';
7.  my $newRecording = 'test.wav';
8.
9.  print header;
10.
11.  open (SAVE, "> $pathToRecordings/$newRecording");
12.    binmode(SAVE);
13.    while (read(param('voiceMessage'),$data,1024))
14.      { print SAVE $data; }
15.  close(SAVE);
16.
17.
18.  # CONFIRM RECORDING WAS SAVED
19.
20.  print <<INSERT_VXML;
21.  <?xml version="1.0"?>
22.
23.  <vxml version="1.0">
24.  <form id="acceptInput">
25.   <block>
26.     Input was $ENV{'CONTENT_LENGTH'} bytes in length.
27.     The recording was processed and saved.
28.    <return/>
29.   </block>
30.  </form>
31.  </vxml>
32.
33.  INSERT_VXML
```

Listing 3.4   Perl script for processing a recording.

The Perl script in Listing 3.4 begins with the path to the Perl interpreter. The path to Perl is platform dependent, so it may be different than that in the example script.

NOTE   **Perl is not stored in the same location on all servers. In addition, many platforms have two versions of Perl running: Perl 4 for server administration and Perl 5 for processing CGI scripts. Check with your server administrator to get the correct path to Perl and the correct naming convention for Perl 5.**

Line 3 imports the Perl CGI module for processing the form data. The CGI module comes standard with Perl 5 implementations. It handles all of the background dirty work for transforming the user input into a useful format for the script to process.

Line 4 disables output buffering. Normally when a Web server is processing data and responding to a request, it will hold the output in a buffer until it has reached a specified quantity of data before sending it back to the browser. With output buffering disabled, the data is sent immediately without being held in the buffer.

Lines 6 and 7 declare variables for the location on your Web server where the recording will be stored. *$pathToRecordings* should be changed to hold the absolute path to a directory on your server. The *$newRecording* scalar variable is initialized with the value of test.wav. The test.wav file will be used to test the application. It will be overwritten on the server each time the script is run. Once we have confirmed that the application is running properly, this value will be replaced with a dynamically generated name, making it possible to have multiple recordings within the recording directory.

VoiceXML uses HTTP protocol for exchanging information between the browser and the server. An HTTP header is output on line 9 using the header method from the CGI.pm module. The header method sets the standard HTTP content-type.

Lines 11 through 15 hold the routine that accepts the data and stores it in a file on the server. Line 11 opens a filehandle called SAVE, which is set to write or overwrite the filename stored in the *$newRecording* variable within the *$pathToRecordings* directory.

Line 12 uses binmode() as a safety mechanism for passing data between a Win32 and Unix system. Win32 file systems distinguish between binary files and ASCII text files. The binmode() function specifies that the file being saved is binary. It does not affect a Unix-to-Unix or Win32-to-Win32 transfer. Its main use in this application is for portability.

The spoken input, passed as the voiceMessage field from the calling application, is read into the *$data* variable on line 13 and saved to the *$newRecording* file on line 14. Line 15 closes the SAVE filehandle.

Though not mandatory, because Perl does automatic garbage collection, it is good practice to close any filehandles that have been opened.

TIP

Lines 20 through 33 use the Perl *print here* method to output a confirmation notice to the user that all went well. Line 23 is a quick check for the developer, testing the length of the message content. Once the script is debugged and functioning properly, this line will be commented out.

Install the Perl script on your Web server. Call your application on the telephone and leave a voice message. Confirm that the message was

HANDS ON **processed and stored on your server by opening a Web browser, accessing your Web site, and listening to the recording. Make several calls to the application to confirm that the message is being replaced with a new recording.**

If you have installed your script on a Unix server, verify that the directory for saving the recordings has write permissions and that the CGI script has
WARNING **execute permissions.**

Dynamically Creating a Filename

In Listing 3.4, the test.wav filename is hardcoded into the *$newRecording* variable, overwriting any previous recording on the server. It is more useful to have a dynamically generated name so that multiple files can be stored on the server. We'll create a short routine that generates a new filename each time the application is called.

Line 1 of Listing 3.5 initializes the value of *$newRecording* with the return value from a subroutine called *createFileName*. The *createFileName* subroutine block on lines 3 through 8 starts with a scalar variable declaration that holds the return from the current localtime() function. localtime() is declared as a scalar value and has the format Weekday Month Monthday hour:minutes:seconds year. The spaces and the colons within the format can cause trouble when used within a filename, so lines 5 and 6 are regular expression substitutions, replacing the spaces with underscores and the colons with hyphens: Thu Jan 24 07:44:17 2002 becomes Thu_Jan_24_07-44-17_2002.

Line 7 appends the .wav extension to the newly created filename. There is no need for an explicit return from the subroutine because the last thing evaluated in a Perl subroutine is automatically returned.

Rewrite your filename variable declaration to accept the return value from a subroutine that generates a unique filename each time your application is
HANDS ON **called. Call your application several times and verify that a new file is created on the server for each call.**

Sound files can take up disk space very quickly. Limit the user input with the *maxtime* attribute and prune the recordings directory on a regular basis.
WARNING

```
1.  my $newRecording = createFileName();
2.
3.  sub createFileName {
4.    my $fileName = localtime();
5.    $fileName =~ s/\s/_/g;
6.    $fileName =~ s/:/-/g;
7.    $fileName = $fileName . '.wav';
8.  }
```

Listing 3.5 Generating a new filename.

Transferring a Call

VoiceXML contains a <transfer> element that allows the application to transfer the phone call to another phone number or extension. In this section, we will add a third option to the menu that transfers the call to a receptionist. Start by adding a third option to the existing menu.

Line 6 of Listing 3.6 adds a prompt line, informing the user that transferring to a receptionist is available as an option. Lines 18 through 24 handle the processing of the request by defining a grammar that will be recognized as the transfer choice. As with the previous two grammars, an extended grammar generated for the transfer choice allows multiple utterances to activate the transfer.

```
1.  <!-- MAIN MENU -->
2.  <menu id="mainmenu">
3.    <prompt>
4.      To hear the address of Mars Colony 7, say "Address".
5.      To leave a voice message, say "Voice".
6.      If you would like to speak with a receptionist,
7.      say "Transfer".
8.    </prompt>
9.
10.   <choice next="#address">
11.     <grammar>[ (address ?please) ]</grammar>
12.     Address
13.   </choice>
14.   <choice next="#voice">
15.     <grammar>[ (voice ?message) voicemail ]</grammar>
16.     Voice
17.   </choice>
18.   <choice next="#transfer">
19.     <grammar>
20.        [ (transfer ?me ?please) receptionist ]
21.     </grammar>
22.     Transfer
23.   </choice>
24.   <nomatch>
25.     Your choices are <enumerate/>
26.     Try again.
27.   </nomatch>
28. </menu>
```

Listing 3.6   Adding a menu option.

The <transfer> Element

After setting up the menu to recognize a request for transferring the call, a form must be built to process the request. The <transfer> element is the foundation for this routine, making it possible to create a connection to another phone without exiting the VoiceXML application.

There are two types of transfers, *bridge* and *blind*. The *blind* transfer disconnects the user from the VoiceXML application while leaving the caller connected to the new telephone. With a *bridge* transfer, the application pauses, waiting for the new connection to terminate, and then returns processing to the VoiceXML application.

The <block> on lines 2 through 4 of Listing 3.7 confirms to the user that the request for a transfer has been understood. The <transfer> element beginning on line 6 carries a series of attributes that set up the configuration for the call transfer. It is set at the field level within a form using a <filled> element to process various returns from the telephone number being called.

```
1.  <form id="transfer">
2.    <block>
3.      Please wait while we wake up the android.
4.    </block>
5.
6.    <transfer
7.      name="reception"
8.      connecttimeout="20s"
9.      maxtime="60s"
10.     bridge="true"
11.     dest="800-555-1212">
12.
13.   <filled>
14.     <if cond="reception == 'busy'">
15.       <prompt>
16.         Hal is busy chatting with Dave.
17.         Please try again later.
18.       </prompt>
19.     <elseif cond="reception == 'far_end_disconnect'"/>
20.       Hal has terminated the call.
21.     <elseif cond="reception == 'noanswer'"/>
22.       <prompt>
23.         Hal is not responding.
24.         Dave might have unplugged him.
25.       </prompt>
26.     </if>
27.   </filled>
28.   </transfer>
29.
30.       <field name="returnToMenu" type="boolean">
```

Listing 3.7 Transferring a call.

```
31.         <prompt>
32.            Would you like to return to the main menu?
33.         </prompt>
34.
35.         <filled>
36.           <if cond="returnToMenu">
37.             <goto next="#mainmenu"/>
38.           <else/>
39.             Thank you for calling. Good bye.
40.             <disconnect/>
41.           </if>
42.         </filled>
43.       </field>
44.    </form>
```

Listing 3.7 Transferring a call. *(continued)*

Attributes of the <transfer> element

Attributes of the <transfer> element control processing during the transfer of the call. The *name* attribute of the <transfer> element is a unique identifier that holds the return results of the transfer. *name* can be used to check the return value from the bridge transfer and process the outcome accordingly. The conditional checks on lines 14 through 26 of Listing 3.7 have appropriate responses based upon whether the return value for the transfer was *busy*, *far_end_disconnect*, or *noanswer*.

For a comprehensive list of available return values, see section 2.3.7 of the VoiceXML 2.0 Working Draft.

NOTE

The *connecttimeout* attribute specifies a time in seconds for the transfer to try to reach the number being called. The default value is determined by the platform. If a connection has not been made in the time alloted, a noanswer value is set in the name attribute. Our application handles the *noanswer* return value on line 21, informing the user that the number called has been reached but has not been connected.

maxtime limits the length of the call once it has been transferred. This attribute is useful for enforcing a maximum time limit on each call. Most voice portals enforce a time limit on transferring calls because of the potential for abuse. BeVocal has a 60-second limit on each transfer.

Because of the possibility of developers abusing the <transfer> function, most major voice portals limit free developer accounts to a maximum of 60 seconds for a transferred call. The time restriction is not part of the VoiceXML specification.

NOTE

The *bridge* attribute specifies whether processing should be sent back to the calling application once the call has been terminated. The default of *bridge* is set to *true* on the BeVocal platform.

By default, all BeVocal transfers are bridge transfers that return control to the calling script.

NOTE

The value of the *dest* attribute is the phone number to be dialed. Long distance phone numbers may be proceeded by an optional 1. The BeVocal platform allows numbers in 5 formats:

phone://8005551212

800-555-1212

phone://800-555-1212

tel:800-555-1212

tel:800-555-1212;postd=123

The last format example dials an extension number after the main number has been reached. Check your platform's documentation for specific formatting requirements.

Checking the Return Results

Once the transfer has been made, error checking is handled within the <filled> element, beginning on line 13. The *cond* attribute uses the name of the <transfer> element as the condition to be checked against. Busy signals, called-party disconnects, and no answers on the receiving end are all handled with descriptive messages to the user followed by an offer to return to the main menu.

<transfer> elements are field-level elements that allow processing to fall through to the next item within the <form>. Once the <filled> element has completed processing on line 27, the *returnToMenu* <field> is automatically accessed. It is set to the type *boolean*, using the built-in true/false grammar provided by the platform. On line 32, a <prompt> is output, offering the user the chance to return to the main menu. A positive response transfers processing to the top of the menu. Otherwise, a courtesy goodbye message is output and the connection is terminated.

Set up a call transfer within your application. Test the application by changing the phone number to access your private voicemail system or a long distance phone.

HANDS ON

Completing the Script

The main sections of the Contact Us script are now completed. To finish the script, we need to add greeting and goodbye forms, global help, and a link for restarting the application, and we will need to add changes to the existing forms to access the new sections. Listing 3.8 shows the completed script.

```
1.  <?xml version="1.0"?>
2.
3.  <vxml version="2.0">
4.  <var name="companyName" expr="'Mars Colony 7'"/>
5.
6.  <!-- START OVER LINK -->
7.  <link next="contact-us.vxml">
8.    <grammar>
9.      <![CDATA[
10.        [(start over)]
11.      ]]>
12.    </grammar>
13. </link>
14.
15. <!-- GLOBAL HELP -->
16. <link event="help">
17.    <grammar root="help">
18.     <rule id="help">
19.      <one-of>
20.        <item>help</item>
21.        <item>help me</item>
22.        <item>i'm lost</item>
23.        <item>where am i</item>
24.      </one-of>
25.     </rule>
26.    </grammar>
27. </link>
28.
29. <!-- GLOBAL HELP OUTPUT -->
30. <help>
31.    <prompt>
32.       You are speaking to the voice system at
33.       <value expr="companyName"/>. Please make
34.       a selection.
35.    </prompt>
36.    <reprompt/>
37. </help>
38.
39. <!-- GREETING -->
40. <form id="greeting">
41.    <block>
42.       You have reached the information center at
43.       <value expr="companyName"/>.
44.       <goto next="#mainmenu"/>
45.    </block>
46. </form>
47.
48. <!-- MAIN MENU -->
```

Listing 3.8 Completed Contact Us script. *(continues)*

```
49.  <menu id="mainmenu">
50.    <prompt>
51.      To hear the address of <value expr="companyName"/>,
52.        say "Address".
53.      To leave a voice message, say "Voice".
54.      If you would like to speak with a receptionist,
55.        say "Transfer".
56.    </prompt>
57.
58.    <choice next="#address">
59.      <grammar>[ (address ?please) ]</grammar>
60.      Address
61.    </choice>
62.    <choice next="#voice">
63.      <grammar>[ (voice ?message) voicemail ]</grammar>
64.      Voice
65.    </choice>
66.    <choice next="#transfer">
67.      <grammar>
68.        [ (transfer ?me ?please) receptionist ]
69.      </grammar>
70.      Transfer
71.    </choice>
72.    <nomatch>
73.      Your choices are <enumerate/>
74.      Try again.
75.    </nomatch>
76.  </menu>
77.
78.  <!-- SNAIL MAIL -->
79.  <form id="address">
80.      <field name="snailMail" type="boolean">
81.
82.        <prompt>
83.          <value expr="companyName"/>
84.          is located on the fourth planet of
85.          the local solar system <break size="small"/>
86.          third quadrant <break size="small"/>
87.          northern section <break size="small"/>
88.        parsec 7891<break size="small"/>
89.        The main intersection is 12th Street and Vine.
90.        Would you like me to repeat the address?
91.      </prompt>
92.
93.    <filled>
94.      <if cond="snailMail">
95.          <clear/>
96.        <else/>
```

Listing 3.8   Completed Contact Us script.

```
97.          <goto next="#goodbye"/>
98.       </if>
99.     </filled>
100.  </field>
101.  </form>
102.
103.  <!-- VOICE MESSAGE -->
104.  <form id="voice">
105.  <record name="voiceMessage"
106.          beep="false"
107.          maxtime="10s"
108.          finalsilence="1.5s"
109.          type="audio/wav">
110.    <prompt>
111.      You will have 10 seconds to record a message.
112.      Please speak after the tone.
113.    </prompt>
114.  </record>
115.
116.  <!-- OFFER TO RECORD AGAIN -->
117.  <field name="processMessage" type="boolean">
118.    <prompt>
119.      Here is your message <value expr="voiceMessage"/>
120.      Is this the message you would like to send to
121.      <value expr="companyName"/>
122.    </prompt>
123.
124.    <filled>
125.      <if cond="processMessage">
126.        Please wait while your message is being saved.
127.      <else/>
128.        Let's try again.
129.        <clear/>
130.      </if>
131.    </filled>
132.  </field>
133.
134.  <!-- SAVE MESSAGE -->
135.  <subdialog name="saveMessage"
136.             src="recording.cgi"
137.             method="post"
138.             enctype="multipart/form-data"
139.             namelist="voiceMessage">
140.    <filled>
141.      <audio>Your message has been sent.</audio>
142.      <goto next="#goodbye"/>
143.    </filled>
144.  </subdialog>
```

Listing 3.8   Completed Contact Us script. *(continues)*

```
145.  </form>
146.
147.  <!-- TRANSFER CALL -->
148.  <form id="transfer">
149.    <block>
150.      Please wait while we wake up the android.
151.    </block>
152.
153.    <transfer
154.       name="reception"
155.       connecttimeout="20s"
156.       maxtime="60s"
157.    bridge="true"
158.    dest="800-555-1212">
159.
160.    <filled>
161.      <if cond="reception == 'busy'">
162.        <prompt>
163.          Hal is busy chatting with Dave.
164.          Please try again later.
165.        </prompt>
166.      <elseif cond="reception == 'far_end_disconnect'"/>
167.        Hal has terminated the call.
168.      <elseif cond="reception == 'noanswer'"/>
169.        <prompt>
170.          Hal is not responding.
171.          Dave might have unplugged him.
172.        </prompt>
173.      </if>
174.      <goto next="#goodbye"/>
175.    </filled>
176.    </transfer>
177.
178.    <field name="returnToMenu" type="boolean">
179.      <prompt>
180.        Would you like to return to the main menu?
181.      </prompt>
182.
183.      <filled>
184.        <if cond="returnToMenu">
185.          <goto next="#mainmenu"/>
186.        <else/>
187.          <goto next="#goodbye"/>
188.        </if>
189.      </filled>
190.    </field>
191.  </form>
```

Listing 3.8 Completed Contact Us script.

```
192.
193.  <!-- GOODBYE -->
194.  <form id="goodbye">
195.    <field>
196.      <prompt>
197.        Enjoy your stay. Good bye.
198.      </prompt>
199.      <grammar>quit</grammar>
200.    </field>
201.  </form>
202.
203.  </vxml>
```

Listing 3.8   Completed Contact Us script. *(continued)*

In Listing 3.8, a global *start over* link has been created starting on line 7. As discussed in Project 2, this link makes it easy for the developer to restart the application with a fresh set of variables without having to disconnect and redial the application. The global *help* template starting on line 16 can be activated from anywhere within the application when the user speaks one of the recognized terms of the help grammar.

The greeting on lines 40 through 46 is contained within its own form to isolate it from the main menu. This is useful for allowing the user to return to the main menu without having to hear the greeting each time. The <goto> element on line 44 transfers processing to the mainmenu form.

The last form in the application, the goodbye form on lines 194 through 201, serves two purposes. It is used as a graceful exit when a user is leaving the application, and it also offers the developer a chance to start the application over by activating the global start over link. Notice that this is an invisible prompt to the end user and is only known by the developer.

A few changes need to be made to the basic script to access the *goodbye* form. Lines 96 and 97 add an <else/> condition to the <if> statement, transferring users to the goodbye form if they do not want to hear a repeat of the company address. The <filled> condition starting on line 140 in the subdialog call now ends with a <goto> element, again sending the user to the goodbye form.

With these additions and changes, the basic Contact Us script is complete.

Final Thoughts

There you have it, a simple, automated answering service. As you develop more complex projects, refer back to Hal, our automated receptionist, and give it more responsibilities. We have only used it to handle the most basic of services, but it would be relatively simple to expand the main menu to cover FAQs, calendar of events, and general company information by using a hierarchy of menus. Project 6 shows how to build a telephone directory system that can easily be incorporated into the Contact Us project.

Another addition to the project would be an extension of the <record> routine, saving the voice messages to private Web pages for each of the recipients. The recipients could access their messages while on the road by logging into the company Web site and retrieving the messages through a VoiceXML interface. The <record> element will be used again in Project 5 when we look at how to modularize pieces of code, making them generic enough to use in multiple applications.

The listings for this project can be downloaded from the BeVocal Web site at cafe.bevocal.com/wiley/10projects. They are saved as text files, useful as templates for creating your own VoiceXML scripts.

The next chapter, Project 4, will complete our look at the basic components of a Web page by developing a login system to validate users.

User Authentication

In the early days of the World Wide Web, the network resembled a close-knit neighborhood. Everyone knew everyone else, free information was available, and anyone could participate. With the advent of e-commerce and online business, the game has changed. Private networks are using the resources of the Internet, allowing access to privileged information such as customer records, proprietary company data, and personalized account information. This project looks at several solutions for validating users through voice authentication procedures.

THE PROBLEM
Web sites need ways to block users from gaining access to private information and to log in users to refine the user's profile.

THE SOLUTION
Create a user authentication system, using multiple ways to confirm the user's identity.

Project Description

Web developers have created login systems for their Web sites, which include requesting usernames and passwords before allowing users to gain access to secure or paid materials. VoiceXML is capable of using those existing resources plus adding voice authentication as another way of verifying the identity of the user. This project develops three levels of security using the caller's phone number, a username/password combination, and a voice print recognition system.

To complete this project, you will:

1. Test the caller's phone number.
2. Activate password protection.
3. Make a voice print.
4. Verify a user through voice recognition.
5. Create an application using the three methods of security.

You Will Need

✔ **BeVocal developer account**

✔ **voicePrintRegistration.vxml**

✔ **login.vxml**

✔ **Download example files: cafe.bevocal.com/wiley/10projects**

VoiceXML Elements Used in This Project

ELEMENT NAME	DESCRIPTION
<assign>	Assigns a variable a value
<block>	A container of (noninteractive) executable code
<catch>	Catches an event
<else>	Used in <if> elements
<field>	Declares an input field in a form
<filled>	An action executed when fields are filled
<form>	A dialog for presenting information and collecting data
<goto>	Go to another dialog in the same or different document
<grammar>	Specifies a speech recognition or DTMF grammar
<if>	Simple conditional logic
<link>	Specifies a transition common to all dialogs in the link's scope

VoiceXML Elements Used in This Project   *(Continued)*

ELEMENT NAME	DESCRIPTION
<prompt>	Queues speech synthesis and audio output to the user
<register>	Accepts voice input for building a sample (proprietary)
<value>	Inserts the value of an expression in a prompt
<var>	Declares a variable
<verify>	Checks user input against stored voice pattern (proprietary)
<vxml>	Top-level element in each VoiceXML document

Source: *VoiceXML 2.0 Working Draft*, section 1.4

Application Call Flow

The authentication application is developed in two parts. The first part, shown in Figure 4.1, is a login sequence, and the second one builds the voice print registration system, as shown in Figure 4.2.

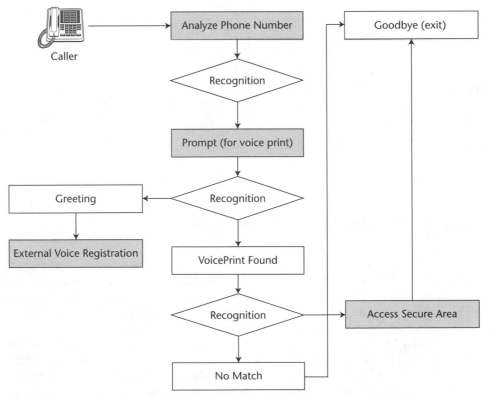

Figure 4.1   Login sequence.

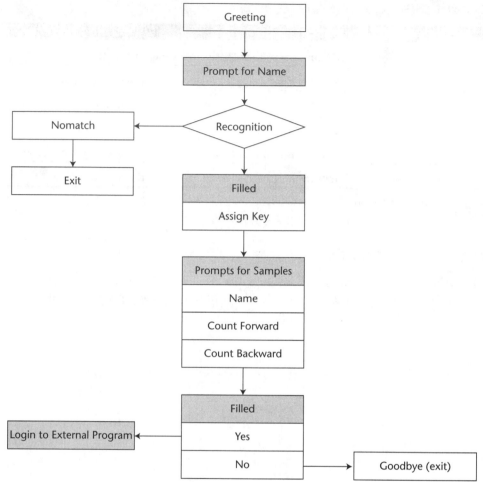

Figure 4.2   Voice print registration.

Testing a Caller's Phone Number

A simple way to begin a secure login is to test the caller's phone number through standard session variables. Session variables make information available to the application such as the caller's phone number, the number the caller dialed, and the type of machine the call was originated from (pay phone, cell phone, prison phone, and so on). A session variable has a value of *undefined* if the service is not supported.

Session variables can be accessed within your VoiceXML application and used for making decisions on how to process a call. Table 4.1 is a list of session variables and the type of information they contain. See section 5.1.4 of the *VoiceXML 2.0 Working Draft* for an extended discussion of the values each variable can hold.

Table 4.1 Session Variables

SESSION VARIABLE	DEFINITION
session.telephone.ani	Automatic number identification
session.telephone.dnis	Dialed number identification service
session.telephone.iidigits	Information indicator digits
session.telephone.uui	User-to-user information
session.telephone.rdnis	Redirect dialed number information service
session.telephone.redirect_reason	Redirect reason

TIP

The environment that processes your VoiceXML script has access to standard session variables that can be used to decide how to process a call.

```
1.  <vxml version="2.0">
2.
3.  <var name="callersPhone" expr="session.telephone.ani"/>
4.
5.  <form id="greeting">
6.   <block>
7.    <if cond="callersPhone == '0' ||
8.             callersPhone == '7183990000' ||
9.             callersPhone == '2124020000'">
10.          <goto next="#mainmenu"/>
11.   <else/>
12.      <prompt>
13.       You are calling from
14.        <say-as type="telephone">
15.           <value expr="callersPhone"/>
16.        </say-as>
17.        You are trying to access a secure area
18.        from a phone that does not have access privileges.
19.        Please disconnect and call from a secure phone.
20.      </prompt>
21.      <goto next="#goodbye"/>
22.    </if>
23.   </block>
24. </form>
25.
26. <form id="mainmenu">
27.     <block>
```

Listing 4.1 Authentication through standard session variables. *(continues)*

```
28.          You have accessed Mars Colony 7
29.          Security Information Center.
30.          <goto next="#goodbye"/>
31.       </block>
32.  </form>
33.
34.  <form id="goodbye">
35.       <block>
36.          Thank you for calling.
37.          Good Bye.
38.       </block>
39.    </form>
40.
41.  </vxml>
```

Listing 4.1 Authentication through standard session variables. *(continued)*

Listing 4.1 is a simple authentication system that verifies the caller's phone number by comparing it to a list of secure phone numbers that are stored as data within the application. If the caller's number is not listed, the call will not be processed.

The *callersPhone* variable on line 3 stores a session variable that has dynamic access to the caller's phone number through the *session.telephone.ani* number session variable. As a reminder, the *expr* attribute of a <var> element dynamically generates a value based upon the return value of the expression. The *session.telephone.ani* variable provides the telephone number of the calling party if the service is supported. When set, *callersPhone* is used to compare against a list of phone numbers that have been approved to access the secure areas of a site.

An <if> condition on lines 7 through 9 tests the caller's phone number against a set of approved numbers. The *cond* attribute compares the value stored in the *callersPhone* variable against the list. The numbers in the secure numbers list are 10 digits (area code plus seven-digit phone number), except for the platform-specific number in the working environment, which is zero.

 When using a VoiceXML portal's scripting environment to test your application, use the *session.telephone.ani* variable to output the caller's phone number. This will show you what the platform is using as a phone number; 0 is used in the current application to accept the phone number from the BeVocal Voice Scripter environment.

TIP

The double pipes, ||, on lines 7 and 8 are used as short-circuit operators to test the numbers in sequence. Starting with the first number in the list, the number is compared to the *callersPhone* variable. If the numbers do not match, processing moves to the next number.

When a number is recognized, comparison checking stops and the user is passed on to the main menu through the <goto> element on line 10. If processing falls through to the end of the list without any number being recognized, the caller does not have approval to access the secured areas and is passed to the <else/> section starting on line 11.

Lines 12 through 19 handle the call if the phone number is not approved for access. The callers are informed that the number they are dialing from is not secure and they should disconnect and call from another phone. Processing is passed to the *goodbye* form for exiting from the script.

<say-as> Elements

Within the TTS output of the <else/> clause is a new element we have not seen before: <say-as>. The <value> element on line 15 is contained within a <say-as> block that controls how the TTS engine will render the output. In the case of a telephone number, the BeVocal platform outputs the <say-as type="telephone"> as a series of prerecorded wav files, as shown in this log output from the Vocal Scripter:

```
** Dialing in progress...
Connection established
OUTPUT -->   You are calling from 0.wav  You are trying to access a
secure area from a phone that does not have access privileges. Please
disconnect and call from a secure phone.
OUTPUT -->   Thank you for calling. Good Bye.
*** Call session ended ***
```

Types may optionally contain a format by inserting a colon followed by the formatting description. As an example, <say-as type="time:hm">1:30:45</say-as> to output the hours, minutes, and seconds. Table 4.2 shows the available values for the <say-as> element.

Table 4.2 Say-as Types

TYPE	OUTPUT
acronym	Pronounced as individual characters.
number	Format values are ordinal and digits.
date	Format values for dates are dmy, mdy, ymd, ym, my, md, y.
time	Format values for time are hm and hms.
duration	Format values for duration are hm, hms, ms, and so on.
currency	Leading and trailing currency symbols are ignored.
measure	A measurement.
telephone	A telephone number.
name	A proper name of a person, organization, and so on.
net	An Internet handle. Format values for net are email and url.
address	A postal address.

Source: The *VoiceXML 2.0 Working Draft*, section 4.1.2.6

Create a simple login procedure that will check the caller's phone number against a list of approved numbers. Be sure to include your own phone number in the list. Call the application to verify that you can access the application from your home phone.

Delete your phone number from the list and verify that access is denied.

Activate Password Protection

Testing whether a phone has been approved for access to a secure area is good as long as the person who is actually using the phone is supposed to have access. This section demonstrates how to ask a user to provide an ID number that will be compared against the phone number for verification of the caller.

Listing 4.2 adds another level of authentication to the *greeting* form in Listing 4.1. If a caller's phone number is recognized, the <goto> element on line 17 transitions to the *password* field on line 32 instead of going directly to the *mainmenu* form. Notice the use of the *nextitem* attribute within the <goto> element, specifying that the location of the item to transition to is within the current dialog.

The password field has four logical areas: a greeting, a grammar, error checking of input, and processing of acceptable input.

```
1.  <?xml version="1.0"?>
2.
3.  <!DOCTYPE vxml
4.    PUBLIC
5.    "-//BeVocal Inc//VoiceXML 2.0//EN"
6.    "http://cafe.bevocal.com/libraries/dtd/vxml2-0-bevocal.dtd">
7.
8.  <vxml version="2.0">
9.
10.   <var name="callersPhone" expr="session.telephone.ani"/>
11.
12.  <form id="greeting">
13.    <block>
14.      <if cond="callersPhone == '0' ||
15.              callersPhone == '7183990000' ||
16.              callersPhone == '2124020000'">
17.              <goto nextitem="password"/>
18.      <else/>
19.        <prompt>
20.           You are calling from
21.         <say-as type="telephone">
22.            <value expr="callersPhone"/>
23.         </say-as>
24.         You are trying to access a secure area
```

Listing 4.2   Verifying a caller's password.

```
25.          from a phone that does not have access privileges.
26.          Please disconnect and call from a secure phone.
27.      </prompt>
28.      <goto next="#goodbye"/>
29.  </if>
30.  </block>
31.
32.  <field name="password">
33.    <audio src="authenticationWelcome.wav"
34.           fetchtimeout="2s">
35.      Welcome. Please speak your password.
36.    </audio>
37.    <grammar>
38.    <![CDATA[
39.      [
40.        vocalscripter  {<password 0>}
41.        (open sez me)  {<password 7183990000>}
42.        (mirror mirror){<password 2124020000>}
43.      ]
44.    ]]>
45.    </grammar>
46.
47.    <nomatch count="1">
48.      Please repeat your password
49.    </nomatch>
50.    <nomatch count="2">
51.      Your password was not recognized.
52.      <log label="UNSUCCESSFUL LOGIN">
53.              Unsuccessful attempt to login from:
54.              <value expr="callersPhone"/>
55.      </log>
56.      <goto next="#goodbye"/>
57.    </nomatch>
58.
59.    <filled>
60.      <if cond="password == callersPhone">
61.        <goto next="#mainmenu"/>
62.      <else/>
63.        Your password was not recognized for the phone
64.        you are calling from.
65.        <goto next="#goodbye"/>
66.      </if>
67.    </filled>
68.  </field>
69.  </form>
70.
71.
72.  <form id="mainmenu">
73.      <block>
```

Listing 4.2   Verifying a caller's password. *(continues)*

```
74.         You have accessed Mars Colony 7
75.         Security Information Center.
76.         <goto next="#goodbye"/>
77.       </block>
78.   </form>
79.
80.   <form id="goodbye">
81.     <block>
82.       Thank you for calling.
83.       Good Bye.
84.     </block>
85.   </form>
86.
87. </vxml>
```

Listing 4.2   Verifying a caller's password. *(continued)*

<audio> Elements

Sometimes it is appropriate to output prerecorded audio in place of a TTS prompt. This is accomplished with the <audio> element. An <audio> element contains a *src* attribute that points to a sound file. If the sound file is not available, the content within the audio tag is output. The *fetchtimeout* attribute specifies a time in seconds for the interpreter to fetch the sound source before it plays the element's content.

Prerecorded audio files can come from many sources. For a simple application, recording your own prompts can be fun and instructive. The GoldWave Player at goldwave.com is a good tool for creating homemade prompts. A production-level application for paying clients should use professional voice recordings.

The greeting on line 35 of Listing 4.2 is contained within an <audio> element. The source file *authenticationWelcome.wav* has 2 seconds to play before the TTS mechanism overrides it and outputs the text content of the <audio> element.

Mapping Grammar Slots

As we have seen in previous projects, grammars are created to compare against user input for appropriate responses. A grammar term or phrase can also be mapped to a specific value. This is useful when multiple terms are synonymous for a single term, where the single term will be used as part of a comparison condition. In our case, a user's password needs to be mapped to a designated phone number and then checked against the caller's phone number.

The grammar of the *password* field in Listing 4.2 consists of a list of password terms or phrases mapped to an approved phone number, as shown on lines 40 through 42. It is assumed that the caller has been assigned a password before making the call. The grammar will recognize three phrases, each mapped to a different phone number. The mapping occurs after each grammar term or phrase is set.

As an example, the second phrase, open sez me, is mapped to the phone number 7183990000. When the speaker inputs the phrase open sez me, the value 7183990000 is stored in the *password* field variable. This value can now be accessed through a call to the variable and compared against the caller's actual phone number.

Error Checking

There are three possibilities for user error when inputting a password. The simple one is the <noinput> event where the user fails to speak. In our application, this is handled by the platform's default *noinput* handler.

A <nomatch> event will be thrown if the caller speaks a password that is not recognized as part of the defined grammar. Attribute values for *count* are set in the <nomatch> elements on lines 47 and 50. When a password is not accepted the first time through, the user is prompted to repeat the input, just in case there was a simple mistake. If it happens a second time, it is assumed that the caller should not be accessing the system and that person is booted off through the <goto> element on line 56, which sends processing to the *goodbye* form.

A third possibility is that the caller will speak a phrase that is recognized as an acceptable password. This will send processing to the <filled> element starting on line 59, which we'll look at in the *Processing the Output* section.

<log> Elements

A new element implemented in the VoiceXML 2.0 specification is the <log> element. With it you can insert messages into the Log Browser to track specific events during calls to your application. It is used in our project to track users who have reached the <nomatch> event twice while trying to login. After a warning to the user is output on line 51 confirming that login was unsuccessful, a message is sent to the log file specifying the Automatic Number Identification of the user.

The *label* attribute of the <log> element precedes the message output to the Log Browser. This is useful when an application is tracking multiple <log> outputs. The <log> element may also carry an *expr* attribute that outputs the content of an ECMAScript expression. Both the *label* and *expr* attributes are optional.

View the log messages through the Log Browser in BeVocal. A snippet from the output of Listing 4.2 follows:

```
FIA: Process Phase
Searching for handler for nomatch; count = 2
Execute Content for <nomatch> at line 50
UNSUCCESSFUL LOGIN:
  Unsuccessful attempt to login from:
  0

GOTO : next attribute is: #goodbye
```

Check the implementation of the <log> element on your platform. Inappropriate attempts to access your secure data should be stored in a log for access by the system administrator.

Processing the Output

The <filled> block on lines 59 through 67 processes the input from the user once it has passed the grammar check. The *cond* attribute of the <if> element compares the *password* field to the *callersPhone* variable. If the two match, the user is authenticated and processing is passed to the *mainmenu* form. When the two do not match, a warning message is output and the *goodbye* form is called for a graceful exit.

Rewrite the greeting form from Listing 4.1 to include a password field. Include the Vocal Scripter number as one of the approved grammars and the phone you will use to test the application. Map each phone number to a word or phrase and then test your application.

Add <log> elements at appropriate places within your script for tracking user errors.

Voice Prints

Most vocal platforms can store a user's voice print and make it available for use during authentication. The implementation will be platform specific, but it is worth learning if your system needs triple-strength security. The BeVocal platform has an implementation of voice print sampling that can be used within the authentication script. In addition to requesting a user password, when the user speaks, the voice can be checked against stored voice patterns for a more secure authentication.

Voice recognition is not defined in the VoiceXML 2.0 specification. However, it is an important enough technology that most vendors have implemented it. Check your vendor's documentation for specifics. The code examples in this chapter are BeVocal specific and may not be applicable for your platform.

Making a Voice Print

Before using voice authentication as a login procedure, the system must be trained to identify the user's voice as a unique item. The script in Listing 4.3 takes several voice samples from the user and combines them into a single voice print.

```
1.  <?xml version="1.0"?>
2.
3.  <!DOCTYPE vxml
4.    PUBLIC
5.    "-//BeVocal Inc//VoiceXML 2.0//EN"
6.    "http://cafe.bevocal.com/libraries/dtd/vxml2-0-bevocal.dtd">
7.
8.  <vxml version="2.0">
9.
10.  <var name="verificationKey"/>
11.
12.    <form id="checkID">
13.      <block>
14.       You have reached the Voice Print Registration System
15.       at Tyrell Corporation on Mars Colony 7.
16.      </block>
17.
18.      <!-- ASSIGN USER A UNIQUE KEY -->
19.      <field name="userID">
20.      <prompt>
21.        Speak your first and last name.
22.      </prompt>
23.        <grammar>
24.          <![CDATA[
25.            [
26.               (rick deckard)      {<userID 1234>}
27.               (roy baitey)        {<userID 2234>}
28.               (rachael tyrell)    {<userID 3234>}
29.               (eldon tyrell)      {<userID 4234>}
30.            ]
31.          ]]>
32.        </grammar>
33.        <nomatch count="1">
34.           Please repeat your first and last name.
35.        </nomatch>
36.        <nomatch count="2">
37.        I'm sorry. You are not authorized to create a voice
38.        print on this system. Please contact the system
39.        administrator if you think you have access to
40.        this system.
41.        <goto next="#goodbye"/>
42.        </nomatch>
43.        <filled>
44.          <assign name="verificationKey" expr="userID"/>
45.        </filled>
```

Listing 4.3   Making a voice print. *(continues)*

```
46.        </field>
47.
48.        <!-- GET VOICE SAMPLES-->
49.        <register name="getName"
50.                  keyExpr="verificationKey"
51.                  mode="delete">
52.          I will create a voice print for you.
53.          You will need the following ID number when
54.          accessing your account
55.          <value expr="userID" />. To start
56.          your voice print, please repeat your first and
57.          last name.
58.          <grammar>
59.            <![CDATA[
60.              [
61.                 (rick deckard)
62.                 (roy baitey)
63.                 (rachael tyrell)
64.                 (eldon tyrell)
65.              ]
66.            ]]>
67.          </grammar>
68.        </register>
69.
70.        <register name="countBackward"
71.                     keyExpr="verificationKey"
72.                     mode="adapt"
73.                     type="digits">
74.          Please count backwards from five to one.
75.        </register>
76.
77.        <register name="countForward"
78.                     keyExpr="verificationKey"
79.                     mode="adapt"
80.                     type="digits">
81.          Please count from 95 to 100.
82.        </register>
83.
84.        <filled>
85.          <prompt>
86.            Your voice print has now been registered
87.            with the Tyrell Corporation.
88.          </prompt>
89.            <goto next="#goodbye"/>
90.        </filled>
91.      </form>
92.
93.      <form id="goodbye">
```

Listing 4.3   Making a voice print.

```
94.        <field name="whereTo" type="boolean">
95.          <prompt>
96.            You are exiting the Tyrell Corporation
97.            Voice Print Registration System.
98.            Please make a note of your new ID number:
99.            <break size="medium"/>
100.            <value expr="verificationKey" />
101.            <break size="large"/>
102.            Would you like to transfer to the Security
103.            Information Center.
104.          </prompt>
105.          <filled>
106.            <if cond="whereTo">
107.              <goto next="authenticate.vxml"/>
108.            <else/>
109.              Good bye.
110.            </if>
111.          </filled>
112.        </field>
113.      </form>
114.
115.    </vxml>
```

Listing 4.3   Making a voice print. *(continued)*

Creating a voice print involves several steps. A unique name must be assigned to the user's print, and the voice print recorder must get an initial sample of the caller's voice. Other samples are then taken and used to form a composite print that is theoretically as identifiable as a fingerprint.

Unique Keys

When a voice print is created, each print must have a unique name, a *key*, attached to it, giving access to the voice print within a calling VoiceXML script when a user needs to be authenticated. Within Listing 4.3, this *key* will also be used to access and refine the user's voice print. Once the print is completed, users will access their print by speaking the unique *key* value.

Line 10 of Listing 4.3 declares a variable named *verificationKey* that will hold the user's unique key once it is assigned.

NOTE

Each voice print must have a unique name, a *key*. This identifies the voice print to a calling application. On the BeVocal platform, all keys within a developer's account are available to every application in that account. Check your platform's documentation for specifics on accessing voice print keys from multiple applications.

As processing enters the *checkID* form in Listing 4.3, users are asked for their first and last name, which if accepted, are then mapped to a *userID* on lines 26 through 29. The mapping assigns a unique identifier to the user. The <nomatch> events are similar to those seen in Listing 4.2. The first <nomatch> asks users to repeat their input, and the second <nomatch> outputs a warning message and terminates the call through the *goodbye* form.

> **User's names and id's can be stored in a database and created dynamically whenever needed. By using an external data source for this information, the VoiceXML application will not have to be changed every time a new user is added to the list.**
>
> **TIP**

<assign> Elements

The <filled> block starting on line 43 contains an <assign> element, assigning a value to the *verificationKey* variable that was declared at the top of the script.

An <assign> element inserts a value into a variable. The *name* attribute is the name of the variable that will receive the assignment, in this case, *verificationKey*. The *expr* attribute is an ECMAScript expression that can generate a value dynamically or insert the value from a previously defined field.

By assigning the user's unique key to the *verificationKey* variable, it can now be used to build and access the user's voice print.

Taking Voice Samples

Several voice samples must be elicited from the user to create an accurate voice print. On the BeVocal platform, the <register> element is used to accept input for the prints.

> **The recording and use of voice samples is a new technology in VoiceXML and may not be implemented the same way on all platforms. Check your platform's documentation for specific details. This project was built using proprietary elements from BeVocal.**
>
> **WARNING**

<register> Elements

To create a voice print, the user needs to supply voice samples. The <register> element is a field-level element that accepts user input for sampling. A prompt is output as content of the <register> element, requesting input from the user. If the user's response is recognized by the field-level grammar within the <register> element, that input is sent to the verifier. The verifier creates a base print from the first sample supplied and uses subsequent samples to refine the base print.

There are three <register> blocks in Listing 4.3 starting on line 49. The first <register> element prompts users to repeat their first and last name. Because this is the first

<register> element in the sequence, it will be used to define the base voice print. A list of names is used for the grammar on lines 61 through 64.

A second and third <register> element occurs on lines 70 and 77, whose input will be used to refine the voice print. The extended request for counting forward and backward is to get as much user input as possible, as quickly as possible. The developer can request other types of input as well.

It is a good idea to decide in advance what users input will be when they are trying to access a secure system and to use that input within a <register> element when creating the voice print. As an example, in this application, the user's name will be used to recognize the user upon entrance to the system; therefore the first <register> element uses that as basis of the voice print.

Create a <register> element that prompts users for a voice sample of the exact phrase they will use when logging in to the voice authentication
TIP **system.**

<register> can carry four attributes:

name: A name for the item

type: Built-in data type supplied by the platform

keyExpr: Unique key value for identifying the voice print

mode: Determines how the sample should be processed

The *name* attribute of a <register> element is a unique field name that holds the recognized input from the user when a sample is taken. Instead of creating a specific grammar for the field, an optional *type* attribute can be used to dynamically construct grammar for *boolean*, *date*, *digits*, and other built-in types, as discussed in Project 1.

The *keyExpr* attribute uses an ECMAScript expression to generate the voice print's unique *key*. The *key* will be needed as a unique identifier for the voice print during an authentication procedure. We will use the *key* in the *Authenticating a User through Voice Recognition* section.

The <register> element carries a *mode* attribute, specifying how the sample should be handled by the verifier. A *mode* can have three values: *delete*, *skip*, or *adapt*.

The *delete* value removes any existing voice print from the application platform that matches the *keyExpr* value. This is used to create a new voice print for the user and should only be used in the first <register> element of the sequence.

Subsequent <register> elements within the form use *adapt* to request more user speech patterns for refining the voice print. A value of *skip* within the *mode* attribute instructs the processor to skip over the <register> element. This is useful within the first <register> element when existing users need to refine their voice print without generating a new *key*.

The *delete* value of the *mode* attribute in <register> should only be used in the first occurrence of the <register> element. If used with other <register>
WARNING **elements, it will delete the existing voice print, not refine it. Use the *adapt* value of *mode* when refining a voice print.**

At this phase in our application development, error checking is handled by the platform, letting users try multiple times if their name is not recognized. Because <register> is a field-level element within a form, <nomatch>, <noinput>, <filled>, and all the child elements of <field> are available to the <register> element.

> **Within a commercial application using voice print recognition for security, the application would explicitly handle <nomatch> and <noinput> responses, transferring the user to a different section of the script after two incorrect entries.**

Completing the Voice Print Sampling

Once the user's voice samples have been taken, the application needs a way to exit gracefully. The <filled> block on lines 84 through 90 confirms to the user that a voice print has been registered and processing is sent to the *goodbye* form. The *goodbye* form reminds users of their newly issued ID number and gives them the chance to return to the secure area of the site.

The <if> condition on lines 106 through 110 handles the transfer to the login script upon a positive response and the termination of the script upon a negative one.

> **Notice the use of the <break> elements on lines 99 and 101. Using pauses when outputting important information gives the user time to absorb what is being said.**

> **Create a new script called voicePrintRegistration.vxml using Listing 4.3 as a template. Create a list of usernames for your application. Assign each user a unique ID number. Insert the usernames and id numbers into the userID field. Test your application by creating voice prints for two or three of your users.**

Authenticating a User through Voice Recognition

Once a voice print of a user has been saved, that voice print can be used to verify that user upon entrance to a secure site. Listing 4.4 changes the login script of Listing 4.2 to accept voice verification as part of the login procedure.

```
1.  <?xml version="1.0"?>
2.
3.  <!DOCTYPE vxml
4.  PUBLIC
5.  "-//BeVocal Inc//VoiceXML 1.0//EN"
6.  "http://cafe.bevocal.com/libraries/dtd/vxml1-0-bevocal.dtd">
```

Listing 4.4 Authenticating a user.

```
7.
8.    <vxml version="2.0">
9.
10.   <var name="callersPhone" expr="session.telephone.ani"/>
11.   <var name="assignedKey"/>
12.
13.     <form id="greeting">
14.       <block>
15.         <if cond="callersPhone == '0' ||
16.                   callersPhone == '7183992000' ||
17.                   callersPhone == '2124020000' ||
18.                   callersPhone == '4155551212'">
19.                 <goto nextitem="userInput"/>
20.           <else/>
21.           You are calling from
22.           <value expr="callersPhone"/>
23.           You are trying to access a secured area from
24.           an insecure phone. Please disconnect and call
25.           from a secure phone.
26.           <goto next="#goodbye"/>
27.         </if>
28.       </block>
29.
30.       <field name="userInput" type="digits">
31.          <prompt>
32.            Speak your four digit ID number.
33.          </prompt>
34.          <filled>
35.            <assign name="assignedKey" expr="userInput"/>
36.          </filled>
37.       </field>
38.
39.       <verify name="userName"
40.              type="digits"
41.              keyExpr="assignedKey">
42.         <prompt>
43.           Speak your first and last name
44.         </prompt>
45.         <grammar>
46.          <![CDATA[
47.            [
48.              (rick deckard)
49.              (roy baitey)
50.              (rachael tyrell)
51.              (eldon tyrell)
52.            ]
53.          ]]>
54.         </grammar>
```

Listing 4.4 Authenticating a user. *(continues)*

```
55.
56.         <catch event="error.verify.keynotfound">
57.           This ID number does not have a voice print.
58.           I will transfer you to the Voice Print
59.           Registration System at the Tyrell Corporation.
60.           <goto next="voicePrintRegistration.vxml"/>
61.         </catch>
62.
63.         <filled>
64.           <if cond="userName$.decision == 'accepted'">
65.             <goto next="#mainmenu"/>
66.           <else/>
67.             Your voice print was not recognized.
68.             <goto next="#goodbye"/>
69.           </if>
70.         </filled>
71.       </verify>
72.     </form>
73.
74.     <form id="mainmenu">
75.       <block>
76.         You have accessed Mars Colony 7
77.         Security Information Center.
78.         <goto next="#goodbye"/>
79.       </block>
80.     </form>
81.
82.     <form id="goodbye">
83.       <field>
84.         <prompt>
85.           Exiting Mars Colony 7 Security Information Center.
86.         </prompt>
87.       </field>
88.     </form>
89.
90.   </vxml>
```

Listing 4.4   Authenticating a user. *(continued)*

When users initially dial into the system, their phone number is checked against a list of approved numbers, just as in the original script. Approved callers are then sent through the voice authentication process instead of being asked to input a password.

When users created a voice print, they were assigned a unique key to identify their voice print. Line 11 of Listing 4.4 creates a variable called *assignedKey* that will hold the user's assigned key. A <field> block on lines 30 through 37 requests the caller's key and assigns the input to the *assignedKey* variable. Processing then falls through to the next field item, the <verify> element, starting the voice authentication process.

<verify> Elements

The <verify> element is a field-level element that accepts user input and compares it against a stored voice print. The content of <verify> is a prompt, requesting spoken input from the user and a grammar for testing the input.

 <verify> is a proprietary element of the BeVocal platform. Check your platform documentation for an applicable element for authentication WARNING using a voice print.

The <verify> element may carry *name*, *type*, and *keyEpr* attributes. The *name* attribute holds the results of the recognition processing, which we will examine in the next section. The *type* attribute is one that we have seen in previous examples when using built-in grammars. A *keyExpr* attribute contains the assigned key that will be used to find a stored copy of the voice print. In this case, it is the value the user has input as his or her assigned key.

In Listing 4.4, the <verify> element starting on line 39 requests the user's name and compares it against a list stored within the <grammar> element. The <catch> or <filled> blocks will handle processing, depending upon whether or not a voice print was found using the value from the *keyExp* attribute.

 It is not mandatory to use a phrase that was input as part of the voice print registration process, but you will get a more accurate reading if you do.
TIP

<catch> Elements

With VoiceXML, it is possible to trap events with a <catch> element and do conditional processing based upon what is found. We have seen examples of the shorthand method of using catch by activating help events with the <help> element and nomatch/noinput events with <nomatch> and <noinput> elements. <catch> allows explicit catching of other types of events.

A <catch> may be set at a document or form level. It carries three attributes: *event*, *count*, and *cond*. We have seen the *count* attribute within the <help>, <nomatch>, and <noinput> elements keeping track of the number of times through the event. The *cond* attribute is optional, forcing a specific ECMAScript condition to be true before the catch element can be entered.

The *event* attribute of a <catch> element specifies the event to be caught. During the verification stage of voice recognition, a unique key provides access to a voice print within the verification engine. If there is no print associated with that key, an error.verify.keynotfound event is thrown within the <verify> element. Line 56 of Listing 4.4 checks for *error.verify.keynotfound*. If the event is found, the content of the <catch> element is executed, outputting an error message and transferring processing to the voicePrintRegistration.vxml script.

If the id number points to a stored voice print, the voice print is compared to the user's spoken input for authentication within the <filled> element on lines 63 through 70.

Shadow Variables

Field-level items may have values attached to them that are made available through a shadow variable. When the verifier returns information to the <verify> element concerning the return value of the voice authentication, it is accessed through the *decision* property of the shadow variable.

 A shadow variable holds additional information about a <field> item or a <verify> element that can be accessed through the field item's name and the shadow variable's properties.

NOTE

To access the value of a shadow variable, begin with the field item's name followed by a dollar sign. A dot separates the element name from the property. Shadow variables are attached to field item variables according to the variable's context. Check your platform's documentation to determine what shadows are available for each type of field item.

The *verify* shadow variable contains three possible values: *accepted*, *rejected*, or *unsure*. When the value of the variable is *accepted*, the verifier confirms the voice print and the spoken input is a match. *rejected* signifies there is no match. If the return value is *unsure*, the verifier cannot guarantee a positive match, but the confidence level is still high enough that it might be a match. The developer can use the return values to decide how to proceed with processing.

In our case, the *userName$.decision* shadow variable accessed on line 64 contains information about the recognition confidence of the user input. It is used in a conditional statement to check the return value from the verifier. If the voice input is *accepted*, processing transitions to the *mainmenu* form. Any other response from the verifier forces a rejection, terminating the call through the *goodbye* form.

For this application, the *mainmenu* form is a placeholder for proof of concept, outputting a confirmation message to the developer and then exiting through the *goodbye* form.

Final Touches to the Application

The authentication application can use a few minor additions such as comments, a *start over* link for developer convenience, optimization of the script by removing the call to the DTD, and a global help menu. Listing 4.5 shows the completedauthentication.vxml script.

```
1.  <?xml version="1.0"?>
2.
3.  <vxml version="2.0">
4.
5.  <var name="callersPhone" expr="session.telephone.ani"/>
6.  <var name="assignedKey"/>
```

Listing 4.5 Completed authentication application.

```
7.
8.   <!-- START OVER -->
9.   <link next="links.vxml">
10.    <grammar>
11.    <![CDATA[
12.    [(start over)]
13.    ]]>
14.    </grammar>
15.  </link>
16.
17.  <!-- GLOBAL HELP LINK -->
18.    <link event="help">
19.      <grammar root="helpVocab">
20.        <rule id="helpVocab">
21.          <one-of>
22.            <item>help</item>
23.            <item>help me</item>
24.            <item>i'm lost</item>
25.            <item>where am i</item>
26.          </one-of>
27.        </rule>
28.      </grammar>
29.    </link>
30.
31.  <!-- GLOBAL HELP OUTPUT -->
32.  <help>
33.    <prompt>
34.      You have reached the Mars Colony 7 tourist info center.
35.      I can help you find your way around the Mars 7 Colony.
36.    </prompt>
37.    <reprompt/>
38.  </help>
39.
40.  <!-- AUTHENTICATION ROUTINES -->
41.  <form id="greeting">
42.
43.    <!-- VALIDATE PHONE NUMBER -->
44.    <block>
45.      <if cond="callersPhone == '0' ||
46.              callersPhone == '7183992000' ||
47.              callersPhone == '2124020000' ||
48.              callersPhone == '4155551212'">
49.              <goto nextitem="userInput"/>
50.      <else/>
51.      You are calling from
52.      <value type="phone" expr="callersPhone"/>
53.      You are trying to access a secured area from
54.      an insecure phone. Please disconnect and call
55.      from a secure phone.
```

Listing 4.5 Completed authentication application. *(continues)*

```
56.        <goto next="#goodbye"/>
57.      </if>
58.  </block>
59.
60.  <!-- RECEIVE USERS VOICE PRINT KEY -->
61.  <field name="userInput" >
62.    <prompt>
63.      Speak your four digit ID number.
64.    </prompt>
65.    <filled>
66.      <assign name="assignedKey" expr="userInput"/>
67.    </filled>
68.  </field>
69.
70.  <!-- VERIFY KEY AND RECEIVE USER INPUT -->
71.  <verify name="userName"
72.          type="digits"
73.          keyExpr="assignedKey">
74.    <prompt>
75.      Speak your first and last name
76.    </prompt>
77.    <grammar>
78.      <![CDATA[
79.        [
80.          (rick deckard)
81.          (roy baitey)
82.          (rachael tyrell)
83.          (eldon tyrell)
84.        ]
85.      ]]>
86.    </grammar>
87.
88.    <!-- VERIFY KEY FOUND AND AVAILABLE -->
89.    <catch event="error.verify.keynotfound">
90.      This ID number does not have a voice print.
91.      I will transfer you to the Voice Print
92.      Registration System at the Tyrell Corporation.
93.      <goto next="voicePrintRegistration.vxml"/>
94.    </catch>
95.
96.    <!-- CHECK RETURN VALUE FROM VERIFIER -->
97.    <filled>
98.      <if cond="userName$.decision == 'accepted'">
99.        <goto next="#mainmenu"/>
100.       <else/>
101.         Your voice print was not recognized for that
102.         id number.
103.         <goto next="#goodbye"/>
```

Listing 4.5 Completed authentication application. *(continued)*

```
104.        </if>
105.      </filled>
106.    </verify>
107.  </form>
108.
109.  <!-- MAIN MENU PLACEHOLDER -->
110.  <form id="mainmenu">
111.   <block>
112.     You have accessed Mars Colony 7
113.     Security Information Center.
114.     <goto next="#goodbye"/>
115.   </block>
116.  </form>
117.
118.  <!-- GOODBYE FORM -->
119.  <form id="goodbye">
120.    <field>
121.      <prompt>
122.        Exiting Mars Colony 7 Security Information Center.
123.      </prompt>
124.      <nomatch><exit/></nomatch>
125.      <noinput><exit/></noinput>
126.    </field>
127.  </form>
128.
129.  </vxml>
```

Listing 4.5   Completed authentication application. *(continued)*

Final Thoughts

The voice authentication routine coupled with a phone number verification list is currently one of the most secure methods of using VoiceXML for verifying a user. Voice recognition interfaces solve problems for the user as well as the system administrator. The caller will not have to remember password and username combinations, and the system administrator will no longer have to maintain and distribute a list of new passwords every month.

An improvement to this project would be to generate the secure phone numbers dynamically from a database instead of hard-coding them into the application.

The listings for this project can be downloaded from the BeVocal Web site at cafe.bevocal.com/wiley/10projects. They are saved as text files, useful as templates for creating your own VoiceXML scripts.

In the first four projects, we developed many of the components that will be needed when developing your own applications. The next project will revisit each of the projects and extract sections of code that can be modularized and stored as separate routines, accessible as modules for all of your VoiceXML applications.

Templates and Multiple Documents

The previous projects each developed specific parts of a Web page and were added to a single document. When building a large Web site, however, it is much more efficient to break up the application into separate components and access them from a single base document. This project will take forms built in the first four projects and store them in separate documents, making it possible for various members of your development team to work on a single component. We will examine techniques for building generic subdialogs that can be used in multiple applications.

THE PROBLEM

As single-document applications develop into larger applications, it is difficult to maintain them and there is a greater chance of code duplication.

THE SOLUTION

Develop a set of common components for generic forms and functions common to most VoiceXML applications.

Project Description

This project uses components from the previous four projects to handle most of the major processing. The user dials into the site and chooses from a menu of three items: hear the company address, leave a recorded voice message, or talk to a receptionist. Each of the responses within the script is stored in a separate document. There is a hidden link within the main menu that allows users to access a secure area if they know the correct grammar.

To complete this project, you will:

1. Create the application root document.

2. Build external placeholder templates.

3. Put content and processing from previous projects into placeholder templates.

4. Access the external templates using the <subdialog> element.

You Will Need

- ✔ **BeVocal developer account**
- ✔ **Previous project files**
- ✔ **Download example files: cafe.bevocal.com/wiley/10projects**

VoiceXML Elements Used in This Project

ELEMENT NAME	DESCRIPTION
<audio>	Plays an audio clip within a prompt
<block>	A container of (noninteractive) executable code
<break>	Forces a pause in output
<choice>	Defines a menu item
<clear>	Clears one or more form item variables
<disconnect>	Disconnects a session
<else>	Used in <if> elements
<elseif>	Used in <if> elements
<exit>	Exits a session
<field>	Declares an input field in a form

VoiceXML Elements Used in This Project   *(Continued)*

ELEMENT NAME	DESCRIPTION
<filled>	An action executed when fields are filled
<form>	A dialog for presenting information and collecting data
<goto>	Go to another dialog in the same or different document
<grammar>	Specifies a speech recognition or DTMF grammar
<if>	Simple conditional logic
<link>	Specifies a transition common to all dialogs in the link's scope
<meta>	Defines a meta data item as a name/value pair
<nomatch>	Catches a nomatch event
<object>	Interacts with a custom extension
<param>	Parameter in <object> or <subdialog>
<prompt>	Queues speech synthesis and audio output to the user
<record>	Records an audio sample
<return>	Returns from a subdialog
<subdialog>	Invokes another dialog as a subdialog of the current one
<transfer>	Transfers the caller to another destination
<value>	Inserts the value of an expression in a prompt
<var>	Declares a variable
<vxml>	Top-level element in each VoiceXML document

Source: *VoiceXML 2.0 Working Draft*, section 1.4

Application Call Flow

The application flow for this project is shown in Figure 5.1. The phone call is answered with a greeting which then transfers the caller to the main menu. The user may then choose to request company address information, leave a voice mail, or have the call transferred to another number. For knowledgeable callers, secure access is hidden within the main menu. Once the call has been completed, it is terminated with a polite goodbye message.

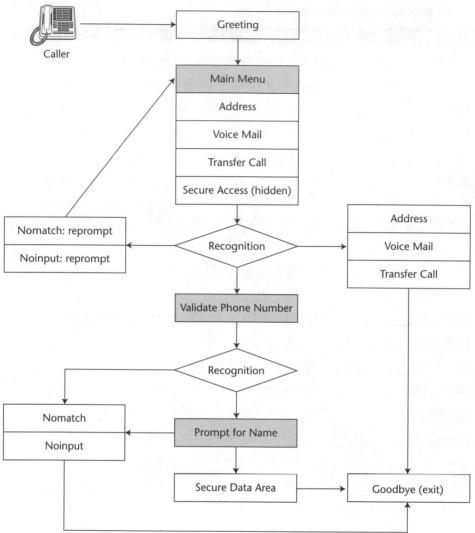

Figure 5.1 Application flow.

Create the Root-Level Document

This project will be created in two phases. First, we will create the base application skeleton, which will contain global variables and links that will be available to all of the documents in the application. The base application is used as an entry point to the rest of the application through calls to subdialogs. The second phase of the project will be to create generic templates for the major components that were created in the first four projects.

```
1.  <?xml version="1.0"?>
2.
3.  <!DOCTYPE vxml
4.    PUBLIC
5.    "-//BeVocal Inc//VoiceXML 2.0//EN"
6.    "http://cafe.bevocal.com/libraries/dtd/vxml2-0-bevocal.dtd">
7.
8.  <vxml version="2.0">
9.
10.    <!-- GLOBAL VARIABLES AND LINKS -->
11.    <var name="companyName" expr="'Mars Colony 7'"/>
12.
13.    <link next="templates.vxml">
14.      <grammar>
15.        <![CDATA[[(start over)]]]>
16.      </grammar>
17.    </link>
18.
19.    <!-- PUBLIC ACCESS -->
20.    <form id="baseApplication">
21.      <subdialog name="getGreeting"
22.                 src="templatesgreeting.vxml"/>
23.      <subdialog name="getMenu"
24.                 src="templatesmainmenu.vxml"/>
25.      <subdialog name="getGoodbye"
26.                 src="templatesgoodbye.vxml"/>
27.    </form>
28.
29.  </vxml>
```

Listing 5.1 Root-level document.

Listing 5.1 is the application root document, the foundation, for the rest of the application. It uses elements and techniques that were developed in the first four projects.

The application begins with an XML declaration and a DOCTYPE declaration for
access to a DTD. The root element, <vxml>, is specified on line 8 with a VoiceXML version number of 2.0. The company name is stored in global variable *companyName* on
line 11, and a convenience link for the developer to restart the application is set on lines
13 through 17.

NOTE

**Remember, global variables and links are available to the complete
application, including the external templates of the application.**

Lines 20 through 27 are calls to the subdialogs that contain the various templates of
the application. The *greeting*, *menu*, and *goodbye* forms from the previous projects have
been turned into standalone templates, accessible through subdialog calls. Each call to

a subdialog contains two attributes: a *name* attribute as a unique identifier and a *src* attribute that holds the URL location of the template to be called.

TIP

Let the platform set the default attributes when making a call to a subdialog unless you need to specifically override a value. See your vendor's documentation for applicable attributes.

HANDS ON

Create an application root document that will be used for accessing multiple templates within your application. At a minimum, have subdialog calls to greeting, menu, and goodbye templates. Include a developer link at the top of the base application for restarting the application.

NOTE

The subdialog calls will not work until the templates are created.

Creating Templates

The base application created in Listing 5.1 is the jumping off point for access to the various templates of the application. To create the templates, we will first make place-holder templates and then add a processing script to each.

Templates versus Objects

VoiceXML has elements that can be used to create reusable components: <subdialog> and <object>. <subdialog> was introduced in Project 2 when discussing links. It gives the developer the option of creating routines within an application that function like subroutines or functions, accepting parameters and returning values based upon those parameters.

<objects> are prebuilt functions provided by the platform to handle complex input processing such as requesting a credit card number or accepting an address. The objects are completely self-contained and do not allow the developer to make adjustments for specific needs of the application. They are platform specific, possibly limiting portability when changing vendors.

As we develop Project 5, when referring to templates, we will be talking about calls to subdialogs. Templates are useful when objects provided by the platform are too restrictive for the task at hand. By creating developer-defined templates, components can be adjusted and tweaked for various applications without having to design the complete template from scratch.

NOTE

Reusable components are prepackaged complex routines that are provided by the platform and are accessed through the <object> element. Templates are created by the developer to isolate sections of the code that are easily customized for use within multiple applications.

Appendix K of the W3C *VoiceXML 2.0 Working Draft* is a discussion of reusable dialog components versus templates and samples. This is not part of the specification of the language; it is a discussion of the concept of building a robust VoiceXML application.

Creating the Placeholder Templates

In this project, we will construct three leaf documents as templates: templatesgreeting.vxml, templatesmainmenu.vxml, and templatesgoodbye.vxml, as shown in Listings 5.2 through 5.4. The placeholders are used for setting up the main structure of the application and confirming processing flow. The templatesgoodbye.vxml placeholder is called within various locations of the other templates as their script is expanded and is used for gracefully exiting the application.

```
1.  <?xml version="1.0"?>
2.
3.  <vxml version="2.0" application="templates.vxml">
4.
5.   <form id="greeting">
6.    <block>
7.       Inside the greeting template.
8.       <return/>
9.    </block>
10.  </form>
11.
12.  </vxml>
```

Listing 5.2 Greeting placeholder.

```
1.  <?xml version="1.0"?>
2.
3.  <vxml version="2.0" application="templates.vxml">
4.
5.   <form id="mainmenu">
6.    <block>
7.      Inside the main menu template
8.      <return/>
9.    </block>
10.   </form>
11.
12.  </vxml>
```

Listing 5.3 Main menu placeholder.

```
1.  <?xml version="1.0"?>
2.
3.  <vxml version="2.0" application="templates.vxml">
4.
5.   <!-- GOODBYE -->
6.   <form id="goodbye">
7.     <block>
8.        Inside the Goodbye placeholder.
9.     </block>
10.   </form>
11.
12.  </vxml>
```

Listing 5.4   Goodbye placeholder.

Each of the placeholders is a complete, standalone Voice XML document that contains an XML declaration, a <vxml> root element, and a single form to handle processing. Line 3, which holds the root element, carries an attribute named *application*. This attribute points to the application root document that holds the global variables and links.

The <block> on lines 6 through 9 of each document, except for the goodbye template, serves two functions. First, it outputs a confirmation message to the developer that this part of the application has been accessed and then, on line 8, it returns processing control to the calling application through the <return> element. The goodbye template implicitly exits the script because processing terminates when the last field-level item of a form is processed and there is no transfer of processing using the <goto>, <submit>, or <subdialog> elements.

HANDS ON

Create the placeholder templates for greeting, mainmenu, and goodbye. Save them as templatesgreeting.vxml, templatesmainmenu.vxml, and templatesgoodbye.vxml. Test your base application, verifying that each leaf within the application can be accessed.

The Greeting Template

The *greeting* template is used to confirm to users that they have entered the called application. Each of our previous projects has contained a greeting that has passed processing to the *maincontent* form of the application.

```
1.  <form id="greeting">
2.     <block>
3.        Welcome to <value expr="companyName"/>.
4.        You have reached the Visitor&apos;s Information Center.
5.        <return/>
6.     </block>
7.  </form>
```

Listing 5.5   Greeting.

Scope of Variables

Listing 5.5 expands the *greeting* form to include the use of the *companyName* variable that was declared as a global variable at the top of the application root document. Variables can also be scoped to more explicit levels within the application.

As we have seen in previous projects, variables can be declared with the <var> element or as a field-level item that can be accessed through the item's name. The scope of the variable is determined by context within the VoiceXML application. *Session* variables are set by the platform and are available as read-only values through *session.telephone.** calls. Project 4 used session variables to access the phone number of the calling party.

Application-level variables are set with the <var> element as children of the application root document, making them globally accessible to all leaves of the application. Leaves within the application may individually contain document-scoped variables that are set as children of the root element of that document. They are in that scope for the time the document is accessible.

Forms and menus limit the scope of their content to the dialog level. Variables may finally be scoped at the anonymous level within a <block>, <catch>, or <filled> element.

 NOTE The *companyName* variable has been declared at an application level. Variables may also be declared at document level for a single document or at dialog level for a single dialog. Section 5.1.2 of the *VoiceXML 2.0 Working Draft* discusses the scope of grammars within variables.

 HANDS ON Expand the greeting in the templatesgreeting.vxml file to include the *companyName* variable. Place a phone call to your application to verify that *companyName* has expanded properly.

The Goodbye Template

Graceful termination of the application is handled through the goodbye template. At various locations within the application, processing is sent to the goodbye dialog to exit the script. This also gives the developer a chance to start over without having to disconnect and place another phone call.

```
1.  <?xml version="1.0"?>
2.
3.  <vxml version="2.0" application="templates.vxml">
4.
5.  <!-- GOODBYE -->
6.  <form id="goodbye">
7.    <field>
8.      <prompt>
9.        Thank you for calling <value expr="companyName"/>
10.        Good Bye.
11.     </prompt>
```

Listing 5.6   Goodbye. *(continues)*

```
12.        <grammar>quit</grammar>
13.        <nomatch><exit/></nomatch>
14.        <noinput><exit/></noinput>
15.      </field>
16.    </form>
17.
18.  </vxml>
```

Listing 5.6   Goodbye. *(continued)*

Listing 5.6 fills in the placeholder template for the *goodbye* form. The company name is output at the end of the Thank you statement, while a <prompt> element waits for input from the developer. As explained in a previous project, the start over <link> at the top of the application can be activated from within this form to clear all variables and reload the application without having to disconnect and redial.

The Menu Template

Isolating an application's menus into separate documents helps with maintenance of the menus and to keep a clear hierarchy of structure. To create the menu shown in Listing 5.7, replace the prompt within the templatesmainmenu.vxml file with the menu that was created in Project 3.

```
1.  <?xml version="1.0"?>
2.
3.  <vxml version="2.0" application="templates.vxml">
4.
5.  <!-- MAIN MENU -->
6.  <menu id="mainmenu">
7.    <prompt>
8.      To hear the address of <value expr="companyName"/>,
9.        say "Address".
10.       To leave a voice message, say "Voice".
11.       If you would like to speak with a receptionist,
12.       say "Transfer".
13.    </prompt>
14.
15.    <choice next="#address">
16.      <grammar>[ (address ?please) ]</grammar>
17.      Address
18.    </choice>
19.    <choice next="#voice">
20.      <grammar>[ (voice ?message) voicemail ]</grammar>
```

Listing 5.7   Main menu.

```
21.      Voice
22.   </choice>
23.   <choice next="#transfer">
24.      <grammar>
25.         [ (transfer ?me ?please) receptionist ]
26.      </grammar>
27.      Transfer
28.   </choice>
29.   <nomatch>
30.      Your choices are <enumerate/>
31.      Try again.
32.   </nomatch>
33. </menu>
34.
35. </vxml>
```

Listing 5.7   Main menu. *(continued)*

In Listing 5.7, the <choice> elements in lines 15 through 23 are still pointing to relative links within the existing document. These links need to be changed to point to the eternal templates that will be created for each link. Listing 5.8 shows the correct path for calling the templates.

The external templates that will be accessed from the main menu are each standalone files. We will build placeholders, as was done before, and then add the relevant processing to each document after the application has been tested.

```
1.  <choice next="templatesaddress.vxml">
2.     <grammar>[ (address ?please) ]</grammar>
3.     Address
4.  </choice>
5.  <choice next="templatesvoice.vxml">
6.     <grammar>[ (voice ?message) voicemail ]</grammar>
7.     Voice
8.  </choice>
9.  <choice next="templatestransfer.vxml">
10.     <grammar>
11.        [ (transfer ?me ?please) receptionist ]
12.     </grammar>
13.     Transfer
14.  </choice>
```

Listing 5.8   Calls to the external templates.

```
1.  <?xml version="1.0"?>
2.
3.  <vxml version="2.0" application="templates.vxml">
4.
5.    <!-- ADDRESS -->
6.    <form id="address">
7.      <block>
8.        Inside Address at third level of application
9.        <return/>
10.   </block>
11.  </form>
12.
13.  </vxml>
```

Listing 5.9   Address placeholder.

Listing 5.9 shows a basic template for the *address* choice. It follows the same format as the other placeholders. Line 3 points back to the base application, templates.vxml, giving access to the global variables and links that were declared two levels above the current template. Line 6 gives an id of *address* to the current form, and line 8 confirms to the developer the location of the current processing context.

The <return> element on line 9 returns execution to a <subdialog>. This has interesting implications within the current context. The *address* template was called from the *mainmenu*, which in turn was called as a subdialog from the application root document. Because <return> relates to the context in which the subdialog was called, processing returns to the application root document context, not the *mainmenu*, when processing is completed within the *address* template.

The <return> element on line 9 of Listing 5.9 returns processing to the routine that called the original subdialog, not the menu item that called this template.

Insert the menu from Project 3 into the menu placeholder template in the current project. Change the links within the <choice> elements to point to the appropriate external files. Create placeholder templates for address, voice, and transfer. Use Listing 5.9 as a model for creating the templatesaddress.vxml, templatesvoice.vxml, and templatestransfer.vxml. Before proceeding to the next section, test the application to verify that processing can access all levels of the application.

The application has three levels at this point: level one is the base application that calls the subdialogs, level two is the main menu that points to external template files for processing each item of the menu, and level three holds the templates that will respond to each of the menu items.

Completing the Templates

Each of the placeholder templates can now be used to process information. We will use the forms created in Project 3 to insert processing into each template, starting with the address template.

The Address Template

Listing 5.10 is the completed address template, filled in with code taken from Project 3. The only changes to the original code are on lines 20 through 26. The original form had an if/else statement in the <filled> element that controlled the process flow, transferring processing to the goodbye form. This has been altered to handle the <return/> element.

```
1.  <?xml version-"1.0"?>
2.
3.  <vxml version="2.0" application="templates.vxml">
4.
5.    <!-- ADDRESS -->
6.    <form id="address">
7.      <field name="snailMail" type="boolean">
8.
9.        <prompt>
10.           <value expr="companyName"/>
11.           is located on the fourth planet of
12.           the local solar system <break size="small"/>
13.           third quadrant <break size="small"/>
14.           northern section <break size="small"/>
15.           parsec 7891<break size="small"/>
16.           The main intersection is 12th Street and Vine.
17.           Would you like me to repeat the address.
18.        </prompt>
19.
20.        <filled>
21.           <if cond="snailMail">
22.              <clear/>
23.           <else/>
24.              <return/>
25.           </if>
26.        </filled>
27.
28.      </field>
29.  </form>
30.
31.  </vxml>
```

Listing 5.10   The address template.

Add content and processing from Project 3 to the templatesaddress.vxml document. Verify that the document processes properly before proceeding HANDS ON to the next section.

The Voice Message Template

The code in Listing 5.11 was taken verbatim from the *voice* form in Project 3 to fill in the voice message template. Notice the change on line 43 where the <return/> element sends processing back to the original subdialog call.

```
1.  <?xml version="1.0"?>
2.
3.  <vxml version="2.0" application="templates.vxml">
4.
5.    <!-- LEAVE VOICE MESSAGE -->
6.    <form id="voice">
7.
8.      <record name="voiceMessage"
9.              beep="false"
10.             maxtime="10s"
11.             finalsilence="1.5s"
12.             type="audio/wav">
13.       <prompt>
14.         You will have 10 seconds to record a message.
15.         Please speak after the tone.
16.       </prompt>
17.     </record>
18.
19.     <!-- OFFER TO RECORD AGAIN -->
20.     <field name="processMessage" type="boolean">
21.       <prompt>
22.         Here is your message <value expr="voiceMessage"/>
23.         Is this the message you would like to send.
24.       </prompt>
25.
26.       <filled>
27.         <if cond="processMessage">
28.           Please wait while your message is being saved.
29.         <else/>
30.           <clear/>
31.         </if>
32.       </filled>
33.     </field>
34.
35.     <subdialog name="saveMessage"
36.                src="recording.cgi"
37.                method="post"
38.                enctype="multipart/form-data"
```

Listing 5.11   The voice message template.

```
39.                 namelist="voiceMessage"
40.                 fetchtimeout="10s">
41.       <filled>
42.          <audio>Your message has been sent.</audio>
43.          <return/>
44.       </filled>
45.     </subdialog>
46.
47.   </form>
48.
49. </vxml>
```

Listing 5.11   The voice message template. *(continued)*

Use the voice form in Project 3 to change the placeholder prompt in templatesvoice.vxml, allowing users to leave a voice message.

HANDS ON

The Transfer Template

The templatesoperator.vxml document in Listing 5.12 uses an explicit <block> element on line 35 to hold the <return/> element because a <return> cannot be a child of a <form>. Processing is exactly as it was in Project 3 for the *transfer* form.

```
1.  <?xml version="1.0"?>
2.
3.  <vxml version="2.0" application="templates.vxml">
4.
5.  <!-- TRANSFER CALL -->
6.   <form id="transfer">
7.      <block>
8.         Please wait while we wake up the android.
9.      </block>
10.
11.     <transfer
12.        name="reception"
13.        connecttimeout="20s"
14.        maxtime="60s"
15.     bridge="true"
16.     dest="800-555-1212">
17.
18.     <filled>
19.        <if cond="reception == 'busy'">
```

Listing 5.12   Transfer template. *(continues)*

```
20.        <prompt>
21.          Hal is busy chatting with Dave.
22.          Please try again later.
23.        </prompt>
24.      <elseif cond="reception == 'far_end_disconnect'"/>
25.        Hal has terminated the call.
26.      <elseif cond="reception == 'noanswer'"/>
27.        <prompt>
28.          Hal is not responding.
29.          Dave might have unplugged him.
30.        </prompt>
31.      </if>
32.    </filled>
33.    </transfer>
34.
35.    <block><return/></block>
36.
37.    </form>
38.
39. </vxml>
```

Listing 5.12   Transfer template. *(continued)*

Use the *transfer* form from Project 3 to fill in the placeholder template in templatestransfer.vxml. Test the application to verify that all three documents can be accessed from the main menu and processing is returned to the application root document from each leaf.

With these three templates completed, the application is now a fully functioning, multidocument application.

Secure Login

In Project 4, a secure login script was created using either a username/password combination or a voice authentication procedure. We will be adding the secure login procedures to the current project along with a hidden link to the login that can only be accessed through the main menu by knowledgeable users.

A link has been added on lines 5 through 9 in Listing 5.13. When the user speaks the words *security access*, processing transfers to the templatesauthenticate.vxml script. Note that the link is only accessible while the menu document is active. The user must know that the link is available because it is not listed as one of the menu options. The idea of security by obscurity is not considered a safe way to access secure material, but because there will be an authentication procedure when the link is activated, this will be adequate for our purposes.

```
1.  <?xml version="1.0"?>
2.
3.  <vxml version="2.0" application="templates.vxml">
4.
5.    <link next="templatesauthenticate.vxml">
6.      <grammar>
7.        <![CDATA[[(security access)]]]>
8.      </grammar>
9.    </link>
10.
11.   <!-- MAIN MENU -->
12.   <menu id="mainmenu" dtmf="true">
13.     <prompt>
14.       To hear the company address, say "Address".
15.       <break size="medium"/>
16.       To leave a voice message, say "Voice".
17.       <break size="medium"/>
18.       To speak with an A.I. receptionist, say "Hal".
19.     </prompt>
20.
21.     <choice next="templatesaddress.vxml">
22.       <grammar>[ address ]</grammar>
23.     </choice>
24.     <choice next="templatesvoice.vxml">
25.       <grammar>[ voice ]</grammar>
26.     </choice>
27.     <choice next="templatesoperator.vxml">
28.       <grammar>[ hal ]</grammar>
29.     </choice>
30.     <nomatch>
31.       I missed that. Try again.
32.       <reprompt/>
33.     </nomatch>
34.   </menu>
35.
36.  </vxml>
```

Listing 5.13   Add a hidden link to the menu.

Hidden links are useful when creating applications for experienced users. They can open a short window of opportunity if callers know they are available and what grammar is needed to activate them. Because there are no prompts to indicate that the link exists, the user must know the location of the prompt in advance. When inserted judiciously into a VoiceXML application, it allows experienced users to bypass instructional messages and hierarchical menus by jumping directly to relevant sections.

Scope of Grammars

Grammars have scope, just as variables do. Scope of grammars can be set by context, as in Listing 5.13, or in some cases set explicitly using the *scope* attribute set to a value of *document* or *dialog*. The hidden link on lines 5 though 9 of Listing 5.13 is only available when the templatesmainmenu.vxml document is active.

Grammars set within links are scoped to the same level as the element that contains the link. We have seen this previously when constructing the *start over* link at the top level of the application root document, creating a grammar that is accessible through the entire application. A link grammar can also be scoped to the *document* level within any leaf of the application, limiting use of that grammar to the current document, as was done in Listing 5.12. The *scope* attribute is not available to a grammar within a link.

Form-level grammars are active while processing is within a <form>. This is considered *dialog* scope and is the default scope of any form. <menu> elements are at the same level as <form> elements, following the same rules of grammar scoping.

A <form> may carry a *scope* attribute set to *document*, overriding the default *dialog* scope of the grammar, forcing it to the document level. If the document containing the <form> is the application root document, the grammar will be available throughout a multidocument application. When a grammar outside of the current <form> or <menu> is recognized and activated, processing of the current <form> or <menu> is terminated, and control is transferred to the <form> or <menu> where the grammar was recognized.

Forms are not limited to containing a single <grammar> element. Within a <form>, each <grammar> element may carry a *scope* attribute, specifying the scope at *dialog* or *document* level. If the <form> and the <grammar> elements both carry a *scope* attribute, the <grammar> element takes precedence.

Grammars set at field level are only active within that field and cannot carry a *scope* attribute.

The security access link is considered document-level scoping. It is limited to being accessed from within the menu document. See the W3C *VoiceXML 2.0 Working Draft*, section 3.1.3, for a detailed overview of grammar scope.

Alter the templatesmenu.vxml file by inserting a hidden link that will access an authentication procedure.

Login Template

The hidden security link in the menu template points to the templatesauthenticate.vxml file. The file is a placeholder, shown in Listing 5.14, for an authentication procedure. Line 8 points to a file or process that contains the secure data, in this case a placeholder template, as shown in Listing 5.15.

```
1. <?xml version="1.0"?>
2.
3. <vxml version="2.0" application="templates.vxml">
4.
5.    <form id="authenticate">
6.      <block>
7.        Inside the authentication template.
8.        <goto next="templatessecuredata.vxml"/>
9.      </block>
10.   </form>
11.
12. </vxml>
```

Listing 5.14   Login template.

Because these templates are not called as subdialogs, the <return> element is not applicable for transferring processing back to the calling dialog. Each uses a <goto> element to explicitly access the next document within the application. In Listing 5.14, once the developer has received confirmation that this part of the application has been accessed, processing transfers to templatessecuredata.vxml, a placeholder area that can contain secure data. The Secure Data Template in Listing 5.15 transfers processing to the templatesgoodbye.vxml document, which will gracefully exit the application.

```
1. <?xml version="1.0"?>
2.
3. <vxml version="2.0" application="templates.vxml">
4.
5.    <form id="securedata">
6.      <block>
7.        Inside the security data template.
8.        <goto next="templatesgoodbye.vxml"/>
9.      </block>
10.   </form>
11.
12. </vxml>
```

Listing 5.15   Secure data template.

Create the templateauthenticate.vxml file and the templatessecuredata.vxml placeholder files. Test the hidden link to verify that the authentication template can be accessed from the menu document and that processing is passed to the templatessecuredata.vxml file.

HANDS ON

Authentication Routine

Project 4 developed a form that can be used for user authentication through a username/password routine. This routine needs to be isolated into its own document, as shown in Listing 5.16.

```
1.  <?xml version="1.0"?>
2.
3.  <vxml version="2.0" application="templates.vxml">
4.  <varname="callersPhone"expr="session.telephone.ani"
5.    <form id="authenticate">
6.      <block>
7.        <if cond="callersPhone == '0' ||
8.                  callersPhone == '7183990000' ||
9.                  callersPhone == '2124020000' ||
10.             callersPhone == '4155551212'">
11.               <goto nextitem="userName"/>
12.         <else/>
13.         You are calling from
14.         <value expr="callersPhone"/>
15.         You are trying to access a secured area from
16.         an insecure phone. Please disconnect and call
17.         from a secure phone.
18.         <goto next="templates.vxml#goodbye"/>
19.       </if>
20.     </block>
21.
22.     <field name="userName">
23.       <prompt>
24.         Speak your first and last name.
25.       </prompt>
26.       <grammar>
27.         <![CDATA[
28.           [
29.             (richard deckard)   {<userName 0>}
30.             (roy baty)          {<userName 7183992000>}
31.             (rachael tyrell)    {<idNumber 2124020000>}
32.             (eldon tyrell)      {<idNumber 4155551212>}
33.           ]
34.         ]]>
35.       </grammar>
36.
37.       <nomatch count="1">
38.         For security purposes, repeat your first
39.         and last name.
40.       </nomatch>
41.       <nomatch count="2">
```

Listing 5.16 Authentication document.

```
42.          You are not registered as a secure user.
43.          <goto next="templates.vxml#goodbye"/>
44.       </nomatch>
45.
46.       <filled>
47.        <if cond="userName == callersPhone">
48.          <goto next="templatessecuredata.vxml"/>
49.        <else/>
50.          ID was not recognized.
51.          <goto next="templatesgoodbye.vxml"/>
52.        </if>
53.       </filled>
54.     </field>
55.   </form>
56.
57. </vxml>
```

Listing 5.16 Authentication document. *(continued)*

You should recognize the code in Listing 5.16 as that created in Project 4. The user's phone number is checked against an approved set of numbers upon entrance to the authentication form. If the phone number is authenticated, the user speaks his or her name, which is compared against the list of phone numbers. When the name and phone number match, the user is passed into the secure data area of the application. The only change is within each <goto> element sending processing to the templates-goodbye.vxml document for terminating the application.

HANDS ON

Add the login sequence to the templatesauthenticate.vxml document. Verify that the hidden link works by activating it during the menu dialog.

Final Thoughts

Don't be deceived by how easy this project was to accomplish. The concepts used were very powerful ones. Isolating generic code into separate documents will help you quickly prototype future projects without having to build each application from scratch. As you continue to develop projects with VoiceXML, keep an eye out for code that can become part of your common components library.

The listings for this project can be downloaded from the BeVocal Web site at cafe.bevocal.com/wiley/10projects. They are saved as text files, useful as templates for creating your own VoiceXML scripts.

This project is the last in the series on building a voice site from an existing Web site. The next five projects will expand on the ideas that have been covered here, examining advanced VoiceXML concepts for use within your applications. We will use the templates to create a personal telephone assistant to access your phone directory through one phone number, a report recorder using Perl, a quiz/survey generator using XML and XSLT, an events calendar with Cold Fusion, and a voice interface to an FAQ engine.

PROJECT
6

Telephone Dialer

How many different places do you have phone numbers stored? If you are like most busy people, you have at least three: a little black book, an online address book, and a PDA. What these methods lack is a way to access those numbers without having to carry them around with you.

This project builds a simple vocal telephone dialer that stores names and phone numbers and allows you to access them through one phone number. You access a phone number in your list by speaking the name of the person you want to call. The application will retrieve the phone number and dial it for you. All you have to do is remember the one phone number that accesses your contact list.

THE PROBLEM

Whenever you need to retrieve a phone number, whether at home, at work, or on the road, you have to find your address book, look up the phone number, and dial it. It is almost impossible to keep track of all telephone resources through one central source.

THE SOLUTION

Create a comprehensive telephone directory that can be accessed by voice through one toll-free telephone number.

173

Project Description

The user inserts a list of phone numbers into the VoiceXML script. Each phone number is associated with a unique user through a defined grammar. The caller dials the phone directory number and speaks the name of the person or business to dial. The program transfers the call to the phone number associated with the business or person.

To complete this project, you will:

1. Build a contact list.

2. Map a name to a telephone number.

3. Confirm user input with implied prompts.

4. Group items in a grammar.

5. Create multiple tokens as a single item in a grammar.

6. Refine the contact list.

7. Allocate multiple phone numbers for one contact.

8. Control data type output.

9. Transfer the call to the contact number.

10. Place another call without disconnecting.

11. Localize help and error messages.

12. Put it all together.

You Will Need

✔ **An account with BeVocal**

✔ **List of phone numbers and locations to call**

✔ **Download example files: cafe.bevocal.com/wiley/10projects**

VoiceXML Elements Used in This Project

ELEMENT NAME	DESCRIPTION
<assign>	Assigns a variable a value
<block>	A container of (noninteractive) executable code
<disconnect>	Disconnects a session

VoiceXML Elements Used in This Project *(Continued)*

ELEMENT NAME	DESCRIPTION
<else>	Used in <if> elements
<elseif>	Used in <if> elements
<field>	Declares an input field in a form
<filled>	An action executed when fields are filled
<form>	A dialog for presenting information and collecting data
<goto>	Go to another dialog in the same or different document
<grammar>	Specifies a speech recognition or DTMF grammar
<help>	Catches a help event
<if>	Simple conditional logic
<link>	Specifies a transition common to all dialogs in the link's scope
<noinput>	Catches a noinput event
<nomatch>	Catches a nomatch event
<prompt>	Queues speech synthesis and audio output to the user
<reprompt>	Plays a field prompt when a field is revisited after an event
<transfer>	Transfers the caller to another destination
<vxml>	Top-level element in each VoiceXML document

Source: *VoiceXML 2.0 Working Draft*, section 1.4

Application Call Flow

Figure 6.1 shows the call flow for this application. The caller is greeted by a standard welcome message and then is prompted for the name of the person to call. The phone number is retrieved from the address book and the call is transferred to the new number. Once the call has been completed, a request for another number is output. The application is terminated with a goodbye message once all calls have been made.

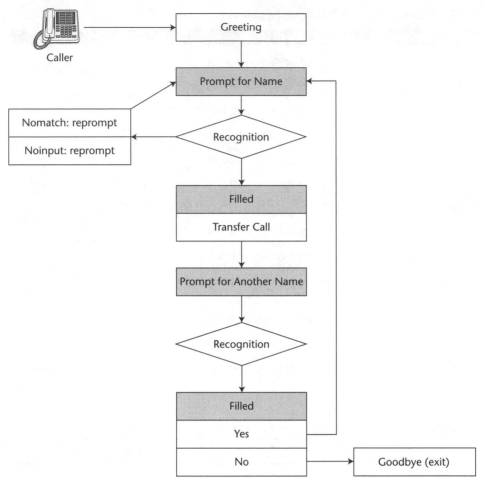

Figure 6.1 Application flow.

Build a Contact List

The phone book application is a list of phone numbers associated with a list of names. We'll start with a simple contact list and then expand to a list of contacts or businesses you would like to be able to access.

The first pass at a simple grammar is a list of fictitious family members. This will give us a chance to deal with groups of people who have the same phone number and people who have multiple phone numbers. The initial contact list is first names only, as shown in Listing 6.1. Later in the project we will develop a more complex grammar that will handle first name duplicates and shortcuts to your most used contacts.

```
1.  <?xml version="1.0"?>
2.
3.  <!DOCTYPE vxml
4.  PUBLIC
5.  "-//BeVocal Inc//VoiceXML 2.0//EN"
6.  "http://cafe.bevocal.com/libraries/dtd/vxml2-0-bevocal.dtd">
7.
8.  <vxml version="2.0">
9.    <form id="getContactName">
10.
11.     <field name="contactList">
12.       <prompt>
13.         Whom would you like to contact?
14.       </prompt>
15.
16.       <grammar>
17.         <![CDATA[
18.           [
19.             rosemary
20.             john
21.             anthony
22.             kristi
23.             cubby
24.             kim
25.             mary
26.             richard
27.             aaron
28.             justin
29.           ]
30.         ]]>
31.       </grammar>
32.
33.       <filled>
34.         <prompt>
35.           You asked for <value expr="contactList"/>
36.         </prompt>
37.       </filled>
38.
39.     </field>
40.   </form>
41.
42. </vxml>
```

Listing 6.1   Initial contact list.

Listing 6.1 contains a single form holding the list of contact names and a confirmation of the name selected. It begins with an optional DTD for validating the VoiceXML syntax. The *contactList* <form> outputs a <prompt>, requesting a name from the caller. The user input is compared to the names on lines 19 through 28. If the user input is recognized, processing passes to the <filled> block, confirming to the user that the name spoken was recognized. Any error messages for <nomatch> or <noinput> are handled by the defaults of the platform.

Select a list of first names that will be used as the basis for building your personal phonebook. Use Listing 6.1 as a template and create a simple application that will respond to the user with the name input. Test your application in the Vocal Scripter or through a telephone call.

HANDS ON

Map a Name to a Telephone Number

The names in your contact list must be mapped, or associated, with a specific telephone number. Mapping input to specific values is done through slots, as shown in Listing 6.2, expanding the grammar section to include the phone numbers for each person.

```
1.  <grammar>
2.  <![CDATA[
3.     [
4.        [rosemary]  { <contactList 7183991234> }
5.        [john]      { <contactList 2012342342> }
6.        [anthony]   { <contactList 2013453453> }
7.        [kristi]    { <contactList 2013453453> }
8.        [cubby]     { <contactList 3343615678> }
9.        [kim]       { <contactList 3343615678> }
10.    [mary]      { <contactList 2079674564> }
11.    [richard]   { <contactList 2079674564> }
12.    [aaron]     { <contactList 2079674564> }
13.    [justin]    { <contactList 2079674564> }
14.    ]
15. ]]>
16. </grammar>
```

Listing 6.2   Using slots to map values.

Filling Slots

In simple grammars, the utterance that is recognized when the user speaks is what is stored in the field variable. Sometimes it is useful to be able to allocate a developer-defined value to the variable based on the user's input instead of inserting the user's input itself. This is helpful when building complex grammar phrases that need to return a single value or when parsing a phrase that will fill several field variables at one time.

slot is an optional attribute of a <field> element. Simple grammars are used to fill the implied *slot* of a <field> element by defaulting to the field name when the *slot* attribute is absent. If the user utterance is recognized, it is input in the field variable. This is how we have constructed grammars in the previous projects. Slots allow the developer to explicitly force a specific value into a field. In the current project, we want to force a specific phone number as a value depending upon the person we wish to call.

The syntax of mapping the contact name to a phone number starts by enclosing each name in square brackets. The square brackets signify a disjunction, meaning *or*. [rosemary mark aurora] means rosemary, or mark, or aurora.

The syntax might look odd upon first viewing. In Listing 6.2, there is one set of square brackets on lines 3 and 14 that surrounds another set of square brackets on lines 4 through 13, each holding a different name. All of that is contained within a CDATA section.

CDATA sections are convenient when the content of the grammar contains the less than (<) character. This is a reserved character in VoiceXML and must either be escaped by using the CDATA section or expanded into it's XML equivalent: <. With each line of the grammar containing a less than character as part of the grammar syntax construction, it is much simpler to enclose the entire grammar in a CDATA section than to replace each of the special characters. Table 6.1 is a list of reserved characters and their entity equivalents.

The disjunction square brackets around each name are not mandatory at this point, but it is good preparation for the time when we will want to expand the names to a group of people, as we will in the next section. The curly braces set up the slot that will hold the field variable value when an utterance is recognized. In our case, the <contactList> field will be filled with a phone number. After each of the disjunction square brackets that hold a contact name from your phone list, the slot name is followed by the value to be assigned to the field variable.

Using white space and line breaks to put each name on a separate line helps keep the structure clear and makes it easier to maintain as we expand the description of each name.

Table 6.1 Special Characters and Their Entity Equivalents

CHARACTER	ENTITY EQUIVALENT
<	&lt;
>	&gt;
'	&apos;
"	&quot;
&	&amp;

HANDS ON   Replace the existing grammar in Listing 6.1 with the newly defined slot-filling grammar in Listing 6.2. Test your application to verify that the phone number of the person to call is output, not his or her name.

Confirm User Input

Voice applications are more natural sounding if confirmation of the user input is implied rather than explicitly stated each time the user speaks. As an example, if the user says "Mary" when asked for a name, instead of confirming with a question, "You said Mary. Is that correct?", the application can respond with a statement, "Calling Mary at 2014564564." This confirms that the user was understood correctly and the phone number was retrieved.

As a general rule, when the system repeats a statement to the user that the user has just spoken, any response from the user should be considered a negative response and caught as an error. Listing 6.3 opens a small 1 1/2-second window for accepting a response from the user.

```
1.  <?xml version="1.0"?>
2.
3.  <!DOCTYPE vxml
4.  PUBLIC
5.  "-//BeVocal Inc//VoiceXML 2.0//EN"
6.  "http://cafe.bevocal.com/libraries/dtd/vxml2-0-bevocal.dtd">
7.
8.  <vxml version="2.0">
9.    <form id="getContactName">
10.
11.    <field name="contactList">
12.      <prompt>
13.      Whom would you like to contact?
14.      </prompt>
15.
16.    <grammar>
17.    <![CDATA[
18.      [
19.        [rosemary] { <contactList 7183991234> }
20.        [john]     { <contactList 2012342342> }
21.        [anthony]  { <contactList 2013453453> }
22.        [kristi]   { <contactList 2013453453> }
23.        [cubby]    { <contactList 3343615678> }
24.        [kim]      { <contactList 3343615678> }
```

Listing 6.3   Confirming user input.

```
25.        [mary]     { <contactList 2079674564> }
26.        [richard]  { <contactList 2079674564> }
27.        [aaron]    { <contactList 2079674564> }
28.        [justin]   { <contactList 2079674564> }
29.     ]
30.    ]]>
31.    </grammar>
32.   </field>
33.
34.   <field name="confirmContactName">
35.     <prompt timeout="1.5s">
36.       Calling <value expr="contactList$.utterance"/>
37.       at <value expr="contactList"/>
38.     </prompt>
39.     <noinput>
40.       <assign name="confirmContactName" expr="'true'"/>
41.     </noinput>
42.     <nomatch>I'm sorry.<clear/></nomatch>
43.   </field>
44.
45.   <block>
46.     Glad to be of service. Good bye.
47.   </block>
48.
49.  </form>
50.
51. </vxml>
```

Listing 6.3   Confirming user input. *(continued)*

The <field> element, *confirmContactName,* starting on line 34, repeats to the caller the name that was recognized and the phone number that is mapped to that name. To access the user's recognized input, reference the *getContactName$.utterance* shadow variable. The field-level shadow variable returns what the user spoke, not what was set as the slot value.

Field-Level Shadow Variables

We briefly touched on shadow variables in Project 4 when verifying the voice print of a caller. Field-level shadow variables are set as part of the grammar recognition system of the VoiceXML platform. They are read-only variables that give access to the platform's analysis of spoken input that can be used to do conditional processing based upon their value.

The *utterance* shadow variable returns the raw input that was understood by the platform to be part of the defined grammar for that field. In the current application, a user speaks a name, the platform checks the input against the available list of names within the grammar, and if a name is recognized, stores the input in the *getContact-Name$.utterance* shadow variable. The platform's confidence level in recognizing the spoken grammar can be accessed through the *getContactName$.confidence* variable, and the *input* mode, whether DTMF or voice, can be accessed through the *getContact-Name$.input* variable.

Check for User Input

There is a 1 1/2-second window of opportunity set in the <prompt> on line 35 of Listing 6.3, giving callers a chance to respond to the prompt, *even though they don't know it exists*. This is a hidden prompt where any response at all is considered an error and is handled by the <nomatch> element on line 42. If there is any response from the user, all fields in the form are cleared through the <clear> element within the <nomatch> block on line 42. The application takes verbal responsibility for the error with output of "I'm sorry" and the FIA returns processing to the first field in the form.

After the 1 1/2-second window closes, it is assumed that there was no reaction from the caller, implying that the person to call is accurate. The <noinput> element assigns a value to the *confirmContactName* field, allowing the FIA to proceed to the next section of the dialog. The <block> beginning on line 45 is a placeholder that will be developed into a *goodbye* form in a later section.

TIP

Using implied and hidden dialogs are a good way to confirm user input without bogging down the exchange with a series of yes-no responses.

HANDS ON

Add a <field> element containing a hidden prompt to your application. Output to the user what was recognized by the VoiceXML platform and if there is any response, clear the form and begin the processing again.

Group Items in a Grammar

The telephone contact list has numbers that are duplicates. Any group of people who have the same phone number can be consolidated into a single list within a set of square brackets. Square brackets act as the equivalent of *or* when setting up a grammar. You can insert a list of names separated by spaces, and each name will be a standalone token. This saves space in the coding and also makes more sense logically when trying to maintain your mini-database. If a family moves and changes its phone number, only one item needs to be changed.

Listing 6.4 consolidates the contacts who have the same phone number into a list and associates each member of the list to a single slot value. White space and line breaks are generally ignored when building grammar structure, so the phone numbers are lined up, making it easy for your eye to scan down the list instead of having to jump back and forth, trying to locate a phone number.

```
 1. <grammar>
 2. <![CDATA[
 3.      [
 4.        [rosemary]                  { < contactList 7183991234> }
 5.        [john]                      { < contactList 2012342342> }
 6.        [anthony kristi]            { < contactList 2013453453> }
 7.        [cubby kim]                 { < contactList 3343615678> }
 8.        [mary richard aaron justin] { < contactList 2079674564> }
 9.      ]
10. ]]>
11. </grammar>
```

Listing 6.4   Grouping for a single slot value.

 If you have duplicate phone numbers in your contact list, consolidate the grammar of your application to handle the group as a single slot value.

HANDS ON

Create Multiple Tokens as a Single Name

Sometimes people have two words as a first name, like Mary Jo or Billy Bob. These can be handled by using parentheses to surround the names, forcing them to be seen as a sequence of single tokens.

Listing 6. 5 makes changes to the existing contacts by changing one user's name to a multiple token string and adding last names to each contact in the list.

```
 1. <grammar>
 2. <![CDATA[
 3.      [
 4.      ( rosemary miller )          { < contactList 7183991234 > }
 5.      ( john caviglia )            { < contactList 2072342342 > }
 6.      ([anthony kristi] caviglia)  { < contactList 2073453453 > }
 7.      ([cubby kim] miller)         { < contactList 3343615678 > }
 8.      ([(mary jo) richard aaron justin] weiss){<contactList 2014564564>}
 9.      ]
10. ]]>
11. </grammar>
```

Listing 6.5   Multiple tokens in a grammar.

Table 6.2 Grammar Operators

OPERATOR	EXAMPLE	DESCRIPTION
( )	(mary jo)	Concatenates content into a single token, each word mandatory and in order.
[ ]	[john tony]	Specifies a disjunction; each word is an individual token.
?	kim ?miller	The token following the operator is optional.
+	(i am +very happy)	There must be at least one or more instances of the token that follows the operator.
*	(i am *very happy)	There may be zero or more instances of the token that follows the operator.

Grammar Operators

Grammars can be more than just simple words or phrases. A complex grammar can contain references to other grammars, tokens representing literal words, a long series of phrases, and conditional operators to make input optional. There are five grammar operators, as shown in Table 6.2. The operators are used to specify optional parts of a grammar and to group words as single tokens.

Listing 6.5 uses the grammar concatenation operator to force full names when requesting a contact. Lines 4 and 5 are simple tokens that just have a first and last name. Line 6 contains a disjunction operator inside of a concatenation operator, forcing the user to choose between *tony* and *kristi* as a first name with a mandatory *caviglia* last name to follow.

Line 8 is a combination of concatenation and disjunction. It starts with the concatenation operator, forcing the complete contents to be seen as a single item with the last name of *weiss*. Within that, the disjunction operator holds a list of four tokens, one of which is a concatenation of *mary jo*.

 Add last names to your list. Check the syntax, save the file, and then run your script. Try different variations of names to confirm that a last name
HANDS ON **must be spoken in order to get output.**

Refine the Contact List

Using last names helps when you have first name duplicates like Tony Miller and Tony Caviglia, but what if you just want to use first names with an optional last name for other listings?

Optional Tokens

The question mark signifies optional in VoiceXML grammar. To make something optional, put a question mark right before the token, as shown in Listing 6.6. The processor will now understand the user's request when a first name is spoken alone or a first name is spoken with a last name. To handle duplicates, leave off the question mark and force the last name.

```
1. <grammar>
2. <![CDATA[
3.     [
4.     ( rosemary ?miller )            { < contactList 7183991234 > }
5.     ( john ?caviglia )              { < contactList 2072342342 > }
6.     ([anthony kristi] ?caviglia) { < contactList 2073453453 > }
7.     ([cubby kim] ?miller)           { < contactList 3343615678 > }
8.     ([(mary jo) richard aaron justin] ?weiss){<contactList 2014564564>}
9.     ]
10. ]]>
11. </grammar>
```

Listing 6.6   Optional last names.

Creating Nicknames

Another way to handle duplicates is just as we do in real life: give one of the dupes a nickname. Anthony's father's first name is also Anthony. When growing up, he got the nickname Ants. When his mother was screaming for him to wash his hands before dinner, there was not any confusion as to which Anthony was really in trouble. Use the same technique (without screaming, of course) to develop a list that has no ambiguity.

```
1. <grammar>
2.  <![CDATA[
3.     [
4.     ( rosemary ?miller )            { < contactList 7183991234 > }
5.     ( john ?caviglia )              { < contactList 2072342342 > }
6.     ( anthony louise ) ?caviglia { < contactList 5105812344 > }
7.     ([ants kristi] ?caviglia)       { < contactList 2073453453 > }
8.     ([cubby kim] ?miller)           { < contactList 3343615678 > }
9.     ([(mary jo) richard aaron justin] ?weiss){<contactList 2014564564>}
10.    ]
11. ]]>
12. </grammar>
```

Listing 6.7   Inserting nicknames.

Listing 6.7 has an added contact line for Anthony and Louise Caviglia. Because this conflict's with Anthony and Kristi Caviglia, the nickname for Anthony Junior is inserted on line 7.

Primary Selections

Most of us have a short list of people we contact on a regular basis. We can give their name priority over other people with the same first name by not designating a last name as part of their token: Leave the last name off the primary contact and force the last name for the duplicates. The user will be able to access the most important member of that set with a single utterance instead of having to speak the complete name.

Lines 4 through 6 of Listing 6.8 set Rosemary as the primary contact by leaving off her last name and forcing the last name for each of the other Rosemarys.

```
 1. <grammar>
 2. <![CDATA[
 3.    [
 4.    rosemary                      { < contactList 7183991234 > }
 5.    ( rosemary oconnor )          { < contactList 3012932394 > }
 6.    ( rosemary clooney )          { < contactList 2124354455 > }
 7.    ( john ?caviglia )            { < contactList 2072342342 > }
 8.    ( anthony louise ) ?caviglia  { < contactList 5105812344 > }
 9.    ([ants kristi] ?caviglia)     { < contactList 2073453453 > }
10. ([cubby kim] ?miller)           { < contactList 3343615678 > }
11. ([[(mary jo) richard aaron justin] ?weiss){<contactList 2014564564>}
12. ]
13. ]]>
14. </grammar>
```

Listing 6.8   Designating a primary selection.

 Check for duplicate names in your list. Verify that there are no possibilities of ambiguity. Designate a primary contact for the people most called in your list. Make it easy to access their numbers through a single word token instead of having to speak their complete name. Verify your changes through the Vocal Scripter or by placing a call to your application.

Allocate Multiple Phone Numbers for One Contact

Many people carry a cell phone in addition to the phone they have at work and at home. We need to set up some kind of system to handle multiple phone numbers for one person. The main problem is one of the caller's memory. The match must be intuitive enough to remember when in a hurry. The grammar operators can help by making certain parts of a phrase optional.

Create a Memorable Token

The location of the phone, home or work, seems like a logical choice when creating multiple numbers for a contact. If there is a cell phone involved, use the words *cell phone*. Put the contact name as the first part of the token, followed by the descriptive word, as shown in Listing 6.9. Surround the phrase with parentheses to force a match on all the words.

```
1.  <grammar>
2.  <![CDATA[
3.    [
4.    ( rosemary work )              { < contactList 7183991234 > }
5.    ( rosemary home )              { < contactList 2124560987 > }
6.    ( rosemarys cellphone )        { < contactList 9173998765 > }
7.    ( rosemary oconnor )           { < contactList 3012932394 > }
8.    ( rosemary clooney )           { < contactList 2124354455 > }
9.    ( john ?caviglia )             { < contactList 2072342342 > }
10. ( anthony louise ) ?caviglia { < contactList 5105812344 > }
11. ([ants kristi] ?caviglia)     { < contactList 2073453453 > }
12. ([cubby kim] ?miller)         { < contactList 3343615678 > }
13. ([[(mary jo) richard aaron justin] ?weiss){<contactList 2014564564>]
14. ]
15. ]]>
16. </grammar>
```

Listing 6.9   Multiple phone listings.

Add Optional Words to the Phrase

You can insert key words that are optional to make a complete phrase. "rosemary work" does not sound as intuitive as "rosemary at work," making the *at* an optional part of the user input. We will use techniques such as these when creating more complex grammars in future projects. Listing 6.10 has optional words added for contacting Rosemary at work or home.

TIP   **When using these methods, be consistent. Your application will be much easier to maintain in the future.**

HANDS ON   **Examine the names in your contact list and add processing for contacts with multiple phones. Add optional words to the grammar phrases to make accessing a listing as intuitive as possible.**

```
 1. <grammar>
 2. <![CDATA[
 3.    [
 4.    ( rosemary ?at work )          { < contactList 7183991234 > }
 5.    ( rosemary ?at home )          { < contactList 2124560987 > }
 6.    ( rosemarys cellphone )        { < contactList 9173998765 > }
 7.    ( rosemary oconnor )           { < contactList 3012932394 > }
 8.    ( rosemary clooney )           { < contactList 2124354455 > }
 9.    ( john ?caviglia )             { < contactList 2072342342 > }
10.    ( anthony louise ) ?caviglia { < contactList 5105812344 > }
11.    ([ants kristi] ?caviglia)     { < contactList 2073453453 > }
12.    ([cubby kim] ?miller)         { < contactList 3343615678 > }
13.    ([(mary jo) richard aaron justin] ?weiss){<contactList 2014564564>}
14.    ]
15. ]]>
16. </grammar>
```

Listing 6.10   Optional words in a phrase.

Control Data Type Speech Output

In Project 4, we looked at the built-in data types of VoiceXML that handle spoken output from the TTS engine. The <say-as> element is helpful in the output of a confirmation message to the user, as shown in Listing 6.11. As a reminder, output data types include *number*, *date*, *time*, *telephone*, and several more types.

The <value> element that outputs the slot value stored in the *contactList* variable is surrounded by <say-as> on line 4. This will force the TTS engine to output a platform-predefined recorded output of the telephone number.

```
 1. <field name="confirmContactName">
 2.     <prompt timeout="1.5s">
 3.        Calling <value expr="contactList$.utterance"/> at
 4.        <say-as type="telephone"><value expr="contactList"/></say-as>
 5.     </prompt>
 6.     <noinput>
 7.        <assign name="confirmContactName" expr="'true'"/>
 8.     </noinput>
 9.     <nomatch>I'm sorry.<clear/></nomatch>
10. </field>
```

Listing 6.11   Using <say-as> speech data type.

Call your account and listen to the output before inserting the <say-as> data type. After inserting the <say-as> element, run your application **HANDS ON** through the Vocal Scripter to see the output and then call your application to hear the output.

Transfer the Call to the Contact Number

Project 3 introduced the concept of call transfer. We will use the model created in that project to transfer the call in the current project to the selected contact from the contact list. Listing 6.12 incorporates the necessary changes into that model to access the phone number the caller has chosen.

```
1.  <field name="confirmContactName">
2.     <prompt timeout="1.5s">
3.       Calling <value expr="contactList$.utterance"/>
4.       at <say-as type="telephone"><value expr="contactList"/></say-as>
5.     </prompt>
6.     <noinput>
7.       <assign name="confirmContactName" expr="'true'"/>
8.     </noinput>
9.     <nomatch>I'm sorry.<clear/></nomatch>
10. </field>
11.
12.   <transfer
13.    name="transferCall"
14.    connecttimeout="20s"
15.    maxtime="60s"
16.    bridge="true"
17.    destexpr="contactList">
18.
19.    <filled>
20.      <if cond="transferCall == 'busy'">
21.        <prompt>
22.          The line is busy
23.          Please try again later.
24.        </prompt>
25.      <elseif cond="transferCall == 'far_end_disconnect'"/>
26.        <prompt>
27.          The party you called has hung up.
28.        </prompt>
29.      <elseif cond="transferCall == 'noanswer'"/>
30.        <prompt>
31.          No one is answering.
32.          Try again later.
33.        </prompt>
34.      <elseif cond="maxtime_disconnect"> 60"/>
```

Listing 6.12 Transfer the call. *(continues)*

```
35.        You were disconnected because the maximum time allowed
36.        for your call was exceeded.
37.      </if>
38.    </filled>
39. </transfer>
40.
41.  <block>
42.     Glad to be of service. Good bye.
43.  </block>
```

Listing 6.12 Transfer the call. *(continued)*

The <transfer> block starting on line 12 receives the *contactList* variable, which holds the selected phone number, as the value of the *destexpr* attribute on line 17. *destexpr* is a BeVocal attribute extension that accepts a value of an ECMAScript, which in this case is the phone number stored in the *contactList* variable.

The call is set to last a maximum of 60 seconds, at which time processing returns to the <filled> element to check on how the call was terminated.

NOTE **Most voice portals have set a limit on the amount of time for a call when using the <transfer> element because of the potential for abuse. The BeVocal platform has a *maxtime* default of 60 seconds.**

The <filled> block starting on line 19 checks to see how the transfer is terminated. A busy signal, no answer on the other end, the user hanging up, and exceeding the maximum call time output verbal feedback. Giving users feedback about what is happening with the system gives them a sense of security, assuring them that everything is working properly.

HANDS ON **Insert a <transfer> block into your application. Check the *VoiceXML 2.0 Working Draft*, section 2.3.7, for transfer attributes that might be applicable when catching events during the transfer.**

Place Another Call without Disconnecting

The application would be much more user friendly if the caller could request another call without having to terminate the application and dial again. Listing 6.13 does a simple boolean check through the *type* attribute on line 5, asking if the user would like to place another call. If there is a positive response, all values in the form are cleared using the <clear> element on line 12. The FIA will then start processing back at the top of the form, requesting a name from the contact list.

```
1. <transfer>
2.   ....
3. </transfer>
4.
5. <field name="anotherCall" type="boolean">
6.   <prompt>
7.     Would you like to call someone else.
8.   </prompt>
9.
10.   <filled>
11.     <if cond="anotherCall">
12.       <clear/>
13.     </if>
14.   </filled>
15. </field>
```

Listing 6.13   Requesting another call.

Modularize the Application

To make the code easier to maintain, we need to isolate the greeting and goodbye routines into their own forms. Listing 6.14 creates each of the forms while adding a *start over* global link for the developer's use within the goodbye form.

```
1. <?xml version="1.0"?>
2.
3. <!DOCTYPE vxml
4.    PUBLIC
5.    "-//BeVocal Inc//VoiceXML 2.0//EN"
6.    "http://cafe.bevocal.com/libraries/dtd/vxml2-0-bevocal.dtd">
7.
8. <vxml version="2.0">
9.
10. <link next="phonebook.vxml getContactName">
11.   <grammar>
12.     <![CDATA[
13.       [(start over)]
14.     ]]>
15.   </grammar>
16. </link>
17.
18. <form id="greeting">
```

Listing 6.14   Modularized code and start over link. *(continues)*

```
19.    <block>
20.      <prompt>
21.        Welcome back, Master.
22.      </prompt>
23.      <goto next="#getContactName"/>
24.    </block>
25.  </form>
26.
27.  <form id="getContactName">
28.
29.    ... [ get the name and transfer the call ] ...
30.
31.  <field name="anotherCall" type="boolean">
32.    <prompt>
33.      Would you like to call someone else.
34.    </prompt>
35.
36.    <filled>
37.      <if cond="anotherCall">
38.        <clear/>
39.      <else/>
40.        <goto next="#goodbye"/>
41.      </if>
42.    </filled>
43.  </field>
44.  </form>
45.
46.  <form id="goodbye">
47.  <field>
48.    <prompt>
49.      Good bye, Master. I'll talk with you again, soon.
50.    </prompt>
51.    <grammar>quit</grammar>
52.    <noinput><exit/></noinput>
53.    <nomatch><exit/></nomatch>
54.  </field>
55.  </form>
56.  </vxml>
```

Listing 6.14 Modularized code and start over link. *(continued)*

The *start over* link on lines 10 through 16 is the same as we have seen in previous projects. It can be activated from anywhere within the application, including within the *goodbye* form, where a <noinput> or <nomatch> event is used to exit the application. Any input other than start over will trigger the exit event.

The main part of the application within the *getContactName* form no longer falls through to exit the script by default. An explicit <else> statement on line 41 transfers processing to the *goodbye* form.

Localize Help and Error Messages

In previous projects, help and error messages were set at the application level, making them global in scope. These may also be set at the form and field levels to scope them locally. Localizing help and error messages is useful for creating context-sensitive messages, giving each <field> or <form> block its own event handlers.

All errors in the application are currently handled by the platform's default responses. Listing 6.15 develops a series of context-sensitive help and error messages to replace the defaults. Because all of the user input for this application is contained within the *getContactName* form, the error checking can be localized within the *contactList* field, instead of creating it at a global level as a child of the <vxml> element.

```
1.  <field name="contactList">
2.
3.    <nomatch count="1">
4.      I do not recognize that name. Please try again
5.      <reprompt/>
6.    </nomatch>
7.
8.    <nomatch count="2">
9.      This is the second time that name was not recognized.
10.     Try one more time.
11.     <reprompt/>
12.   </nomatch>
13.
14.   <nomatch count="3">
15.     Sorry! You have not entered that name in your book yet.
16.     <goto nextitem="anotherCall"/>
17.   </nomatch>
18.
19.   <noinput count="1">
20.     I did not hear you say a name.
21.     <reprompt/>
22.   </noinput>
23.
24.   <noinput count="2">
25.     Please speak a name to access your contact list.
26.   </noinput>
27.
28.   <noinput count="3">
29.       There must be something wrong with the connection.
30.       Please call back on a better phone line.
31.     <disconnect/>
32.   </noinput>
33.
```

Listing 6.15 Help and error messages. *(continues)*

```
34.    <help count="1">
35.      You are trying to access names within your phonebook.
36.      Speak the name of the person you would like to call.
37.    </help>
38.
39.    <help count="2">
40.      If you are having a problem, the name you are requesting
41.      might not be in your phonebook or it could be stored under
42.      a nickname. Try a different name.
43.      <reprompt/>
44.    </help>
45.
46.    <prompt>
47.      Whom would you like to contact?
48.    </prompt>
49.
50. <grammar>
51.   <![CDATA[
52.     [
53.       ( rosemary ?at work )          { < contactList 7183991234 > }
54.       ( rosemary ?at home )          { < contactList 2124560987 > }
55.       ( rosemarys cellphone )        { < contactList 9173998765 > }
56.       ( rosemary oconnor )           { < contactList 3012932394 > }
57.       ( rosemary clooney )           { < contactList 2124354455 > }
58.       ( john ?caviglia )             { < contactList 2072342342 > }
59.       ( anthony louise ) ?caviglia { < contactList 5105812344 > }
60.       ([ants kristi] ?caviglia)      { < contactList 2073453453 > }
61.       ([cubby kim] ?miller)          { < contactList 3343615678 > }
62. ([(mary jo) richard aaron justin] ?weiss){<contactList 2014564564>}
63.     ]
64.   ]]>
65. </grammar>
66.
67.  </field>
```

Listing 6.15   Help and error messages. *(continued)*

A series of three <nomatch> elements begins on line 3. When the user input is not recognized as a name within the grammar of the contact list, the caller is asked to repeat the input. Each <nomatch> message gets a little more adamant about what is needed and why the current input is not working. The third time a nomatch event is thrown, starting on line 14, a final error message is output and processing is transferred to the *anotherCall* field with the <goto> element on line 16.

If the user does not speak any input, the three <noinput> elements on lines 19 through 32 prompt the user for a name from the contact list. The first <noinput> is a simple prompt in case the user did not hear the initial prompt. The second <noinput> is a clarification of what is expected from the user. If the third <noinput> event is reached, it is assumed there is a problem with the telephone system and the user is disconnected from the application.

There are two <help> elements in Listing 6.15 that respond to a user's request for help. The first message, starting on line 34, is a simple message reminding the user about what application is running and what is expected as input. The second help message assumes that users are speaking a name they think is in their contact list but might not be available because it has been stored as a nickname. Line 60 uses the nickname Ants to access Anthony. The user might have forgotten about the nickname and needs a reminder.

The <reprompt> element on line 43 repeats the original prompt from the field that called the help message.

Insert localized help and error messages into your application. Set them at field or form level, depending upon what is most applicable.

Insert Meta Data

When other applications, such as search robots, access a voice site, they will use the meta data in the project to get information about the content of the application. Project 1 included a discussion of the <meta> element and the recommendations of the W3C for including it in your projects. The six basic properties and placeholder values for the current project are shown in Listing 6.16.

```
1. <meta name="author" content="Peter Altamuro"/>
2. <meta name="copyright" content="Copyright 2002, Peter Altamuro"/>
3. <meta name="description" content="Telephone Voice Dialer"/>
4. <meta name="keywords" content="voicexml, dialer"/>
5. <meta name="maintainer" content="pete.altamuro@yourdomain.com"/>
6. <meta name="robots" content="all"/>
```

Listing 6.16 Meta data for this project.

Put the six W3C recommended <meta> elements at the top of the script, inserting values that are appropriate for your application.

Put It All Together

The complete script, as shown in Listing 6.17, is a fully functioning telephone directory with context-sensitive error checking and help messages built in.

```
1.  <?xml version="1.0"?>
2.
3.  <!DOCTYPE vxml
4.  PUBLIC
5.  "-//BeVocal Inc//VoiceXML 2.0//EN"
6.  "http://cafe.bevocal.com/libraries/dtd/vxml2-0-bevocal.dtd">
7.
8.  <vxml version="2.0">
9.
10. <meta name="author" content="Peter Altamira"/>
11. <meta name="copyright" content="Copyright 2002, Peter Altamira"/>
12. <meta name="description" content="Telephone Voice Dialer"/>
13. <meta name="keywords" content="voicexml, dialer"/>
14. <meta name="maintainer" content="pete.altamuro@yourdomain.com"/>
15. <meta name="robots" content="all"/>
16.
17. <!-- GLOBAL START OVER -->
18. <link next="phonebook.vxmlgetContactName">
19.   <grammar>
20.     <![CDATA[
21.       [(start over)]
22.     ]]>
23.   </grammar>
24. </link>
25.
26. <!-- GREETING -->
27. <form id="greeting">
28.   <block>
29.     <prompt>
30.       Welcome back, Master.
31.     </prompt>
32.     <goto next="#getContactName"/>
33.   </block>
34. </form>
35.
36. <!-- MAIN PROCESSING -->
37. <form id="getContactName">
38.
39. <field name="contactList">
40.
41.   <!-- LOCALIZED NOMATCH EVENTS -->
42.   <nomatch count="1">
```

Listing 6.17 Complete telephone dialer script.

```
43.      I do not recognize that name. Please try again
44.      <reprompt/>
45.    </nomatch>
46.
47.    <nomatch count="2">
48.      This is the second time that name was not recognized.
49.      Try one more time.
50.      <reprompt/>
51.    </nomatch>
52.
53.    <nomatch count="3">
54.      Sorry! You have not entered that name in your book yet.
55.      <goto nextitem="#anotherCall"/>
56.    </nomatch>
57.
58.    <!-- LOCALIZED NOINPUT EVENTS -->
59.    <noinput count="1">
60.      I did not hear you say a name.
61.      <reprompt/>
62.    </noinput>
63.
64.  <noinput count="2">
65.      Please speak a name to access your contact list.
66.    </noinput>
67.
68.    <noinput count="3">
69.        There must be something wrong with the connection.
70.        Please call back on a better phone line.
71.      <disconnect/>
72.    </noinput>
73.
74.    <!-- LOCALIZED HELP EVENTS -->
75.    <help count="1">
76.      You are trying to access names within your phonebook.
77.      Speak the name of the person you would like to call.
78.    </help>
79.
80.    <help count="2">
81.      If you are having a problem, the name you are requesting
82.      might not be in your phonebook or it could be stored under
83.      a nickname. Try a different name.
84.      <reprompt/>
85.    </help>
86.
87.    <prompt>
88.      Whom would you like to contact?
89.    </prompt>
90.
```

Listing 6.17   Complete telephone dialer script. *(continues)*

```
91.  <grammar>
92.  <![CDATA[
93.     [
94.     ( rosemary ?at work )          { < contactList 7183991234 > }
95.     ( rosemary ?at home )          { < contactList 2124560987 > }
96.     ( rosemarys cellphone )        { < contactList 9173998765 > }
97.     ( rosemary oconnor )           { < contactList 3012932394 > }
98.     ( rosemary clooney )           { < contactList 2124354455 > }
99.     ( john ?caviglia )             { < contactList 2072342342 > }
100. ( anthony louise ) ?caviglia { < contactList 5105812344 > }
101. ([ants kristi] ?caviglia)     { < contactList 2073453453 > }
102. ([cubby kim] ?miller)         { < contactList 3343615678 > }
103. ([[(mary jo) richard aaron justin] ?weiss){<contactList 2014564564>}
104. ]
105. ]]>
106. </grammar>
107.
108. </field>
109.
110. <!-- CONFIRMATION OF INPUT -->
111. <field name="confirmContactName">
112.    <prompt timeout="1.5s">
113.      Calling <value expr="contactList$.utterance"/>
114.      at <value expr="contactList"/>
115.    </prompt>
116.    <noinput>
117.      <assign name="confirmContactName" expr="'true'"/>
118.    </noinput>
119.    <nomatch>I'm sorry.<clear/></nomatch>
120. </field>
121.
122. <!-- TRANSFER THE CALL -->
123. <transfer
124.  name="transferCall"
125.  connecttimeout="20s"
126.  maxtime="60s"
127.  bridge="true"
128.  destexpr="contactList">
129.
130.  <!-- CONFIRM CALL TERMINATION -->
131.  <filled>
132.    <if cond="transferCall == 'busy'">
133.      <prompt>
134.        The line is busy
135.        Please try again later.
136.      </prompt>
137.    <elseif cond="transferCall == 'far_end_disconnect'"/>
138.      <prompt>
139.        The party you called has hung up.
```

Listing 6.17   Complete telephone dialer script.

```
140.          </prompt>
141.        <elseif cond="transferCall == 'noanswer'"/>
142.          <prompt>
143.            No one is answering.
144.            Try again later.
145.          </prompt>
146.        <elseif cond="maxtime_disconnect > 60"/>
147.            You were disconnected because the maximum time allowed
148.            for your call was exceeded.
149.        </if>
150.      </filled>
151. </transfer>
152.
153. <!-- REQUEST ANOTHER CONTACT -->
154. <field name="anotherCall" type="boolean">
155.   <prompt>
156.     Would you like to call someone else.
157.   </prompt>
158.
159.   <filled>
160.      <if cond="anotherCall">
161.        <clear/>
162.      <else>
163.        <goto next="#goodbye"/>
164.      </if>
165.   </filled>
166. </field>
167. </form>
168.
169. <form id="goodbye">
170. <field>
171.   <prompt>
172.     Good bye, Master. I'll talk with you again, soon.
173.   </prompt>
174.   <grammar>quit</grammar>
175.   <noinput><exit/></noinput>
176.   <nomatch><exit/></nomatch>
177. </field>
178. </form>
179.
180. </vxml>
```

Listing 6.17   Complete telephone dialer script. *(continued)*

Final Thoughts

You now have a simple telephone dialer that contains names and phone numbers that are accessible from any telephone. As the complexity of the projects in the book progresses, consider coming back and applying some modifications.

There is still much that could be done to make this a more useful application. The names and phone numbers that are hard-coded into the application could be stored in an external file or dynamically generated from a database. Another nice touch would be to update a phone number in the grammar list through a vocal administrative interface.

The listings for this project can be downloaded from the BeVocal Web site at cafe.bevocal.com/wiley/10projects. They are saved as text files, useful as templates for creating your own VoiceXML scripts. Join us in the online discussion board for this project and tell us how you will be using the project. If you create a form that would make this project work better, it might be incorporated into the project code online so that others can use it.

Report Recorder

I lived in Hawaii for two years. Waves of nostalgia break over me every once in a while and I just have to know what the break is like at North Shore. www.surfline.com has Web cams and reporters set up at beaches around the world. The reporters log in and type a surf report each day for the Web site, but that doesn't do much good when all you have is a telephone. That's where the idea came from for this project. A special thanks is offered to Tim Chandler and his crew at Surfline.com for making the surf data available for this project.

THE PROBLEM

Multiple sources of information need to be recorded and stored on a daily basis. The people making the reports should be able to call in their reports over any telephone.

THE SOLUTION

A voice recorder that stores reports in .wav file format will allow the remote reporters to log in, make their reports, and have the reports accessible to users through a telephone call or a link on the Web site.

Project Description

Recordings are made daily through direct telephone access. The reporters call in, are validated with a username and id number, choose a beach for reporting, and then record a report. The report is played back to the reporter for verification. Once the reporter has verified the recording, it is saved as a .wav file for access from the public site.

To create this project, you will:

1. Develop a simple grammar.
2. Limit login attempts.
3. Develop an external grammar file.
4. Map reporters to beach names.
5. Record a report.
6. Save the recording.
7. Access the recordings.

You Will Need

✔ **A BeVocal developer account**

✔ **Sound recordings for prompts**

✔ **Web server for processing and storing recorded reports**

✔ **Download example files: cafe.bevocal.com/wiley/10projects**

VoiceXML Elements Used in This Project

ELEMENT NAME	DESCRIPTION
<assign>	Assigns a value to a variable
<audio>	Plays recorded sound
<block>	Holds executable content
<clear>	Sets field names within the current scope to undefined
<else>	Final possibility within an <if> element
<elseif>	A conditional possibility within an <if> element

VoiceXML Elements Used in This Project *(Continued)*

ELEMENT NAME	DESCRIPTION
<field>	Accepts input from user
<filled>	Processes if field input has been accepted
<form>	Contains prompts and fields for collecting user input
<goto>	Controls process flow of the application
<grammar>	Acceptable utterances
<if>	Checks whether a condition is true or false
<noinput>	Handles process if user does not enter input
<nomatch>	Handles process if user does not input valid data
<prompt>	Output to user to request input or give information
<record>	Accepts and records speech as input
<var>	Variable declaration
<vxml>	Root element

Source: *VoiceXML 2.0 Working Draft*, section 1.4

Application Call Flow

Figure 7.1 shows the call flow for this application. The reporter calls in and is prompted for his or her name. Once a name is recognized, a prompt for an id is issued. The reporter name and id are used to verify identity before a beach name is requested. The report for the beach is then recorded and saved on the Web server.

Develop a Simple Grammar

The Report Recorder project has two major sections. First, the user must be validated against a list of approved users. Then a recording must be made and saved for access through the Web site. We will start by developing grammars that will recognize *reporterName* and *reporterId*.

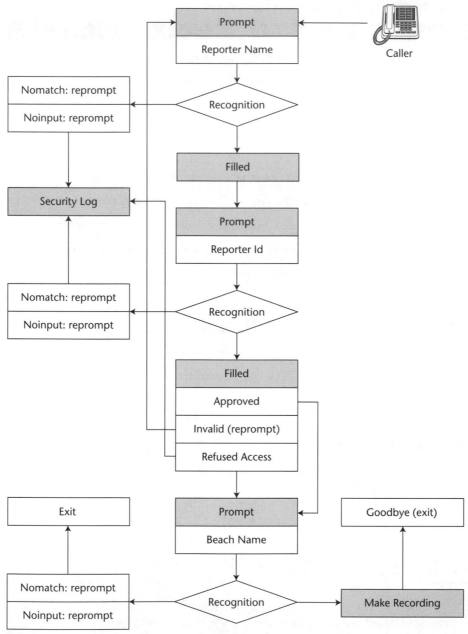

Figure 7.1 Application flow.

reporterName and reporterId Grammars

Listing 7.1 is a simple *reporterName/reporterId* validation similar to that developed in Project 4.

```
1. <?xml version="1.0"?>
2.
3. <!DOCTYPE vxml
4.   PUBLIC
5.   "-//BeVocal Inc//VoiceXML 2.0//EN"
6.   "http://cafe.bevocal.com/libraries/dtd/vxml2-0-bevocal.dtd" >
7.
8.
9. <vxml version="2.0">
10.
11. <form id="validation">
12.
13. <!-- REPORTER NAME -->
14. <field name="reporterName">
15.    <grammar>
16.       <![CDATA[
17.          [
18.             [(mark ?miller)]  {<reporterName A1234>}
19.             [(tim ?chandler)] {<reporterName B4321>}
20.          ]
21.       ]]>
22.    </grammar>
23.    <audio src="speak-your-name.wav">
24.       Please speak your name.
25.    </audio>
26.    <filled/>
27. </field>
28.
29. <!-- REPORTER ID -->
30. <field name="reporterId">
31.    <grammar>
32.       <![CDATA[
33.          [
34.          [hawaii]     {<reporterId A1234>}; Mark Miller
35.          [california] {<reporterId B4321>}; Tim Chandler
36.          ]
37.       ]]>
38.    </grammar>
39.       <audio src="reporter-id.wav">
40.          Reporter ID?
41.       </audio>
42.
43. <!-- VALIDATE -->
44. <filled>
45.
46.    <!-- VALID COMBINATION -->
47.    <if cond="reporterName == reporterId">
48.       <audio src="welcome-back.wav">
```

Listing 7.1 Authenticate a user. *(continues)*

```
49.        Welcome back.
50.     </audio>
51.     <goto next="#recordReport"/>
52.
53.    <!-- INVALID COMBINATION -->
54.    <else/>
55.      <clear namelist="reporterName reporterId"/>
56.      <audio src="invalid-login.wav">
57.    That Reporter Name and ID combination weren't valid.
58.    Try it again.
59.   </audio>
60.  </if>
61.
62. </filled>
63. </field>
64.
65. </form>
66.
67. <form id="recordReport">
68.    <block>
69.        Inside the report recorder.
70.    </block>
71. </form>
72.
73. </vxml>
```

Listing 7.1 Authenticate a user. *(continued)*

The *reporterName* field starting on line 14 contains a grammar that maps a user's name to a specific id number by filling the slot value for *reporterName* if a name is identified. Slots were covered in Project 4.

The *reporterName* value starts with an uppercase letter because we will be using the id number as the name for a grammar rule later in the project, and grammar rules must start with a capital letter. The use of the question mark on lines 18 and 19 makes the last name of the user optional during login. This is useful when there are no duplicates of first names, but as the database of reporters grows, the last names might become mandatory.

Line 23 contains an <audio> element with an *src* attribute pointing to a sound file. If the sound file is available, it will be played as a prompt to the user; otherwise, the content within the <audio> element will be output by the TTS engine. To create a professional user interface for your finished application, all prompts should be prerecorded and played through the <audio> element. TTS prompts are mainly used to output dynamic data that cannot be recorded in advance or for quickly prototyping a project, as we are doing here.

The *reporterId* grammar on lines 34 and 35 maps the user ids to the same set of unique identifiers as in the *reporterName* grammar, setting them up to be used by the comparison operator on line 47. Each slot allocation in the grammar ends with a semicolon, specifying that what is to follow on that line will be a comment. In this case, the reporter's names are added as a comment to each unique id, making the grammar easier to maintain when adding or deleting reporters.

Slot Comparison for Authentication

Comparison of the *reporterName* and *reporterId* takes place in the <filled> block on lines 44 through 62. If the *reporterName* and *reporterId* slot values are exactly the same, a welcome message is output and processing is transferred to the *recordReport* form.

The <else> element on line 54 handles processing if the two field values do not match. The user hears an error message stating that the reporter's name and id combination were not valid. This check is necessary because of the way the grammar functions. The recognition engine will recognize *any* reporter id that is part of the grammar. As an example, if *mark* logs in and then says "california" as his id, california is recognized as an acceptable input for the *reporterId* grammar and processing proceeds. The script must force a comparison to make sure the user's name matches the id.

All field values in the <form> are cleared with the <clear> element on line 55, forcing the FIA to reprocess the form. We will add processing that will limit the number of times a user may try to log in in another section.

Create a VoiceXML file called report-recorder.vxml. Build a set of fields and grammars that will authenticate a user through the reportername/id sequence. Verify that the application works before proceeding.

HANDS ON

Limit Login Attempts

For increased security, the user is limited to two login attempts before being disconnected from the application. A message containing the caller's phone number and phone type is printed to a log file if the user cannot be authenticated.

Listing 7.2 contains variables and error checking during the authentication routine. Login attempts need to be checked in three locations. The *reporterName* field must limit access to those reporters whose name is in the grammar, the *reporterId* field checks to verify that the id input is part of the id grammar, and the <filled> block of *reporterId* verifies that the *reporterName* and *reporterId* slots match.

```
1.  <?xml version="1.0"?>
2.
3.  <!DOCTYPE vxml
4.  PUBLIC
5.  "-//BeVocal Inc//VoiceXML 2.0//EN"
6.  "http://cafe.bevocal.com/libraries/dtd/vxml2-0-bevocal.dtd">
7.
8.  <vxml version="2.0">
9.
10. <form id="validation">
11.
12. <!-- VARIABLES -->
13. <var name="phoneNumber"
14.         expr="session.telephone.ani"/>
15. <var name="phoneType"
16.         expr="session.telephone.iidigits"/>
17. <var name="accessAttempts" expr="1"/>
18.
19. <!-- REPORTER NAME -->
20. <field name="reporterName">
21.   <grammar>
22.     <![CDATA[
23.       [
24.           [(mark ?miller)]  {<reporterName A1234>}
25.           [(tim ?chandler)] {<reporterName B4321>}
26.       ]
27.     ]]>
28.   </grammar>
29.
30.   <!-- PROMPT -->
31.   <audio src="speak-your-name.wav">
32.      Please speak your name.
33.   </audio>
34.   <filled/>
35.
36.   <!-- ERROR CHECKING -->
37.   <catch event="nomatch noinput" count="1">
38.      <prompt>I missed that.</prompt>
39.      <reprompt/>
40.   </catch>
41.
42.   <catch event="nomatch noinput" count="2">
43.      <prompt>
```

Listing 7.2 Limit login attempts.

```
44.            There seems to be a problem with your log in.
45.            Please contact the systems administrator.
46.        </prompt>
47.        <disconnect/>
48.        <submit next="securityLog.cgi"
49.                namelist="phoneNumber phoneType"/>
50.    </catch>
51. </field>
52.
53. <!-- REPORTER ID -->
54. <field name="reporterId">
55.   <grammar>
56.    <![CDATA[
57.      [
58.        [(hawaii)]    {<reporterId A1234>}; Mark Miller
59.        [california] [<reporterId B4321>]; Tim Chandler
60.      ]
61.    ]]>
62.   </grammar>
63.
64.   <audio src="reporter-id.wav">
65.      Reporter ID?
66.   </audio>
67.
68.   <!-- CATCH ERRORS -->
69.   <catch event="nomatch noinput" count="1">
70.      <prompt>I missed that.</prompt>
71.      <reprompt/>
72.   </catch>
73.
74.   <catch event="nomatch noinput" count="2">
75.      <prompt>
76.         There seems to be a problem with your log in.
77.         Please contact the systems administrator.
78.      </prompt>
79.      <disconnect/>
80.      <submit next="securityLog.cgi"
81.              namelist="phoneNumber phoneType"/>
82.   </catch>
83.
84. <!-- AUTHENTICATION -->
85. <filled>
86.
87.   <!-- VALID COMBINATION -->
88.   <if cond="reporterName == reporterId">
89.     <audio src="welcome-back.wav">
90.        Welcome back.
91.     </audio>
92.     <goto next="#recordReport"/>
```

Listing 7.2   Limit login attempts. *(continues)*

```
93.
94.   <!-- INVALID COMBINATION -->
95.   <elseif cond="accessAttempts > 1"/>
96.      Please contact the system admin
97.      to confirm you should
98.      have access to this system.
99.      <disconnect/>
100.      <submit next="securityLog.cgi"
101.             namelist="phoneNumber
102.                       phoneType
103.                       reporterName
104.                       reporterId"/>
105.   <else/>
106.      <audio src="invalid-login.wav">
107.        That Reporter Name and ID combination
108.        was not valid. Try it again.
109.      </audio>
110.      <assign name="accessAttempts"
111.              expr="accessAttempts+1"/>
112.      <clear namelist="reporterName reporterId"/>
113.   </if>
114.
115. </filled>
116. </field>
117.
118. </form>
119.
120. <form id="recordReport">
121.    <block>
122.       Inside the report recorder.
123.    </block>
124. </form>
125.
126. </vxml>
```

Listing 7.2   Limit login attempts. *(continued)*

Set the Variables

Variables set on lines 13 through 17 will be used for logging an unsuccessful access attempt. The Automatic Number Identification (session.telephone.ani) from the standard session variables sets the *phoneNumber* variable, and the Information Indicator Digits (session.telephone.iidigits) sets the *phoneType* variable.

The *accessAttempts* variable keeps track of the number of times the authentication routine is accessed. Its original value is set to 1. If there is a failure during the first attempt when comparing the *reporterName* and *reporterId* slots, the value will be incremented by 1. We will examine the increment when creating the authentication routine.

Error Check Field Input

Input to each <field> must be checked at field level during each stage of the login. Lines 37 through 49 and lines 69 through 81 of Listing 7.2 use the <catch> element to check for nomatch and noinput conditions.

In previous projects, the catch events have each had their own separate counters, letting the user have multiple attempts for each condition. These have been consolidated into one *event* attribute of the *catch* field, making it possible to use the *count* value of the catch event to act upon the nomatch and noinput conditions simultaneously. The new approach forces tighter security by allowing only a single input error for each field.

If an input error is thrown the first time through a field, a simple <prompt> requests a repeat of the input. The second time through the field, an error message is output to the user, the call is disconnected, and the user's phone number and phone type are sent to the security log script for processing.

Develop an Eternal Grammar File

The grammars that were created in previous projects were all relatively simple single-token grammars. Grammars can also be built as a set of rules that can be accessed through a rule name. It is possible to isolate the grammars in external files and then reference them using the *src* or *expr* attribute of the <grammar> element. This creates the possibility of storing large sets of precompiled grammars and accessing them dynamically. In this project, the grammar will be stored in an eternal text file and accessed through rule names.

Create a List of Beach Names

There are three places within the Report Recording application that need grammars: *reporterName*, *reporterId*, and *beachName*. The *reporterName* and *reporterId* grammars have already been set and need to be related to *beachName* so that the application can tell which reporter should have access to a specific set of beaches. We will develop a set of grammar rules to map the *reporterId* to the specific *beachName*.

The grammar for *beachName* needs to be a little flexible when accepting input because some of the beaches contain optional words. Listing 7.3 shows a first pass at setting up the *beachName* grammar.

```
1. <form id="recordReport">
2.
3. <field name="beachName">
4.    <audio src="which-beach.wav">
5.      Which beach are you making a report for?
6.    </audio>
7.
8. <grammar>
```

Listing 7.3 List of beach names. *(continues)*

```
 9. <![CDATA;]
10. [
11. (ventura ?point ?beach)    {<beachName venturaPoint>}
12. (county line)              {<beachName countyLine>}
13. (huntington ?beach)        {<beachName huntingtonBeach>}
14. (manhattan ?beach)         {<beachName manhattanBeach>}
15. (pipeline)                 {<beachName pipeline>}
16. (south shore)              {<beachName southShore>}
17. (blackpoint) (cromwells) {<beachName blackPoint>}
18. (richardsons)              {<beachName richardsons>}
19. ]
20. ]]>
21. </grammar>
22.
23. <filled/>
24. </field>
25.
26. </form>
```

Listing 7.3   List of beach names. *(continued)*

The *beachName* slot in the *recordReport* form holds a list of beaches as the grammar. Several of the beach vocabulary strings contain a question mark, indicating that the word following is an optional part of the utterance.

When a beach listed in the grammar is recognized, a value is assigned to the *beachName* slot. The slot value will be used to map a reporter to a specific beach and to generate a name for the surf report recording later. We will create grammar rules to hold sets of beach names and then map each rule to a *reporterId*.

Grammar Rules

If you know your surfing spots, you will see right away that the *beachName* grammar mixes beaches in Southern California and Hawaii. The *beachName* grammar can be divided, applying a rule name to each set of beaches.

A grammar rule allows you to give a set of data a single name, like an alias, that can access all the members of a specific set. The name can then be used to build complex grammars by referring to the set within other rules. Listing 7.4 creates a rule name for each of the surf regions.

SouthernCalifornia and *Hawaii* on lines 13 and 20 are rule names, defining a set of beach names. A rule name must begin with a capital letter and define the content of the grammar within square brackets. The content of the rule is accessible to other grammars through the use of the rule name.

```
 1. <form id="recordReport">
 2.
 3. <field name="beachName">
 4.   <audio src="which-beach.wav">
 5.     Which beach are you making a report for?
 6.   </audio>
 7.
 8. <grammar>
 9. <![CDATA[
10.
11. AllBeaches [ SouthernCalifornia Hawaii ]
12.
13. SouthernCalifornia [
14.   (ventura ?point ?beach)   {<beachName venturaPoint>}
15.   (county line)            {<beachName countyLine>}
16.   (huntington ?beach)      {<beachName huntingtonBeach>}
17.   (manhattan ?beach)       {<beachName manhattanBeach>}
18. ]
19.
20. Hawaii [
21.   (pipeline)               {<beachName pipeline>}
22.   (south shore)            {<beachName southShore>}
23.   (blackpoint) (cromwells) {<beachName blackPoint>}
24.   (richardsons)            {<beachName richardsons>}
25. ]
26.
27. ]]>
28. </grammar>
29.
30. <filled>
31.   You said <value expr="beachName$.utterance"/>
32. </filled>
33. </field>
34.
35. </form>
```

Listing 7.4 Define beach names through grammar rules.

Using the region name for each set makes future expansion and development of the region sets extremely simple. We can easily create a grammar rule for beaches in Florida, Mexico, and South Africa. The content of a rule is the grammar for each beach followed by an assignment command filling the *beachName* slot. The value in the assignment will be used later when creating a name for the recording, such as venturaPoint.wav.

A rule name must begin with a capital letter and be unique so that it can be used as an identifier among multiple rule names.

NOTE

Line 11 of Listing 7.4 creates a rule called *AllBeaches* that uses the *SouthernCalifornia* and *Hawaii* grammars as its definition. When the *AllBeaches* grammar rule is accessed, the rule names contained within the grammar definition are expanded to the complete set of utterances available for each rule name. As a placeholder before mapping reporters to beaches, the *AllBeaches* grammar allows every reporter access to all beaches for reporting.

Refine the *beachName* grammar to contain a grammar rule for three or four sets of beaches on the surfline.com site. Include each grammar rule as part of the vocabulary of the *AllBeaches* grammar.

External Grammar Files

Grammar rules that are internal to the VoiceXML file cannot be accessed through an *src* or *expr* attribute within the <grammar> element. This limits the current application, making it incapable of mapping a *reporterId* to a specific set of beaches.

External grammar files are simple text files that hold sets of grammar rules. The file may be accessed from multiple applications and is useful for building common grammars. Another advantage of an external grammar is that rules can be set for accessing only specific parts of the grammar. In this project, we want to develop a rule that limits a reporter to a specific set of beaches.

Listing 7.5 contains the two grammar rules that hold beach names, stored in an external text file. *AllBeaches* on line 1 references all of the beaches available within the two rules.

CDATA sections are not included in an external grammar file. Because the grammar is not part of the VoiceXML file being parsed, the CDATA sections are not necessary for escaping special characters.

```
1. AllBeaches [ SouthernCalifornia Hawaii ]
2.
3. SouthernCalifornia [
4.   (ventura ?point ?beach)    {<beachName venturaPoint>}
5.   (county line)             {<beachName countyLine>}
6.   (huntington ?beach)       {<beachName huntingtonBeach>}
7.   (manhattan ?beach)        {<beachName manhattanBeach>}
8. ]
9.
10. Hawaii [
11.   (pipeline)                {<beachName pipeline>}
12.   (south shore)             {<beachName southShore>}
13.   (blackpoint) (cromwells)  {<beachName blackPoint>}
14.   (richardsons)             {<beachName richardsons>}
15. ]
```

Listing 7.5 External grammar file.

Move the *beachName* field grammar to an external file and save it as beachnames.grammar. Save it as a plain text file.

HANDS ON

Calling an External Grammar

Once a grammar has been stored in an external file, it is accessed through the *src* or *expr* attribute of the <grammar> element. The attribute accepts a URI as its value; the URI points to the external file.

The location of the grammar can be hard-coded in the *src* attribute or generated dynamically through the *expr* attribute. In Listing 7.6, the URI points directly to the beachnames.grammar file. A fragment identifier points to the *AllBeaches* rule, giving all reporters access to all beaches. The next section shows how to dynamically map a reporter's id to a specific grammar rule.

As error checking, the reporter is given two chances to input a beach name. The first <nomatch> asks for a repeat of the input in case there was a simple mistake, and the second <nomatch> outputs an error message followed by an <exit> element to terminate the script.

```
1.  <form id="recordReport">
2.
3.  <field name="beachName">
4.    <audio src="which-beach.wav">
5.      Which beach are you making a report for?
6.    </audio>
7.
8.  <grammar src="beachnames.grammar#AllBeaches"/>
9.
10. <nomatch count="1">
11.     Please repeat the beach name.
12. </nomatch>
13.
14. <nomatch count="2">
15.     Please contact surfline dot com to confirm
16.     your reporter status
17.     <exit/>
18. </nomatch>
19.
20.   <filled>
21.     You said <value expr="beachName$.utterance"/>
22.   </filled>
23. </field>
24.
25. </form>
```

Listing 7.6   Calling an external grammar.

Alter the <grammar> element in your application to carry an *src* attribute that points to the beachnames.grammar file. Test your application to verify that the external file is accessible and outputting the expected results.

Dynamically Generate a URI

Now that the external beachname.grammar file is defined and accessible, a *reporterId* must be associated with a specific set of beaches. Mark in Oahu should have access to all the beaches in Hawaii, whereas Tim in San Juan Capistrano should have access to all the beaches in Southern California. This takes a two-step process. First, dynamically create the URI within the *expr* attribute of the <grammar> element, and then map the *reporterId* to a rule name within the external grammar.

The external beachnames.grammar is available through the *expr* attribute of the <grammar> element, but we need to be able to selectively choose the grammar rule that applies to the reporter who is calling in. This is done in three steps: (1) define a global variable for *reporterId* that can be accessed from any form in the script, (2) assign the reporter's *reporterId* to the variable, and (3) concatenate the variable name onto the call to the grammar.

Define a Global Variable

In previous projects, we have seen that variables are holders of information. The information stored in the variable can be accessed as long as the variable is in scope. Global variables are declared as children of the <vxml> element, making them available to any <form> or <field> within the application.

By convention, global variables are stored at the top of a script so that if any changes are needed, they will be easy to find. Listing 7.7 declares the variable *confirmedReporterId* at the top of the script and leaves its value undefined. When a *reporterId* is confirmed within the authentication process, the *expr* attribute will be filled with the new value.

Declare a global variable with the name of *confirmedReporterId* at the top of your application. Do not assign it a value.

```
1. <?xml version="1.0"?>
2.
3. <!DOCTYPE vxml
4. PUBLIC
5. "-//BeVocal Inc//VoiceXML 2.0//EN"
6. "http://cafe.bevocal.com/libraries/dtd/vxml2-0-bevocal.dtd">
7.
8. <vxml version="2.0">
9.
10. <var name="confirmedReporterId"/>
```

Listing 7.7 Completed authentication and beach selection script.

```
11.
12. <form id="validation">
13.
14. <!-- VARIABLES -->
15. <var name="phoneNumber"
16.          expr="session.telephone.ani"/>
17. <var name="phoneType"
18.          expr="session.telephone.iidigits"/>
19. <var name="accessAttempts" expr="1"/>
20.
21. <!-- REPORTER NAME -->
22. <field name="reporterName">
23.   <grammar>
24.     <![CDATA[
25.       [
26.             [(mark ?miller)]  {<reporterName A1234>}
27.             [(tim ?chandler)]  {<reporterName B4321>}
28.       ]
29.     ]]>
30.   </grammar>
31.
32.   <!-- PROMPT -->
33.   <audio src="speak-your-name.wav">
34.     Please speak your name.
35.   </audio>
36.   <filled/>
37.
38.   <!-- ERROR CHECKING -->
39.   <catch event="nomatch noinput" count="1">
40.     <prompt>I missed that.</prompt>
41.     <reprompt/>
42.   </catch>
43.
44.   <catch event="nomatch noinput" count="2">
45.     <prompt>
46.        There seems to be a problem with your log in.
47.        Please contact the systems administrator.
48.     </prompt>
49.     <disconnect/>
50.     <submit next="securityLog.cgi"
51.             namelist="phoneNumber phoneType"/>
52.   </catch>
53. </field>
54.
55. <!-- REPORTER ID -->
56. <field name="reporterId">
57.   <grammar>
58.     <![CDATA[
59.       [
```

Listing 7.7 Completed authentication and beach selection script. *(continues)*

```
60.          [(hawaii)]   {<reporterId A1234>}; Mark Miller
61.          [california] {<reporterId B4321>}; Tim Chandler
62.      ]
63.    ]]>
64.    </grammar>
65.
66.    <audio src="reporter-id.wav">
67.        Reporter ID?
68.    </audio>
69.
70.    <!-- CATCH ERRORS -->
71.    <catch event="nomatch noinput" count="1">
72.        <prompt>I missed that.</prompt>
73.        <reprompt/>
74.    </catch>
75.
76.    <catch event="nomatch noinput" count="2">
77.        <prompt>
78.            There seems to be a problem with your log in.
79.            Please contact the systems administrator.
80.        </prompt>
81.        <disconnect/>
82.        <submit next="securityLog.cgi"
83.                namelist="phoneNumber phoneType"/>
84.    </catch>
85.
86. <!-- AUTHENTICATION -->
87. <filled>
88.
89.    <!-- VALID COMBINATION -->
90.    <if cond="reporterName == reporterId">
91.      <assign name="confirmedReporterId"
92.              expr="reporterId"/>
93.      <audio src="welcome-back.wav">
94.        Welcome back.
95. </audio>
96.      <goto next="#recordReport"/>
97.
98.    <!-- INVALID COMBINATION -->
99.    <elseif cond="accessAttempts > 1"/>
100.      Please contact the system admin
101.      to confirm you should
102.      have access to this system.
103.      <disconnect/>
104.      <submit next="securityLog.cgi"
```

Listing 7.7 Completed authentication and beach selection script. *(continues)*

```
105.                  namelist="phoneNumber
106.                          phoneType
107.                          reporterName
108.                          reporterId"/>
109.    <else/>
110.      <audio src="invalid-login.wav">
111.        That Reporter Name and ID combination
112.        were not valid. Try it again.
113.      </audio>
114.      <assign name="accessAttempts"
115.             expr="accessAttempts+1"/>
116.      <clear namelist="reporterName reporterId"/>
117.    </if>
118.
119. </filled>
120. </field>
121.
122. </form>
123.
124. <form id="recordReport">
125. <field name="beachName">
126.   <audio src="which-beach.wav">
127.     Which beach are you making a report for?
128.   </audio>
129.
130. <grammar expr="'beachnames.grammar#' +
131.                 confirmedReporterId"/>
132.
133. <nomatch count="1">
134.    Please repeat the beach name.
135. </nomatch>
136.
137. <nomatch count="2">
138.    Please contact surfline dot com to confirm
139.    your reporter status
140.    <exit/>
141. </nomatch>
142.
143.   <filled>
144.   You said <value expr="beachName$.utterance"/>
145.   </filled>
146. </field>
147.
148.  </form>
149. </vxml>
```

Listing 7.7 Completed authentication and beach selection script. *(continued)*

Generate a URI

The *confirmedReporterId* variable declared at the top of Listing 7.7 is assigned a value on lines 91 and 92. The <if> condition on line 90 compares the *reporterName* slot to the *reporterId* slot and assigns the variable if the comparison condition is true. With the *confirmedReporterId* variable set, it can now be used to generate a URI for accessing a specific set of beaches in the external grammar file.

The <form> on lines 124 through 148 is a placeholder for the recording and processing of the surf reports. It begins with a request for a beach name that is used to compare to the list of beaches available in the beachnames.grammar file. An ECMAScript concatenation operator is used on lines 130 and 131 to place a call to the external grammar file with a fragment identifier. The call to the grammar file is in single quotes, signifying that it is a literal string that is then concatenated with the *confirmedReporterId* variable. When the variable name is not in quotes, it indicates to the processor that this is not literal text being processed, but a variable that needs to be expanded to its value. When the grammar file is accessed, it will look for a rule named after the *confirmedReporterId*, which we will set up in the next section.

Line 144 is a placeholder that confirms to the developer the input that was recognized. This will be replaced with a recording routine in the next section.

Generate a call to a specific grammar rule in the external grammar file. The fragment identifier should point to a rule that has the same name as the reporter's id. The next section will actually create the names for those rules in the grammar file.

Map Reporters to Beaches' Names

The external grammar shown in Listing 7.8 has changed the *AllBeaches* grammar rule to multiple sets of grammars that are mapped to a *reporterId*. Each *reporterId* is mapped with a grammar that will specify which beaches are available for reporting.

Comments within grammars are made with semicolons, not the usual comment tags. Lines 1 and 2 end with a comment to remind the maintainer of the script of the reporter's names that are associated with each of the regions.

Grammars cannot contain the usual comment tags (<!– comment –>). To include comments in grammars, use a semicolon. Anything on the line after the semicolon will be considered a comment.

A reporter could cover more than one region by inserting another grammar rule within the square brackets for that reporter. As an example, if there are beaches in Baja, Mexico, that Tim Chandler can cover, along with the beaches in Southern California, the grammar rule for Baja, Mexico, can be inserted as grammar for the B4321 rule:

```
B4321 [SouthernCalifornia BajaMexico]
```

```
1. A1234 [ Hawaii ]              ; Mark Miller
2. B4321 [SouthernCalifornia] ; Tim Chandler
3.
4. SouthernCalifornia [
5.    (ventura ?point ?beach) {<beachName venturaPoint>}
6.    (county line)           {<beachName countyLine>}
7.    (huntington ?beach)     {<beachName huntingtonBeach>}
8.    (manhattan ?beach)      {<beachName manhattanBeach>}
9.    ]
10.
11. Hawaii [
12.    (pipeline)                 {<beachName pipeline>}
13.    (south shore)              {<beachName southShore>}
14.    (blackpoint) (cromwells)   {<beachName blackPoint>}
15.    (richardsons)              {<beachName richardsons>}
16. ]
```

Listing 7.8 Map a *reporterId* to a *beachName* grammar rule within the external grammar file.

The *expr* attribute within a grammar tag is a BeVocal proprietary extension. If you are not using the BeVocal environment, check with the documentation WARNING of your platform to see if this is available.

Delete the *AllBeaches* grammar rule from the beachnames.grammar file and replace it with reporter id's that are mapped to specific regions. Test your HANDS ON application before proceeding.

Record a Report

In Project 3, a recording was made when the caller wanted to leave a voice message. We will use that as a starting point for creating the recordings for the surf reports, as shown in Listing 7.9.

```
1. <form id="recordReport">
2.    <field name="beachName">
3.      <audio src="which-beach.wav">
4.        Which beach are you making a report for?
```

Listing 7.9 Make a recording. *(continues)*

```
5.       </audio>
6.
7.     <grammar expr="'beachnames.grammar#' +
8.                    confirmedReporterId"/>
9.
10.    <nomatch count="1">
11.       Please repeat the beach name.
12.    </nomatch>
13.
14.    <nomatch count="2">
15.       Please contact surfline dot com to confirm
16.       your reporter status
17.       <exit/>
18.    </nomatch>
19. </field>
20.
21. <!-- MAKE THE RECORDING -->
22. <record   name="theReport"
23.          beep="true"
24.          maxtime="30s"
25.          finalsilence="1.5s"
26.          type="audio/wav">
27.    <audio src="thirty-seconds.wav">
28.       You will have 30 seconds to record your report
29.       for <value expr="beachName$.utterance"/>.
30.       Start speaking after the tone.
31.    </audio>
32. </record>
33.
34. <!-- PLAYBACK -->
35. <field name="confirm" type="boolean">
36.    <audio src="playback.wav">
37.        Let me play back what you recorded:
38.    </audio>
39.    <prompt>
40.       <value expr="theReport"/>
41.    </prompt>
42.
43. <!-- CONFIRMATION FROM USER -->
44. <audio src="keep-it.wav">
45.    Would you like to keep it?
46. </audio>
47. <filled>
48.    <if cond="confirm">
49.       <assign name="nameOfRecording"
50.              expr="beachName + '.wav'"/>
51.       <audio src="saved.wav">
52.          Please wait while your report is being saved.
53.          The recording name will be
```

Listing 7.9   Make a recording.

```
54.                <value expr="nameOfRecording"/>
55.            </audio>
56.      <else/>
57.          <audio src="re-record.wav">
58.              Let's start over.
59.          </audio>
60.          <clear/>
61.  </if>
62.  </filled>
63.  </field>
64.
65.  <subdialog name="saveMessage"
66.              src="http://localhost/cgi-bin/recording.cgi"
67.              method="post"
68.              enctype="multipart/form-data"
69.              namelist="theReport nameOfRecording">
70.     <filled>
71.        <audio>
72.            Your report has been saved as file
73.            <value expr="nameOfRecording"/>
74.        </audio>
75.     </filled>
76.  </subdialog>
77.
78.  <!-- ANOTHER REPORT? -->
79.  <field name="anotherReport" type="boolean">
80.    <audio src="another-report.wav">
81.      Would you like to file a report for a
82.      different beach?
83.    </audio>
84.    <filled>
85.        <if cond="anotherReport">
86.            <clear/>
87.            <goto next="#recordReport"/>
88.        </if>
89.    </filled>
90.  </field>
91.
92.  <!-- EXIT/DISCONNECT -->
93.  <field name="goodbye">
94.    <audio src="thank-you.wav">
95.        Thanks for helping out.
96.        See you next time.
97.    </audio>
98.    <catch event="noinput nomatch">
99.        <exit/>
100.   </catch>
101. </field>
102. </form>
```

Listing 7.9 Make a recording. *(continued)*

The recording <form> starts with the *beachName* field that requests the name of a beach and confirms it against the grammar stored in the beachnames.grammar file. The *reporterId* is concatenated onto the URI as a fragment identifier as described in a previous section, *External Grammar Files*. When a beach name is recognized as a valid utterance, processing falls through to the *theReport* field.

Processing within the *theReport* field is controlled by the attributes of the <record> element. A user-friendly beep is output to confirm to the user that the recording has begun. The maximum length of time for a recording is set to 30 seconds, and a silence of 1½ seconds signals to the processor that the recording is completed. Simple <nomatch> error checking is handled on lines 10 through 18.

The content of the <record> element is output before the recording begins. Within the audio output is a <value> element on line 29 that repeats to the speaker the word or phrase that was recognized as input.

A <field> element named *confirm* is set as a boolean type beginning on line 35. This forces a yes or no response when users are asked if they would like to save the recording after hearing it played back through the <value> element on line 40. The <filled> block starting on line 48 sets up a conditional statement, checking to see if the *confirm* field recognized a positive response from the user. If so, the *nameOfRecording* variable is set to the *beachName* concatenated with the .wav extension, creating a filename that will be passed to the processing script in the following <subdialog> call.

Lines 56 through 60 handle processing if the confirmation was not positive. A simple <audio> prompt tells the user that the recording process is starting over. The <clear> element on line 60 carries no attributes, so by default all <field> values within the current form are cleared and the FIA revisits each field, starting at the top of the form.

Once the user has confirmed that a recording should be saved, processing falls through to the <subdialog> call starting on line 65. The <subdialog> element is used to send processing to another location and wait for a return value. At the same time, it can pass variable and field name values to the subdialog for processing.

The attributes of the <subdialog> include the *src* for the location of the script that will process the input; the HTTP method for processing type; the encoding type, or *enctype*, for how the data should be passed; and a name list that contains the name of the variables and field names that are passed to the subdialog. Processing reverts to the <filled> element on line 70 when the subdialog has concluded processing, confirming to the user that the report has been saved.

The field beginning on line 79 offers the reporter a chance to record a report for another beach. This is handy when a reporter has multiple beach reports to input, making it unnecessary to make a separate call for each individual report. Again, a boolean type is set for the *anotherReport* field, asking if the reporter would like to make another report. A positive response clears all field name variables through the <clear> element on line 86, and processing begins again at line 2 by requesting a beach name. The reporter may make as many reports as desired with a single phone call.

When the user input is a negative response, processing falls to the *goodbye* <field> for a quick goodbye message. The <catch> block on lines 98 through 100 can be used to access a global *start over* link if it is available. The <audio> element acts as a prompt, waiting for user input. If anything other than "start over" is spoken, the nomatch event triggers the exiting of the script. We will add the *start over* link when putting the finishing touches on the script in the final section.

Use Listing 7.9 as a template for setting up the recording block. Verify that the script is valid VoiceXML by running it through the VoiceXML Checker on HANDS ON the BeVocal site.

Save the Recording

All that is left is to save the recording so that it can be accessed from the public site when someone requests a beach report.

Pass Field Names and Variables to the Subdialog

In the <subdialog> call on line 65 of Listing 7.9, the *src* attribute holds a link to the script that processes the report and stores it on your Web server. As we have seen, the *namelist* attribute is a list of the variables and field names that are received and processed by the subdialog. *theReport* holds the actual spoken input from the user, and *nameOfRecording* is the variable that holds the dynamically generated filename from the <assign> element on line 49.

Process the Recording

VoiceXML does not provide a method for saving a recording. It must be handled dynamically, just as any other call to a CGI script on your Web server would be. Listing 7.10 provides a simple Perl script for saving the recording on your Web server, but you may use any processing language you choose to get the same results.

```
1. #! /usr/bin/perl -w
2.
3. use CGI qw(:standard);
4.
5. $pathToRecordings = "./recordings";
6. $nameOfRecording  = param("nameOfRecording");
7. $theReport        = param("theReport");
8.
9. $|++;
10.
11.
12. open (SAVE, "> $pathToRecordings/$nameOfRecording")
13.     or die "Could not open file for saving: $!";
14.
15.    binmode(SAVE);
16.    while (read(param('theReport'),$data,1024))
17.      { print SAVE $data; }
18.
19. close(SAVE);
```

Listing 7.10   Processing the recording. *(continues)*

```
20.
21. print "Content-Type: text/xml\n\n";
22.
23.
24. # CONFIRM RECORDING WAS SAVED
25.
26. print <<INSERT_VXML;
27. <?xml version="1.0"?>
28.
29. <vxml version="2.0">
30. <form id="acceptInput">
31.
32.  <block>
33.    Input was $ENV{'CONTENT_LENGTH'} bytes in length.
34.    The $nameOfRecording surf report was processed
35.    and saved.
36.  <return/>
37.  </block>
38. </form>
39. </vxml>
40.
41. INSERT_VXML
```

Listing 7.10   Processing the recording. *(continued)*

The Perl script begins with a call to the Perl interpreter. Perl may be installed in a different location on your Web server, so check with your systems administrator to verify the location. The -w switch at the end of line 1 turns on warning messages that might help debug your script if things aren't working properly.

Line 3 pulls in the CGI module that will handle all the heavy-duty processing with a few simple method calls and autoflushes the buffer, sending output immediately to standard out. Variables that will be concatenated to form the path and the filename of the recording are set in lines 5 through 7.

The *$pathToRecordings* variable stores the recordings in a directory below the current directory that the script is running in. *$nameOfRecording* and *$theReport* accept the input from the *namelist* attribute that called the subdialog. The rest of the script is a rehash of the recording section of Project 3, using the *theReport* parameter as the input to the SAVE filehandle.

The final VoiceXML output from the script is contained within the print statements on lines 26 through 41. Line 33 is mainly for developer information and gives an idea of how large the recording content is that was passed to the script. It can be removed once the script has been tested and is running properly.

Test the Script

We need to verify that the script is running properly by making a recording and then saving it. You must have a Web server that allows CGI script processing to run the test. If you currently have a Web hosting account that allows CGI processing, load the script to the server and test your application.

For those without a hosting account, a simple way to run the test is to install an Apache Web server on your local machine and have the <subdialog> call point to the script within the cgi-bin. Running the VoiceXML through the Vocal Scripter at BeVocal will allow you to test your application without having to use the phone. This even works for the CGI processing if you are pointing to your local server. There are a couple caveats, however.

First, you must change the *beep* attribute on the <record> element to *false* or the Vocal Scripter will throw an error. Second, the <subdialog> call must point to an IP address, which is currently set to *localhost* on line 64 of Listing 7.9. To find your IP address, open a DOS window and, at the prompt, enter ipconfig. The output will include the IP address that has been allocated for the current online session.

You can test the results of your Perl script locally by installing the Apache Web server on your local machine and pointing to a script on the server as the subdialog. This makes it easy to change the CGI script while your VoiceXML script is running.

TIP

Install the recording.cgi script on your Web server. Change the path within the <subdialog> call of the VoiceXML application to point to the script. Test the application to confirm that it is saving the recordings to your Web server.

HANDS ON

Access the Recordings

Now that the recordings have been stored on the Web server, there needs to be a way to generate a list of the surf reports and make them available through a Web page or telephone call. Listing 7.11 is a short Perl script that will dynamically create a listing of all the recorded files in the recordings directory.

Line 1 specifies the path to Perl on the Web server. The *use strict* pragma on line 3 forces declaration of all variables; this is not mandatory in Perl. Line 4 imports the File::Basename module for use when extracting the ending filename from a long string. Line 8 uses the *glob* function in Perl to grab all the files in a specified directory that end with .wav and return the names as an array.

```
1.  #! /usr/bin/perl -w
2.
3.  use strict;
4.  use File::Basename;
5.
6.  print "Content-type: text/html \n\n";
7.
8.  my @reports = glob "./recordings/*.wav";
9.
10. foreach my $report (@reports) {
11.     my $fileName = basename $report;
12.     $fileName =~ s#.wav##;
13.     print qq!<a href="$report">$fileName</a><br>!;
14. }
```

Listing 7.11   Listing the report files.

The *foreach* loop starting on line 10 accesses each name within the array and outputs it as a link to an HTML Web page. Line 11 uses the *basename* method from the File::Basename module to extract the filename and store it in the $fileName scalar variable. A regular expression substitution removes the .wav extension from the file so that only the beach names will be visible on the Web page. Line 13 constructs the HTML link that, when clicked on, will activate the sound file to be played within the browser.

HANDS ON

Install Listing 7.11 on your Web server and verify that you have access to the sound recordings that were created for each of the surf reports.

reportRecorder.vxml

Listing 7.12 is the final script for the Report Recorder project. The DOCTYPE reference has been removed to optimize performance, a global *start over* link is at the top of the script, and all developer test print statements have been removed. Line 93 greets reporters by name once they have been authenticated. With these changes, the script can now be used for creating surf reports from anywhere there is telephone access.

```
1.  <?xml version="1.0"?>
2.
3.  <vxml version="1.0">
4.
5.  <link next="listing9-11.vxml">
6.    <grammar>(start over)</grammar>
7.  </link>
```

Listing 7.12   Completed report recorder script.

```
8.
9.  <var name="confirmedReporterId"/>
10. <var name="nameOfRecording"/>
11.
12. <form id="validation">
13.
14. <!-- VARIABLES -->
15. <var name="phoneNumber"
16.          expr="session.telephone.ani"/>
17. <var name="phoneType"
18.          expr="session.telephone.iidigits"/>
19. <var name="accessAttempts" expr="1"/>
20.
21. <!-- REPORTER NAME -->
22. <field name="reporterName">
23.   <grammar>
24.     <![CDATA[
25.         [
26.             [(mark ?miller)]  {<reporterName A1234>}
27.             [(tim ?chandler)] {<reporterName B4321>}
28.         ]
29.     ]]>
30.   </grammar>
31.
32.   <!-- PROMPT -->
33.   <audio src="speak-your-name.wav">
34.     Please speak your name.
35.   </audio>
36.   <filled/>
37.
38.   <!-- ERROR CHECKING -->
39.   <catch event="nomatch noinput" count="1">
40.     <prompt>I missed that.</prompt>
41.     <reprompt/>
42.   </catch>
43.
44.   <catch event="nomatch noinput" count="2">
45.     <prompt>
46.       There seems to be a problem with your log in.
47.       Please contact the systems administrator.
48.     </prompt>
49.     <disconnect/>
50.     <submit next="securityLog.cgi"
51.             namelist="phoneNumber phoneType"/>
52.   </catch>
53. </field>
54.
55. <!-- REPORTER ID -->
56. <field name="reporterId">
```

Listing 7.12 Completed report recorder script. *(continues)*

```
57.    <grammar>
58.     <![CDATA[
59.      [
60.         [(hawaii)]    {<reporterId A1234>}; Mark Miller
61.         [california] {<reporterId B4321>}; Tim Chandler
62.      ]
63.     ]]>
64.    </grammar>
65.
66.    <audio src="reporter-id.wav">
67.       Reporter ID?
68.    </audio>
69.
70.    <!-- CATCH ERRORS -->
71.    <catch event="nomatch noinput" count="1">
72.       <prompt>I missed that.</prompt>
73.       <reprompt/>
74.    </catch>
75.
76.    <catch event="nomatch noinput" count="2">
77.       <prompt>
78.          There seems to be a problem with your log in.
79.          Please contact the systems administrator.
80.       </prompt>
81.       <disconnect/>
82.       <submit next="securityLog.cgi"
83.               namelist="phoneNumber phoneType"/>
84.    </catch>
85.
86. <!-- AUTHENTICATION -->
87. <filled>
88.
89.    <!-- VALID COMBINATION -->
90.    <if cond="reporterName == reporterId">
91.      <assign name="confirmedReporterId" expr="reporterId"/>
92.      <audio src="welcome-back.wav">
93.        Welcome back, <value expr="reporterName$.utterance"/>
94.      </audio>
95.      <goto next="#recordReport"/>
96.
97.    <!-- INVALID COMBINATION -->
98.    <elseif cond="accessAttempts > 1"/>
99.       Please contact the system admin
100.      to confirm you should
101.      have access to this system.
102.      <disconnect/>
103.      <submit next="securityLog.cgi"
104.              namelist="phoneNumber
105.                          phoneType
```

Listing 7.12   Completed report recorder script. *(continues)*

```
106.                          reporterName
107.                          reporterId"/>
108.   <else/>
109.     <audio src="invalid-login.wav">
110.       That Reporter Name and ID combination
111.       was not valid. Try it again.
112.     </audio>
113.     <assign name="accessAttempts"
114.             expr="accessAttempts+1"/>
115.     <clear namelist="reporterName reporterId"/>
116.   </if>
117.
118. </filled>
119. </field>
120.
121. </form>
122.
123. <form id="recordReport">
124.   <field name="beachName">
125.     <audio src="which-beach.wav">
126.       Which beach are you making a report for?
127.     </audio>
128.
129.     <grammar expr="'beachnames.grammar#' +
130.                 confirmedReporterId"/>
131.
132.     <nomatch count="1">
133.        Please repeat the beach name.
134.     </nomatch>
135.
136.     <nomatch count="2">
137.        Please contact surfline dot com to confirm
138.        your reporter status
139.        <exit/>
140.     </nomatch>
141.   </field>
142.
143. <!-- MAKE THE RECORDING -->
144. <record  name="theReport"
145.          beep="false"
146.          maxtime="30s"
147.          finalsilence="1.5s"
148.          type="audio/wav">
149.     <audio src="thirty-seconds.wav">
150.        You will have 30 seconds to record your report
151.        for <value expr="beachName$.utterance"/>.
152.        Start speaking after the tone.
153.     </audio>
154. </record>
```

Listing 7.12   Completed report recorder script. *(continues)*

```
155.
156.  <!-- PLAYBACK -->
157.  <field name="confirm" type="boolean">
158.    <audio src="playback.wav">
159.        Let me play back what you recorded:
160.    </audio>
161.    <prompt>
162.        <value expr="theReport"/>
163.    </prompt>
164.
165.  <!-- CONFIRMATION FROM USER -->
166.  <audio src="keep-it.wav">
167.      Would you like to keep it?
168.  </audio>
169.  <filled>
170.    <if cond="confirm">
171.        <assign name="nameOfRecording" expr="beachName + '.wav'"/>
172.        <audio src="saved.wav">
173.            Please wait while your report is being saved.
174.            The recording name will be <value expr="nameOfRecording"/>
175.        </audio>
176.    <else/>
177.        <audio src="re-record.wav">
178.            Let's start over.
179.        </audio>
180.        <clear/>
181.  </if>
182.  </filled>
183.  </field>
184.
185.  <subdialog name="saveMessage"
186.              src="http://your-server/cgi-bin/recording.cgi"
187.              method="post"
188.              enctype="multipart/form-data"
189.              namelist="theReport nameOfRecording">
190.    <filled>
191.        <audio>Your report has been saved.</audio>
192.    </filled>
193.  </subdialog>
194.
195.  <!-- ANOTHER REPORT? -->
196.  <field name="anotherReport" type="boolean">
197.    <audio src="another-report.wav">
198.      Would you like to file a report for a different beach?
199.    </audio>
200.    <filled>
201.        <if cond="anotherReport">
```

Listing 7.12 Completed report recorder script. *(continues)*

```
202.         <clear/>
203.         <goto next="#recordReport"/>
204.      </if>
205.    </filled>
206. </field>
207.
208. <!-- EXIT/DISCONNECT -->
209. <field name="goodbye">
210.    <audio src="thank-you.wav">
211.       Thanks for helping out.
212.       See you next time.
213.    </audio>
214.    <catch event="noinput nomatch">
215.       <exit/>
216.    </catch>
217. </field>
218. </form>
219.
220. </vxml>
```

Listing 7.12 Completed report recorder script. *(continued)*

Final Thoughts

The Report Recorder is well on the way to becoming a multiuse recording service. Instead of reporters and beach names, a caller could request a specific person or department and leave a message.

Listing 7.11 can be used as a template for creating a dynamic listing of surf reports. The user calls the service, requests a beach by name, and hears the report. Look at the enumerated lists from previous projects to get an idea of how to create a menu by using a list of items. Instead of outputting to a Web page, output to VoiceXML and create it on the fly.

The listings for this project can be downloaded from the BeVocal Web site at cafe.bevocal.com/wiley/10projects. They are saved as text files, useful as templates for creating your own VoiceXML scripts. Join us in the online discussion board for this project and tell us how you will be using the project. If you create a form that would make this project work better, it might be incorporated into the project code online so that others can use it.

The next project uses XML and XSLT to generate surveys and quizzes. Keep the Report Recorder in mind as a possible tool for changing recorded instructions for each of the surveys.

Quiz Generator

Telephone game quizzes and adventure hints are natural extensions to online games. The Quiz Generator project came about when I discovered a site on the Internet that contains over 18,000 sound files from the *Star Trek* series. I thought it would be fun to insert some of the character voices into a game format and have people guess which character was speaking. A special thank you goes to Dave Wythe at Star Trek in Sound and Vision for providing the sound files for this project.

THE PROBLEM

Most companies have multiple sets of data, stored in structured format, that need to be output to different formats. The data is hand-coded into a preset template, causing input errors and wasting valuable time. Once the data has been input into the template, it is no longer available for other applications to use.

THE SOLUTION

Isolate the data from the formatting. Store the data in a nonproprietary format, such as XML. Use XSLT as a generic formatting mechanism, outputting VoiceXML on the fly, while leaving the data source untouched.

Project Description

This project creates a game called the "Star Trek Quotation Game." The user calls the game phone, hears quotations from the original *Star Trek* series, and guesses who is speaking. The techniques in this project show how to integrate sound recordings into VoiceXML telephone output, create localized error messages, integrate multiple grammars into a single form by use of scoping, and dynamically generate content from an XML data source. The data is completely isolated from the formatting, so any number of quizzes, surveys, or games can be run from the same XML/XSLT processing script.

Although a Java work environment is needed to run the advanced part of the project, no Java programming experience is necessary. The same goes for the XML/XSLT programming.

To create this project you will:

1. Create a simple quiz.

2. Add questions to the quiz.

3. Insert recorded prompts.

4. Record the prompts.

5. Complete the VoiceXML template.

6. Set up the XML/XSLT work environment.

7. Create the data file (XML).

8. Build the stylesheet (XSLT).

9. Test the basic application.

10. Insert XSLT templates into the stylesheet.

11. Test the completed XSLT stylesheet.

 ## You Will Need

✔ **A developer account with BeVocal (cafe.bevocal.com)**

✔ **VoiceXML 1.0 Specification (www.w3.org.voice)**

✔ **TextPad or any simple text editor (www.textpad.com)**

✔ **Java Development Kit (www.sun.com)**

✔ **Xerces XML Parser (xml.apache.org)**

✔ **Xalan XSL Processor (xml.apache.org)**

✔ **GoldWave Sound Recorder (www.goldwave.com)**

✔ **Recordings of prompts**

✔ ***Star Trek* Sound Files (www.stinv.com)**

✔ **Source code for this project (cafe.bevocal.com/wiley/10projects)**

VoiceXML Elements Used in This Project

ELEMENT NAME	DESCRIPTION
<assign>	Assigns a variable a value
<audio>	Plays an audio clip within a prompt
<block>	A container of (noninteractive) executable code
<catch>	Catches an event
<exit>	Exits a session
<field>	Declares an input field in a form
<filled>	An action executed when fields are filled
<form>	A dialog for presenting information and collecting data
<goto>	Go to another dialog in the same or different document
<grammar>	Specifies a speech recognition or DTMF grammar
<help>	Catches a help event
<link>	Specifies a transition common to all dialogs in the link's scope
<noinput>	Catches a no-input event
<nomatch>	Catches a no-match event
<reprompt>	Plays a field prompt when a field is revisited after an event
<vxml>	Top-level element in each VoiceXML document

Source: *VoiceXML 2.0 Working Draft*, section 1.4

Application Call Flow

Figure 8.1 shows the call flow for this application. A welcome message greets the caller and then a set of instructions for using the quiz is output. A series of questions is asked, each question allowing two chances for a correct response before giving the correct answer and moving to the next question. At the end of the quiz, the application terminates with a goodbye message.

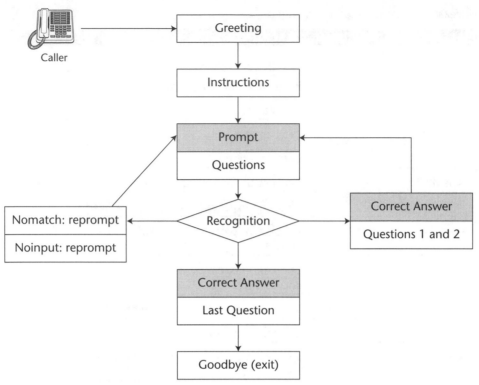

Figure 8.1   Application flow.

Create a Simple Quiz

The Quiz Generator project is built in three phases. First, we'll create a simple quiz to use as a template for adding the questions. Once the questions have been generated, voice prompts are recorded for replacing the TTS prompts. The final phase is to create an XML/XSLT application that will be able to access data dynamically to create any number of quizzes.

The Basic Template

A simple quiz format is shown in Listing 8.1. It contains three forms for creating dialogs: *greeting*, *questions*, and *goodbye*. We have seen the *greeting* and *goodbye* forms in most of the previous projects. The *greeting* form holds a prompt that welcomes the user to your quiz, survey, or game. The prompt should announce the name of the application and give any other information users need to confirm that they are in the right place. The *goodbye* form is used as a graceful exit from the program, confirming verbally that processing has completed, disconnecting from the caller, and closing all open tags.

```
1.  <?xml version="1.0"?>
2.  <!DOCTYPE  vxml
3.     PUBLIC
4.     "-//BeVocal Inc//VoiceXML 2.0//EN"
5.     "http://cafe.bevocal.com/libraries/dtd/vxml2-0-bevocal.dtd">
6.
7.  <vxml version="2.0">
8.
9.  <!-- GREETING -->
10. <form id="greeting">
11.     <block>
12.        <prompt>
13.           Welcome to the Star Trek Quotation Game.
14.        </prompt>
15.        <goto next="#questions"/>
16.     </block>
17. </form>
18.
19. <!-- QUESTIONS -->
20. <form id="questions">
21.
22.     <noinput count="1">
23.        I didn't hear anything. Please try again.
24.     </noinput>
25.     <noinput count="2">
26.        You must say Spock, Kirk, or McCoy to participate.
27.     </noinput>
28.     <noinput count="3">
29.        This is your last chance, Buddy.
30.        You better say something.
31.     </noinput>
32.     <noinput count="4">
33.        Oh, well, it's your loss.
34.        <goto next="#goodbye" />
35.     </noinput>
36.
37.     <block>
38.        You will hear a quotation from a Star Trek
39.        character. You must answer with Spock, Kirk,
40.        or McCoy. Here is the first quotation.
41.     </block>
42.
43.     <field>
44.        <prompt>
45.           I'm a doctor, not a bricklayer.
46.        </prompt>
47.        <grammar>
```

Listing 8.1 A simple quiz. *(continues)*

```
48.          <![CDATA[
49.            [ mccoy bones doc doctor ]
50.          ]]>
51.          </grammar>
52.          <nomatch count="1">
53.              Incorrect. Here is a hint.
54.              He supposedly didn't get along well with Spock.
55.          </nomatch>
56.          <nomatch count="2">Try again</nomatch>
57.          <nomatch count="3">
58.              Incorrect. The answer is "McCoy".
59.          <goto next="#goodbye" />
60.          </nomatch>
61.          <filled>
62.              Correct!
63.              <goto next="#goodbye" />
64.          </filled>
65.      </field>
66.  </form>
67.
68.  <form id="goodbye">
69.      <block>
70.          <prompt>
71.              Thank you for playing StarTrek Quotations.
72.              Live Long and Prosper.
73.          </prompt>
74.          <disconnect />
75.      </block>
76.  </form>
77.  </vxml>
```

Listing 8.1   A simple quiz. *(continued)*

The *questions* form beginning on line 20 can hold as many fields as desired, each <field> containing a single question and its answer. The <prompt> element outputs the questions, and the <grammar> contains the correct answer. The grammar should hold all of the possible answers a user might say that would be considered correct for that question.

All of the questions in the quiz have error checking at two levels. The <form> starting on line 20 begins with <noinput> error checking that is scoped at form level, allowing access from all the fields within the *questions* form. The *count* attribute of <noinput> is incremented each time it is accessed. Helpful prompts are output, trying to give the caller an indication that some kind of input is required.

The first <noinput> starting on line 22 holds a basic courtesy message, and the second is a short summary of the instructions, just in case the user is lost and isn't sure what to do. The third message is a warning, followed by an exit from the program if there is no response after the fourth try. On the fourth attempt to get input from the user, a <goto> element on line 34 transfers processing to the goodbye form for termination of the call.

The second level of error checking is within each <field> that contains a question. A set of <nomatch> elements with count attributes compares the user input to the defined grammar. The grammar is constructed from the correct answer to the question. The first <nomatch> condition outputs a hint to the correct answer, and the second, a simple "Try again" encouragement. On the third <nomatch> attempt for each question, the correct answer is given and processing is passed to the *goodbye* form.

When the user answers the question correctly, the <filled> block starting on line 61 confirms the answer and transfer processing to the goodbye form. As the project develops, more questions will be added and processing will fall through to a new question whenever there is a correct answer.

Create a basic quiz template in your BeVocal account and name it quiz.vxml. We will use this to expand the current application to contain multiple HANDS ON questions.

Add Questions to the Quiz

The first question in the quiz can now be used as a template. The *questions* form can hold any number of questions, coded as <field> items. In our application, there will be three questions.

Process the First Field

In Listing 8.2, processing of fields within a single form progresses linearly starting with the first <field> in the <form>. When a <field> is <filled> with a recognizable utterance, processing automatically proceeds to the next <field>.

```
1.  <form id="questions">
2.
3.    <noinput count="1">
4.       I didn't hear anything. Please try again.
5.    </noinput>
6.    <noinput count="2">
7.       You must say Spock, Kirk or McCoy to participate.
8.    </noinput>
9.    <noinput count="3">
10.      This is your last chance, Buddy.
11.      You better say something.
12.   </noinput>
13.   <noinput count="4">
```

Listing 8.2 Multiple questions within a form. *(continues)*

```
14.           Oh, well, it's your loss.
15.  <goto next="#goodbye" />
16.      </noinput>
17.
18.      <block>
19.         You will hear a quotation from a Star Trek
20.         character. You must answer with Spock, Kirk
21.         or McCoy. Here is the first quotation.
22.      </block>
23.
24.      <field name="question1">
25.         <prompt>
26.             I'm a doctor, not a bricklayer.
27.         </prompt>
28.         <grammar>
29.         <![CDATA[
30.             [ mccoy bones doc doctor ]
31.         ]]>
32.         </grammar>
33.         <nomatch count="1">
34.             Incorrect. Here is a hint.
35.             He supposedly didn't get along well with Spock.
36.         </nomatch>
37.         <nomatch count="2">Try again</nomatch>
38.         <nomatch count="3">
39.             Incorrect. The answer is "McCoy".
40.             <assign name="question1" expr="'incorrect'"/>
41.         </nomatch>
42.         <filled>
43.             Correct!
44.         </filled>
45.      </field>
46.
47.      <block>
48.         Here is your next quotation.
49.      </block>
50.
51.  <field name="question2">
52.         <prompt>
53.             Captain, I suggest the Vulcan mind probe.
54.         </prompt>
55.         <grammar>
56.         <![CDATA[
57.             [ (?mister spock) ]
58.         ]]>
59.         </grammar>
60.         <nomatch count="1">
61.             Incorrect. Here is a hint.
62.             He was an extremely logical creature.
```

Listing 8.2 Multiple questions within a form. *(continues)*

```
63.        </nomatch>
64.        <nomatch count="2">Try again</nomatch>
65.        <nomatch count="3">
66.           Incorrect. The answer is "Spock".
67.           <assign name="question2" expr="'incorrect'"/>
68.        </nomatch>
69.        <filled>
70. Correct! You are doing very well.
71. </filled>
72.     </field>
73.
74.    <block>
75.       Here is your final quotation.
76.    </block>
77.
78.    <field name="question3">
79.        <prompt>
80.           Scotty. Beam me up.
81.        </prompt>
82.        <grammar>
83.        <![CDATA[
84.            [ ?(?captain ?(james ?t) ?jim kirk) ]
85.        ]]>
86. </grammar>
87.        <nomatch count="1">
88.           Incorrect. Here is a hint.
89.           The big guy. The one and only.
90.        </nomatch>
91.        <nomatch count="2">Try again</nomatch>
92.        <nomatch count="3">
93.           Incorrect. The answer is "Kirk".
94.           <assign name="question3" expr="'incorrect'"/>
95.        </nomatch>
96.        <filled>
97.           Correct! That was your final quotation.
98.        </filled>
99.     </field>
100. </form>
```

Listing 8.2   Multiple questions within a form. *(continued)*

The first question about McCoy contains changes that help control the flow of processing. The <goto> elements have been removed from the nomatch and filled events in Listing 8.2 between lines 33 and 44. Within the nomatch event starting on line 38, an <assign> element has replaced the <goto>, forcing a value of *incorrect* into the *question1* <field>. We do not want to keep prompting callers if it was obvious they did not know the answer to *question1*. The third time an utterance is recognized as part of the grammar, the <assign> tag is used to assign a value to the *question1* <field> so that the quiz can continue.

The <assign> element assigns a value to a variable or a <field> item. It carries two mandatory attributes: *name* and *expr*. The *name* attribute is the name of the item to be filled. The *expr* attribute is the value or expression that should be used to fill the field. By assigning a value to *question1*, the FIA sees that that field is filled and moves on to the next phase in processing.

Be careful with the quotation marks when using an <assign> element. A literal word such as McCoy must be surrounded with double quotes and single quotes at the same time. The outside double quotes are interpreted as the mandatory quotes of the XML specification, whereas the single quotes specify that the value is a literal string, not a variable or expression to be interpreted.

When the user inputs an utterance that is recognized by the FIA as part of the acceptable grammar, the <field> is filled and processing continues to the next <form> item, which may be another <field>, <block>, or <subdialog> call. If the field-level item is the last in the form, and there is no transition using a <goto> element, the application is terminated.

Use Blocks for Transitions and Multiple Outputs

Sometimes it is desirable to output a verbal message without it being used as a prompt. The messages within the <block> elements between questions 1 and 2 in Listing 8.2 are a case in point. When a user has completed a question, either by providing a correct answer or by guessing incorrectly three times, a comment is inserted into the output to give users an idea of where they are within the structure of the application and where the transition is taking them.

Verbal clues during transitions between questions are useful when the verbal output of multiple events within a <field> use the same results. As an example, the nomatch event starting on line 38 could hold the "next quotation" transition comment, but then it would also be necessary to insert the same statement into the <filled> output when the user correctly guesses the answer. Using the <block> content on line 48 creates a logical transition between fields while providing output that is appropriate for the nomatch and filled events.

Add Questions

The second <field> starting on line 51 of Listing 8.2 outputs a quotation from Spock. The grammar is a simple one, using an optional *mister* before *spock*. The <assign> element is used again to assign a value to the field so that processing can progress with three wrong answers or a single correct answer.

The final question has a more complex grammar than the previous one. The grammar uses a question mark, signifying that what follows is optional, and also parentheses to force a string of tokens to be spoken as a single phrase. Now the user can say "captain kirk," "james kirk," "captain james kirk," or "kirk" as a correct response. For those on a personal basis with the captain, they may say "jim kirk."

This brings up an interesting subject relating to user responses. The original instructions for the quiz gave the three possible answers as "Kirk," "Spock," or "McCoy." The grammar for each of the questions does not assume that the user will stick with the specific choices offered. When possible, extend the grammar to include every possible choice a user might utter that would be considered a correct response. This will make your application more user friendly and give the impression that it is relatively intelligent when it comes to understanding spoken input.

Insert Recorded Prompts

Using the TTS-generated prompts is a good way to test an application, but recorded prompts make a vocal interface much more user friendly. The <audio> tag is used to point to a prerecorded sound file that can be used as a prompt. The *src* attribute is the name of the location of the sound file. Content for the <audio> tag should be text that will be used if the sound file is not available.

There are two types of sound files recommended by the VoiceXML specification: Raw (headerless) and WAV (RIFF header). The types of acceptable files are platform specific. The most widely accepted format is *.wav. Check your platform's documentation to see what type of sound files can be processed.

Download the *Star Trek* Sound Files

Star Trek resource files for this project can be found at www.stinsv.com, Star Trek in Sound and Vision; Figure 8.2 shows its home page. Dave Wythe, owner of the site, asks that you download the files needed for your project, not point to them on his site. With over 18,000 files available, you can see why he asks. Please read his "Terms of Use" before using any of his files.

Go to www.stinsv.com and download your favorite sound files to use as quotations in your project. You can rename the files to make them easier to remember, but you must keep the same file extension (.wav). When uploading files to the BeVocal environment, all names are forced into lowercase letters, so you might as well name them in lowercase to begin with.

Insert <audio> Elements

The <audio> element is useful for replacing <prompt> tags with recorded input. <audio> is more versatile than <prompt>, allowing an *src* attribute to point to a sound file that can be played as a prompt while also allowing the TTS interpreter to speak the content of the element if the source sound file is not available.

The <audio> element can carry an optional *expr* attribute in place of the *src* attribute. An *expr* value is generated by an ECMAScript expression that evaluates to a URI or an array of URIs that will be played in turn. The *fetchtimeout* attribute is also available to force a timeout for fetching the sound resource. By default, the timeout is set to 60 seconds, which will be too long for our application. The *fetchtimeout* attributes on lines 3, 11, and 19 of Listing 8.3 are set to 1500 milliseconds, forcing the TTS to speak if the sound file cannot be retrieved quickly. If the sound prompt cannot be accessed within that amount of time, the content of the <audio> element will be output by the TTS engine.

Change the quotation prompts in your application into <audio> elements that point to the files downloaded from the Star Trek in Sound and Vision site. Test your application to verify the output.

HANDS ON

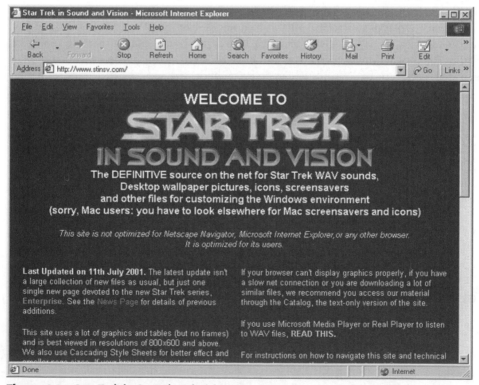

Figure 8.2   Star Trek in Sound and Vision.

```
1.  <field name="question1">
2.      <audio src="mccoy-bricklayer.wav"
3.          fetchtimeout="1500">
4.       I'm a doctor, not a bricklayer.
5.      </audio>
6.  ...
7.  </field>
8.
9.  <field name="question2">
10.     <audio src="spock-mindprobe.wav"
11.         fetchtimeout="1500">
12.       Captain, I suggest the Vulcan mind probe.
13.     </audio>
14. ...
15. </field>
16.
17. <field name="question3">
18.     <audio src="kirk-beammeup.wav"
19.         fetchtimeout="1500">
20.       Scotty. Beam me up.
21.     </audio>
22. ...
23. </field>
```

Listing 8.3   Sound prompts for quotations.

Record the Prompts

Using the Sound Recorder that is provided as an accessory in the Program Files, you can record .wav files on your local Windows desktop. These recordings are useful for building your initial prototype, but a production-level application should have professionally recorded prompts.

Sound files are included with the download package for the current project. They will help you get up and running quickly, but your project will be more personalized if you record your own prompts. The GoldWave sound recorder from GoldWave, Inc., at www.goldwave.com, is a nice intermediate tool to have for recording your own prompts. The recorded vocal prompts needed to complete this project are listed in Table 8.1.

HANDS ON

Make recordings for each of the prompts listed in Table 8.1. Upload the recordings to your BeVocal account.

Table 8.1   Vocal Prompts and Their Content

NAME	CONTENT
startrek-correct.wav	Correct!
startrek-encourage1.wav	You are doing very well.
startrek-hint	Here is a hint.
startrek-incorrect.wav	Incorrect.
startrek-instructions.wav	You will hear a quotation from a Star Trek character. You must answer with Spock, Kirk or McCoy. Here is the first quotation.
startrek-nextquotation.wav	Here is your next quotation.
startrek-noinput1.wav	I didn't hear anything. Please try again.
startrek-noinput2.wave	You must say Spock, Kirk or McCoy to participate.
startrek-noinput3.wav	This is your last chance, Buddy. You better say something.
startrek-noinput4.wav	Oh, well, it's your loss.
startrek-thankyou.wav	Thank you for playing the Star Trek Quotation Game.
startrek-tryagain.wav	Try again.
startrek-welcome.wav	Welcome to the Star Trek Quotation Game.

Complete the VoiceXML Template

Listing 8.4 is the completed VoiceXML script for the Quiz Generator that will be used as a template when creating the XSLT stylesheet in the next section. It includes audio links to all of the recorded prompts as well as a global *start over* link and a global help response.

```
1. <?xml version="1.0"?>
2. <!DOCTYPE  vxml
3.   PUBLIC
4.   "-//BeVocal Inc//VoiceXML 2.0//EN"
5.   "http://cafe.bevocal.com/libraries/dtd/vxml2-0-bevocal.dtd">
6.
7. <vxml version="2.0">
8.
9. <!-- START OVER LINK -->
10. <link next="quiz-generator.vxml">
```

Listing 8.4   Completed quiz generator script.

```
11.      <grammar>(start over)</grammar>
12.  </link>
13.
14.  <!-- GLOBAL HELP -->
15.  <help>
16.     <audio src="startrek-help.wav">
17.         Listen to a quotation from a Star Trek character.
18.         Say the name of the character.
19.         Your three choices are Spock, Kirk or McCoy.
20.     </audio>
21.     <reprompt/>
22.  </help>
23.
24.  <!-- GREETING -->
25.  <form id="greeting">
26.     <block>
27.         <audio src="startrek-theme.wav"
28.                 fetchhint="stream"/>
29.         <audio src="startrek-welcome.wav"
30.                 fetchtimeout="2000">
31.            Welcome to the Star Trek Quotation Game.
32.         </audio>
33.         <goto next="#questions"/>
34.     </block>
35.  </form>
36.
37.  <!-- QUESTIONS -->
38.  <form id="questions">
39.
40.     <!-- FORM SCOPED NOINPUT HANDLERS -->
41.     <noinput count="1">
42.         <audio src="startrek-noinput1.wav"
43.                 fetchtimeout="1000">
44.            I didn't hear anything. Please try again.
45.         </audio>
46.     </noinput>
47.     <noinput count="2">
48.         <audio src="startrek-noinput2.wav"
49.                 fetchtimeout="1000">
50.           You must say Spock, Kirk or McCoy to participate.
51.         </audio>
52.     </noinput>
53.     <noinput count="3">
54.         <audio src="startrek-noinput3.wav"
55.                   fetchtimeout="1000">
56.            This is your last chance, Buddy.
57.            You better say something.
58.         </audio>
59.     </noinput>
```

Listing 8.4 Completed quiz generator script. *(continues)*

```
60.      <noinput count="4">
61.         <audio src="startrek-noinput4.wav"
62.                 fetchtimeout="1000">
63.            Oh, well, it's your loss.
64.         </audio>
65.         <goto next="#goodbye" />
66.      </noinput>
67.
68.      <!-- INSTRUCTIONS -->
69.      <block>
70.         <audio src="startrek-instructions.wav"
71.                 fetchtimeout="1000">
72.            You will hear a quotation from a Star Trek
73.            character. You must answer with Spock, Kirk
74.            or McCoy.
75.         </audio>
76.      </block>
77.
78.      <!-- CONFIRM BEGINNING -->
79.      <block>
80.         <audio src="startrek-confirmbeginning.wav">
81.            Here is the first quotation.
82.         </audio>
83.      </block>
84.
85.      <!-- QUESTION 1 -->
86.      <field name="question1">
87.         <audio src="startrek-mccoy-bricklayer.wav"
88.                 fetchtimeout="2000">
89.            I'm a doctor, not a bricklayer.
90.         </audio>
91.         <grammar>
92.         <![CDATA[
93.            [ mccoy bones doc doctor ]
94.         ]]>
95.         </grammar>
96.
97.         <!-- NOMATCH HANDLERS -->
98.         <nomatch count="1">
99.            <audio src="startrek-incorrect.wav"
100.                 fetchtimeout="1000">
101.               Incorrect.
102.            </audio>
103.            <audio src="startrek-hint.wav"
104.                 fetchtimeout="1000">
105.               Here is a hint.
106.            </audio>
```

Listing 8.4   Completed quiz generator script. *(continues)*

```
107.          <prompt>
108.              He supposedly did not get along well with Spock.
109.          </prompt>
110.      </nomatch>
111.      <nomatch count="2">
112.          <audio src="startrek-tryagain.wav"
113.              fetchtimeout="1000">
114.            Try again
115.          </audio>
116.      </nomatch>
117.      <nomatch count="3">
118.          <audio src="startrek-incorrect.wav"
119.              fetchtimeout="1000">
120.            Incorrect.
121.          </audio>
122.          <prompt>
123.              The answer is "McCoy".
124.          </prompt>
125.          <assign name="question1" expr="'incorrect'"/>
126.      </nomatch>
127.      <filled>
128.          <audio src="startrek-correct.wav"
129.              fetchtimeout="1000">
130.            Correct!
131.          </audio>
132.      </filled>
133.  </field>
134.
135.  <!-- CONFIRM NEXT QUOTATION -->
136.  <block>
137.      <audio src="startrek-nextquotation.wav"
138.          fetchtimeout="1000">
139.        Here is your next quotation.
140.      </audio>
141.  </block>
142.
143.  <!-- QUESTION 2 -->
144.  <field name="question2">
145.      <audio src="startrek-spock-mindprobe.wav"
146.          fetchtimeout="1500">
147.        Captain, I suggest the Vulcan mind probe.
148.      </audio>
149.      <grammar>
150.      <![CDATA[
151.        [ (?mister spock) ]
152.      ]]>
153.      </grammar>
```

Listing 8.4 Completed quiz generator script. *(continues)*

```
154.
155.        <!-- NO MATCH HANDLERS -->
156.        <nomatch count="1">
157.          <audio src="startrek-incorrect.wav"
158.              fetchtimeout="1000">
159.            Incorrect.
160.          </audio>
161.          <audio src="startrek-hint.wav"
162.              fetchtimeout="1000">
163.            Here is a hint.
164.          </audio>
165.          <prompt>
166.            He was an extremely logical creature.
167.          </prompt>
168.        </nomatch>
169.        <nomatch count="2">
170.          <audio src="startrek-tryagain.wav"
171.              fetchtimeout="1000">
172.            Try again
173.          </audio>
174.        </nomatch>
175.        <nomatch count="3">
176.          <audio src="startrek-incorrect.wav"
177.              fetchtimeout="1000">
178.            Incorrect.
179.          </audio>
180.          <prompt>
181.            The answer is "Spock".
182.          </prompt>
183.          <assign name="question2" expr="'incorrect'"/>
184.        </nomatch>
185.        <filled>
186.          <audio src="startrek-correct.wav"
187.              fetchtimeout="1000">
188.            Correct!
189.          </audio>
190.          <audio src="startrek-encourage1.wav"
191.              fetchtimeout="1000">
192.            You are doing very well.
193.          </audio>
194.        </filled>
195.      </field>
196.
197.      <!-- CONFIRM NEXT QUOTATION -->
198.      <block>
199.        <audio src="startrek-nextquotation.wav"
200.            fetchtimeout="1000">
201.          Here is your next quotation.
202.        </audio>
```

Listing 8.4 Completed quiz generator script. *(continues)*

```
203.    </block>
204.
205.    <!-- QUESTION 3 -->
206.    <field name="question3">
207.       <audio src="startrek-kirk-beammeup.wav"
208.            fetchtimeout="1500">
209.          Scotty. Beam me up.
210.       </audio>
211.       <grammar>
212.       <![CDATA[
213.          [ ?(?captain ?(james ?t) ?jim kirk) ]
214.       ]]>
215.       </grammar>
216.
217.       <!   NOMATCH HANDLERS -->
218.       <nomatch count="1">
219.          <audio src="startrek-incorrect.wav"
220.              fetchtimeout="1000">
221.            Incorrect.
222.          </audio>
223.          <audio src="startrek-hint.wav"
224.              fetchtimeout="1000">
225.            Here is a hint.
226.          </audio>
227.          <prompt>
228.             The big guy. The one and only.
229.          </prompt>
230.       </nomatch>
231.       <nomatch count="2">
232.          <audio src="startrek-tryagain.wav"
233.              fetchtimeout="1000">
234.            Try again
235.          </audio>
236.       </nomatch>
237.       <nomatch count="3">
238.          <audio src="startrek-incorrect.wav"
239.              fetchtimeout="1000">
240.            Incorrect.
241.          </audio>
242.          <prompt>
243.             The answer is "Kirk".
244.          </prompt>
245.          <assign name="question3" expr="'incorrect'"/>
246.       </nomatch>
247.       <filled>
248.          <audio src="startrek-correct.wav"
249.              fetchtimeout="1000">
250.            Correct!
251.          </audio>
```

Listing 8.4 Completed quiz generator script. *(continues)*

```
252.        </filled>
253.      </field>
254.
255.      <block>
256.        <audio src="startrek-finalquotation">
257.           That was your final quotation.
258.        </audio>
259.        <goto next="#goodbye"/>
260.      </block>
261. </form>
262.
263. <form id="goodbye">
264.      <block>
265.        <audio src="startrek-thankyou.wav"
266.               fetchtimeout="1000">
267.           Thank you for playing the Star Trek Quotation Game.
268.        </audio>
269.      </block>
270.
271.      <field name="exit">
272.        <audio src="startrek-spock-livelong.wav"
273.               fetchtimeout="1000">
274.           Live Long and Prosper.
275.        </audio>
276.        <catch event="noinput nomatch">
277.           <exit/>
278.        </catch>
279.      </field>
280.
281. </form>
282. </vxml>
```

Listing 8.4   Completed quiz generator script. *(continued)*

On line 28, a *fetchhint* attribute is added to the <audio> element. *fetchhint* specifies to the VoiceXML interpreter when or how the sound resource should be accessed. By setting the value to *stream*, the sound recording will begin playing as soon as the resource starts downloading, instead of waiting for the complete file to download.

Notice the transitions between questions. The blocks starting on lines 136 and 198 isolate the transition messages from the confirmation messages within each question. This allows for more granular control over the output messages when building various scenarios.

HANDS ON **Insert audio links for each of the prompts in your application. Add a** *start* *over* **link and a help prompt to the top of your script. Place a phone call to your application to check the output. Listen for clarity in the prompts. Check the sound volumes to make sure the sound levels are correct and the articulation is clear.**

At this point, you have a fully functioning script that can be used as a quiz template. The next section will show how to use this template to generate hundreds of quizzes by using one, central XSLT script.

VoiceXML Script Generation with XML and XSLT

The VoiceXML Quiz Generator file has the data hard-coded as part of the application. It would be much more usable if there were a way to isolate the data from the application that is processing it. The implications are astounding. We could now have any number of quizzes, even into the thousands, that could be processed by a single application. Point the data at the application and out pops the VoiceXML script. A combination of XML and XSLT technologies can be used to construct such an application.

There are two major reasons XML has been accepted so quickly in the data processing community: nonproprietary exchange of data between applications and standardized data structure. We will use a standardized data structure to expand the capabilities of the quiz application.

The application will consist of two documents: the data, which is an XML file holding the questions and answers to the quiz, and a processing script, which is the XSLT script for transforming and formatting the data into a VoiceXML file. Using the *Star Trek* Quotation Game as a template, we will build both documents and then process the data to show how to create the VoiceXML output.

Set Up the XML/XSLT Work Environment

There are two ways to run an XML/XSLT application: through a local processor that generates the VoiceXML script or by creating the VoiceXML output dynamically through a VoiceXML browser. At this time, VoiceXML browsers do not handle dynamic XSLT output, so the VoiceXML file will be built locally and then uploaded to your developer account.

The XML processing environment is 100 percent Java. The good news is that you will not have to have any Java programming skills to make the pieces work.

You will need to download and install a Java Development Kit from Sun Microsystems and the Xerces XML parser and the Xalan XSLT processor from Apache. If you do not have the environment installed on your machine, now is a good time to get it set up. The installations are very simple on the Window's platform. As your programming experience grows, you will find this combination of software an invaluable resource.

Links to these resources can be found in Project 8 on the cafe.bevocal.com/wiley/ 10projects site.

Create the Data File (XML)

Creating a robust XML application involves separating the data from the formatting of the data. In the Quiz Generator application, the data for each quiz is stored in an XML file. It is marked up with a set of predefined tags that define what the data is. When examining the quiz application in Listing 8.4, a definite structure can be found. Each question, or quotation in our case, has the following items: a quotation, a set of answers, and a hint. The answer items will be used as the correct responses we are looking for from the user, in other words, the grammar.

Let's walk through the process of building an XML file from an existing source of data. We are trying to build a generic application that will handle any quiz or survey data source by isolating data from the formatting of the data. The XML file will hold the data, and the XSL file will hold the formatting.

 For simplicity, the data in this project is stored in a text file. It could also have been generated dynamically from a database or from a combination of NOTE multiple data sources.

Analyze the Data

The data for the *Star Trek* Quotation Game is embedded within the VoiceXML file created as the first part of this project. Listing 8.5 is an outline of the various elements and attributes of that file and how they are related in a hierarchical structure. The value of looking at the hierarchy this way is that it helps to define what the structure of the XML document should be without having to worry about data.

The <vxml> element contains three elements at the child level: <link>, <help>, and <form>. Everything else in the file is a child or descendent of one of those three elements. <link> and <help> are relatively simple elements. <link> carries a single attribute and grammar to define what utterances will activate the link. The <help> element is basically audio output with text as content in case the source sound file can't be fetched in time.

The bulk of the structure of the document is within the <form> element. <form> has three child elements that each contain multiple levels of other elements. We will break down each of the main elements as we develop the XSLT stylesheet in the next section.

```
1.  <vxml>
2.
3.      <link>
4.          src (attribute)
5.          <grammar>
6.
7.      <help>
8.          <audio>
9.              src (attribute)
10.         fetchtimeout (attribute)
```

Listing 8.5 Hierarchical structure of quiz game data.

```
11.        text (content)
12.        <reprompt>
13.
14.    <form>
15.
16.        id (attribute)
17.
18.        <block>
19.           <audio>
20.              src (attribute)
21.              fetchtimeout (attribute)
22.              text (optional content)
23.              <goto> (optional)
24.                 next (attribute)
25.
26.        <noinput>
27.           count (attribute)
28.           <audio>
29.              src (attribute)
30.              text (content)
31.           <goto> (optional)
32.              next (attribute)
33.
34.        <field>
35.           name (attribute)
36.
37.           <audio>
38.              src (attribute)
39.              text (cotent)
40.
41.           <grammar>
42.
43.           <nomatch>
44.              count (attribute)
45.              <audio>
46.                 fetchtimeout (attribute)
47.                 src (attribute)
48.                 text (content)
49.              <prompt> (optional)
50.                 text (content)
51.              <assign> (optional)
52.                 name (attribute)
53.                 expr (attribute)
54.              <goto> (optional)
55.                 next (attribute)
56.              <catch> (optional)
57.                 event (attribute)
58.                 <exit>
59.
```

Listing 8.5   Hierarchical structure of quiz game data. *(continues)*

```
60.          <filled>
61.             <audio>
62.                src (attribute)
63.                fetchtimeout (attribute)
64.                text (content)
```

Listing 8.5   Hierarchical structure of quiz game data. *(continued)*

Create an XML Skeleton

The first step in creating the XML file is to create the basic skeleton that will hold the data. Listing 8.6 shows a skeleton that contains the XML declaration as its first line. The root element *quiz* is declared with a *quizFileName* attribute. The *quizFileName* will be used by the XSLT stylesheet to create the start over link. Line 5 closes the XML document. All content within the XML file will be contained within the *quiz* root element.

```
1. <?xml version="1.0"?>
2.
3. <quiz quizFileName="quiz-startrek.vxml">
4.
5. </quiz>
```

Listing 8.6   The XML skeleton.

 Create a new Projects folder on your local hard drive. Build the XML skeleton shown in Listing 8.6 and save it as quiz-startrek.xml in the Projects HANDS ON directory.

Define a Link

Analyzing the VoiceXML file in Listing 8.4 shows that the <link> element is the first child of the <vxml> root element. The XML data file can define the structure of the <link> element as shown in Listing 8.7 starting on line 5. The <link> must contain a <next> element that holds the URI of the location the link will transfer to when activated. The <grammar> element holds the simple grammar that will activate the link.

```
1.  <?xml version="1.0"?>
2.
3.  <quiz quizFileName="quiz-startrek.vxml">
4.
5.  <link>
6.     <next>quiz-startrek.vxml</next>
7.     <grammar>start over</grammar>
8.  </link>
9.
10. </quiz>
```

Listing 8.7 Define <link>.

Define a Help Message

The VoiceXML file next contains a global help message that must be defined in the XML file. Looking back at the data structure in Listing 8.5, we can see that <audio> is used within the <help> message and that it is also contained in several locations within the <form> element. We need to define element names that will be appropriate in all locations within the XML file so that the XSLT processor will recognize common structures.

The <help> element holds two child elements: <audio> and <reprompt>. The <audio> element in the VoiceXML file has an attribute that points to a sound file and an attribute that defines how long to wait before playing the text prompt if the sound file can't be fetched. Lines 14 through 20 of Listing 8.8 define those attributes and insert a <textPrompt> element to hold the content of the <audio> element.

```
1.  <?xml version="1.0"?>
2.
3.  <quiz quizFileName="quiz-startrek.vxml">
4.
5.  <!-- START OVER -->
6.  <link>
7.     <next>quiz-startrek.vxml</next>
8.     <grammar>start over</grammar>
9.  </link>
10.
11. <!-- HELP -->
```

Listing 8.8 Define <help>. *(continues)*

```
12. <help>
13.   <audio>
14.     <soundSource>startrek-help.wav</soundSource>
15.     <timeout>2000</timeout>
16.     <textPrompt>
17.        Listen to a quotation from a Star Trek character.
18.        Say the name of the character.
19.        Your three choices are Spock, Kirk or McCoy.
20.     </textPrompt>
21.   </audio>
22. </help>
23.
24. </quiz>
```

Listing 8.8   Define <help>. *(continued)*

Greeting Block

The next section within the VoiceXML file is a *greeting* <form>. It contains two sets of <audio> information. The first one starting on line 2 of Listing 8.9 is a simple sound file that does not have a text prompt alternative. The second, starting on line 6, is typical of the <audio> data we have examined so far. The XSLT stylesheet will have to be able to accommodate more than one <audio> element per block.

```
1. <greeting>
2.   <audio>
3.     <soundSource>startrek-theme.wav</soundSource>
4.     <fetchhint>stream</fetchhint>
5.   </audio>
6.   <audio>
7.     <soundSource>startrek-welcome.wav</soundSource>
8.     <timeout>2000</timeout>
9.     <textPrompt>
10.        Welcome to the Star Trek Quotation Game.
11.     </textPrompt>
12.   </audio>
13. </greeting>
```

Listing 8.9   Define greeting.

Define Questions <form>

The *questions* <form> of the VoiceXML file starts with a list of <noinput> handlers, followed by general instructions for using the program and a confirmation to the user that the quiz has begun. Finally the questions are inserted. We will handle each section in turn.

noInput Messages

The VoiceXML file contains numerous <noinput> event handlers within the *questions* <form>. Listing 8.10 shows the <noinput> elements grouped together within an <errorNoInput> block. Each handler contains an <audio> source and a text prompt.

 Keep in mind that the XML file is the not final output to the VoiceXML interpreter. The XML will be transformed by the XSLT stylesheet to output the final results. It is coincidental that some of the tags in the data are also tags in the final output.

NOTE

Notice there are no *count* attributes in the <noinput> event handlers. This is in anticipation of the XSLT stylesheet adding those attributes dynamically. Not including *count* attributes within the XML data makes the application more robust and expandable.

```
1.  <errorNoInput>
2.   <noinput>
3.      <audio>
4.         <soundSource>startrek-noinput1.wav</soundSource>
5.         <timeout>1000</timeout>
6.         <textPrompt>
7.             I didn't hear anything. Please try again.
8.         </textPrompt>
9.      </audio>
10.   </noinput>
11.
12.   <noinput>
13.      <audio>
14.         <soundSource>startrek-noinput2.wav</soundSource>
15.         <timeout>1000</timeout>
16.         <textPrompt>
17.             You must say Spock, Kirk or McCoy to participate.
18.         </textPrompt>
19.      </audio>
20.   </noinput>
21.
```

Listing 8.10 Define <noinput>. *(continues)*

```
22.  <noinput>
23.    <audio>
24.      <soundSource>startrek-noinput3.wav</soundSource>
25.      <timeout>1000</timeout>
26.      <textPrompt>
27.          This is your last chance, Buddy.
28.          You better say something.
29.      </textPrompt>
30.    </audio>
31.  </noinput>
32.
33.  <noinput>
34.    <audio>
35.      <soundSource>startrek-noinput3.wav</soundSource>
36.      <timeout>1000</timeout>
37.      <textPrompt>
38.          Oh, well, it's your loss.
39.      </textPrompt>
40.    </audio>
41.  </noinput>
42.
43.  </errorNoInput>
```

Listing 8.10   Define <noinput>. *(continued)*

Insert Instructions

The general instructions for using the application are inserted within the <instructions> element in Listing 8.11. It is a typical <audio> element containing a URL to a sound file and the duration to wait for a timeout, and ending with a text prompt. The <instructions> block is inserted into the XML file beneath the <errorNoInput> block.

```
1.  <instructions>
2.    <audio>
3.      <soundSource>startrek-instructions.wav</soundSource>
4.      <timeout>1000</timeout>
5.      <textPrompt>
6.        You will hear a quotation from a Star Trek
7.        character. You must answer with Spock, Kirk
8.        or McCoy.
9.      </textPrompt>
10.   </audio>
11. </instructions>
```

Listing 8.11   Insert instructions.

Beginning Confirmation

Before the questions can be inserted into the XML file, a confirmation to the user that the quiz is about to begin must be registered. Listing 8.12 generates a <confirmBeginning> element that holds another <audio> output.

```
1. <confirmBeginning>
2.    <audio>
3.       <soundSource>startrek-confirmbeginning.wav</soundSource>
4.       <timeout>1000</timeout>
5.       <textPrompt>
6.          Here is the first quotation.
7.       </textPrompt>
8.    </audio>
9. </confirmBeginning>
```

Listing 8.12   Confirm quiz is about to begin.

Insert the Questions

The next data within the XML file is the set of questions that will be asked in the quiz. Line 1 of Listing 8.13 begins a <seriesOfQuestions> block that contains all of the questions and answers for the quiz. Each question is stored within a <set> element that contains all of the information about that question: the question, the possible answers for grammar development, and a hint to the correct answer.

Each <question> tag carries a *recording* attribute that holds the name of the .wav file that will be output as the quotation. The <answer> tags each hold a possible utterance that the user might speak that would be considered a correct answer to the question. These will be used to dynamically generate a grammar for each field when the XSLT file transforms the data to VoiceXML output.

```
1.  <!-- QUESTIONS -->
2.  <seriesOfQuestions>
3.
4.     <!-- QUESTION 1 -->
5.     <set>
6.        <question recording="mccoy-bricklayer.wav">
7.           I'm a doctor, not a bricklayer.
8.        </question>
9.
10.       <answers>
11.          <answer>mccoy</answer>
12.          <answer>doc</answer>
13.          <answer>bones</answer>
```

Listing 8.13   Insert the question. *(continues)*

```
14.           <answer>doctor mccoy</answer>
15.        </answers>
16.
17.        <hint>
18.            He, supposedly, did not get along with Spock.
19.        </hint>
20.
21.     </set>
22.
23.     <!-- QUESTION 2 -->
24.     <set>
25.        <question recording="spock-mindprobe.wav">
26.            Captain, I suggest the Vulcan mind probe.
27.        </question>
28.
29.        <answers>
30.           <answer>spock</answer>
31.           <answer>the vulcan</answer>
32.        </answers>
33.
34.        <hint>
35.           James T. Kirk's best friend.
36.           He was extremely logical.
37.        </hint>
38.
39.     </set>
40.
41.     <!-- QUESTION 3 -->
42.     <set>
43.        <question recording="kirk-beammeup.wav">
44.            Scottie, beam me up.
45.        </question>
46.
47.        <answers>
48.           <answer>kirk</answer>
49.           <answer>captain kirk</answer>
50.           <answer>james kirk</answer>
51.           <answer>james t kirk</answer>
52.           <answer>jim</answer>
53.        </answers>
54.
55.        <hint>
56.            The big guy. The one and only.
57.        </hint>
58.     </set>
59. </seriesOfQuestions>
```

Listing 8.13   Insert the question. *(continued)*

Define Goodbye <form>

The final data to place within the XML file are the audio prompts for the *goodbye* <form>. Listing 8.14 shows the data for the two <audio> elements.

```
1.  <goodbye>
2.     <audio>
3.        <soundSource>startrek-thankyou.wav</soundSource>
4.        <timeout>1000</timeout>
5.        <textPrompt>
6.           Thank you for playing the Star Trek Quotation Game.
7.        </textPrompt>
8.     </audio>
9.     <audio>
10.       <soundSource>startrek-spock-livelong.wav</soundSource>
11.       <timeout>1000</timeout>
12.       <textPrompt>
13.          Live Long and Prosper.
14.       </textPrompt>
15.    </audio>
16. </goodbye>
```

Listing 8.14   Goodbye <form>.

The Final XML Data File

Listing 8.15 shows the completed XML data file. Examine the file and you will see there is no formatting using VoiceXML elements; it is purely a data file. Any use of elements with names that have meaning within VoiceXML is coincidental. We can now begin construction of the XSLT stylesheet to transform the data into a VoiceXML application.

```
1.  <?xml version="1.0"?>
2.  <quiz quizFileName="quiz-startrek.vxml">
3.  <!-- START OVER -->
4.  <link>
5.     <next>quiz-startrek.vxml</next>
6.     <grammar>start over</grammar>
7.  </link>
8.  <!-- HELP -->
9.  <help>
10.    <audio>
11.       <soundSource>startrek-help.wav</soundSource>
12.       <timeout>2000</timeout>
```

Listing 8.15   *Star Trek* quiz data file. *(continues)*

```
13.        <textPrompt>
14.           Listen to a quotation from a Star Trek character.
15.           Say the name of the character.
16.           Your three choices are Spock, Kirk or McCoy.
17.        </textPrompt>
18.      </audio>
19.  </help>
20.  <!- GREETING ->
21.  <greeting>
22.    <audio>
23.       <soundSource>startrek-theme.wav</soundSource>
24.       <fetchhint>stream</fetchhint>
25.    </audio>
26.    <audio>
27.       <soundSource>startrek-welcome.wav</soundSource>
28.       <timeout>2000</timeout>
29.       <textPrompt>
30.          Welcome to the Star Trek Quotation Game.
31.       </textPrompt>
32.    </audio>
33.  </greeting>
34.  <!- NOINPUT HANDLERS ->
35.  <errorNoInput>
36.    <noinput>
37.      <audio>
38.       <soundSource>startrek-noinput1.wav</soundSource>
39.       <timeout>1000</timeout>
40.       <textPrompt>
41.          I didn't hear anything. Please try again.
42.       </textPrompt>
43.      </audio>
44.    </noinput>
45.    <noinput>
46.      <audio>
47.       <soundSource>startrek-noinput2.wav</soundSource>
48.       <timeout>1000</timeout>
49.       <textPrompt>
50.          You must say Spock, Kirk or McCoy to participate.
51.       </textPrompt>
52.      </audio>
53.    </noinput>
54.    <noinput>
55.      <audio>
56.       <soundSource>startrek-noinput3.wav</soundSource>
57.       <timeout>1000</timeout>
58.       <textPrompt>
59.          This is your last chance, Buddy.
60.          You better say something.
61.       </textPrompt>
```

Listing 8.15 *Star Trek* quiz data file.

```
62.      </audio>
63.   </noinput>
64.   <noinput>
65.      <audio>
66.         <soundSource>startrek-noinput3.wav</soundSource>
67.         <timeout>1000</timeout>
68.         <textPrompt>
69.            Oh, well, it's your loss.
70.         </textPrompt>
71.      </audio>
72.   </noinput>
73. </errorNoInput>
74. <!-- QUESTIONS -->
75. <seriesOfQuestions>
76. <!-- INSTRUCTIONS -->
77. <instructions>
78.      <audio>
79.         <soundSource>startrek-instructions.wav</soundSource>
80.         <timeout>1000</timeout>
81.         <textPrompt>
82.            You will hear a quotation from a Star Trek
83.            character. You must answer with Spock, Kirk
84.            or McCoy.
85.         </textPrompt>
86.      </audio>
87. </instructions>
88. <confirmBeginning>
89.      <audio>
90.         <soundSource>startrek-confirmbeginning.wav</soundSource>
91.         <timeout>1000</timeout>
92.         <textPrompt>
93.            Here is the first quotation.
94.         </textPrompt>
95.      </audio>
96. </confirmBeginning>
97.      <!-- QUESTION 1 -->
98.      <set>
99.         <question recording="mccoy-bricklayer.wav">
100.           I'm a doctor, not a bricklayer.
101.        </question>
102.        <answers>
103.           <answer>mccoy</answer>
104.           <answer>doc</answer>
105.           <answer>bones</answer>
106.           <answer>doctor mccoy</answer>
107.        </answers>
108.        <hint>
109.           He, supposedly, did not get along with Spock.
110.        </hint>
```

Listing 8.15 *Star Trek* quiz data file. *(continues)*

```
111.   </set>
112.   <!— QUESTION 2 —>
113.   <set>
114.      <question recording="spock-mindprobe.wav">
115.         Captain, I suggest the Vulcan mind probe.
116.      </question>
117.      <answers>
118.         <answer>spock</answer>
119.         <answer>the vulcan</answer>
120.      </answers>
121.      <hint>
122.         James T. Kirk's best friend.
123.         He was extremely logical.
124.      </hint>
125.   </set>
126.   <!— QUESTION 3 —>
127.   <set>
128.      <question recording="kirk-beammeup.wav">
129.         Scottie, beam me up.
130.      </question>
131.      <answers>
132.         <answer>kirk</answer>
133.         <answer>captain kirk</answer>
134.         <answer>james kirk</answer>
135.         <answer>james t kirk</answer>
136.         <answer>jim</answer>
137.      </answers>
138.      <hint>
139.         The big guy. The one and only.
140.      </hint>
141.   </set>
142. </seriesOfQuestions>
143. <goodbye>
144.    <audio>
145.       <soundSource>startrek-thankyou.wav</soundSource>
146.       <timeout>1000</timeout>
147.       <textPrompt>
148.          Thank you for playing the Star Trek Quotation Game.
149.       </textPrompt>
150.    </audio>
151.    <audio>
152.       <soundSource>startrek-spock-livelong.wav</soundSource>
153.       <timeout>1000</timeout>
154.       <textPrompt>
155.          Live Long and Prosper.
156.       </textPrompt>
157.    </audio>
158. </goodbye>
159. </quiz>
```

Listing 8.15   *Star Trek* quiz data file. *(continued)*

Create an XML data file by analyzing the VoiceXML file in Listing 8.4. Use Listing 8.15 as a template.

HANDS ON

Build the Stylesheet (XSLT)

XSLT can be used to select and transform XML data. For the Quiz Generator application, an XSLT script will be used to format the quiz-startrek.xml file into VoiceXML for output by the voice browser.

Listing 8.16 shows a generic stylesheet that can process any XML file. It isn't very useful in its current condition, but when used to transform a file, it will confirm that the processing environment is set up correctly and files are available for processing. By default, an XSLT stylesheet will output all text nodes within an XML file.

```
1. <?xml version="1.0"?>
2.
3. <xsl:stylesheet
4.     xmlns:xsl="http://www.w3.org/1999/XSL/Transform"
5.     version="1.0">
6.
7. <xsl:output method="xml" indent="yes" />
8. <xsl:strip-space elements="*" />
9.
10. </xsl:stylesheet>
```

Listing 8.16 Basic XSLT stylesheet.

Stylesheets must adhere to the rules of XML syntax by starting with an XML declaration and a root element. An XSL stylesheet uses the <stylesheet> tag as the root element, as shown on line 3. The *xsl* namespace is declared within the tag on line 4. The URI specified as the value of the namespace is mandatory according to the XML specification. It must be the exact string ""http://www.w3.org/1999/XSL/Transform" or the application will not compile.

By declaring a namespace, any tags within the stylesheet that are preceded by *xsl* will be processed by the XSLT processor as instructions. Those tags that do not have the namespace prefix will be output as literal text. This is how the VoiceXML tags will be output.

VoiceXML elements displayed within an XSLT stylesheet will be output as literal elements because they are not preceded by the *xsl* namespace.

NOTE

The <xsl:output> element on line 7 carries a *method* attribute to give an indication to the XSLT processor of the type of data that will be output. The *indent* attribute is set to *yes* so that indentation will automatically be incorporated into the output. This makes the output readable by humans. When the project is ready for production, change the *indent* attribute to *no*, optimizing the output for more efficient reading by a machine.

Line 8 strips white space only nodes from all of the elements.

An XSLT file is made up of templates. Each tag within the XML file can have its own template, defining the formatting for that tag. Processing will jump back and forth between the templates, depending upon which element is being accessed at that time.

Save the XSLT stylesheet from Listing 8.8 within the Project folder that contains the quiz-startrek.xml file. Save it as quizFormatter.xsl. The next section shows how to apply the stylesheet to the data.

Test the Basic Application

The XSLT file is now ready to apply to the XML data. Start by creating a batch file. This file will hold a single line that instantiates the Java interpreter and outputs the VoiceXML file. The batch file can be created with any simple text editor. I suggest using TextPad, which can be downloaded at www.textpad.com, but you can use Notepad, VI, Simple Text, or any other type of text editor available on your machine.

Listing 8.17 shows the contents of the batch file. Note that everything following the word *java* in the code should be on one line. The text is wrapped here because of the width of the page.

The content of Listing 8.17, starting at line 2, should all be on one line.

The first line, *cls*, clears the DOS window of any input. Line 2 makes a call to the Java compiler, indicating that an XSLT process is needed using the Xalan processor. This is followed by three switches, -in, -xsl, and -out, indicating the filenames being used. quiz-startrek.vxml will be generated by pulling in quiz-startrek.xml and formatting it with quizFormatter.xsl.

Save Listing 8.17 as buildQuiz.bat in your projects folder. Start the batch file by opening a DOS window. Change directories to your projects folder. Type *buildQuiz* at the command prompt and press the Enter key. The DOS window will clear and you will receive information about the processing of your files. If there are errors, read the messages carefully. They are usually pretty accurate and will give you a filename and line number for tracking down any problems. Most errors will occur because tags or quotation marks were not closed properly in the XML or XSL files.

```
1. cls
2. java org.apache.xalan.xslt.Process
3.      -in quiz-startrek.xml
4.      -xsl quizFormatter.xsl
5.      -out quiz-startrek.vxml
```

Listing 8.17   Batch file for processing the XML data.

The output of the application will be the quiz-startrek.vxml file. Open the file and you will see that all plain text within the XML file has been output. This is the result of the default template in Listing 8.16. The next section applies specific XSLT templates to selected elements within the XML file. When all the templates have been inserted, a complete VoiceXML file will be generated automatically when running the batch file.

Insert XSLT Templates into the Stylesheet

The basic framework for the XSLT processor is now in place and verified, so we can begin adding templates to process each element in the XML file. Templates are used within an XSLT file to access specific elements of the data. The template accesses the data and applies formatting according to the developer's specifications.

The elements within the XML file hold data that can be output in a specific format to the VoiceXML file. Begin construction of the XSLT stylesheet by starting at the top of the XML file. We will work down through each element and design a template for the data's output. Keep in mind that we are building a generic output template. At no time should there be any reference to specific *Star Trek* data within the XSLT stylesheet. The stylesheet should be able to format any source of data into a VoiceXML document as long as that data uses the XML template created above.

TIP

During your first application development process with XSLT, each time a template is added to the quizFormatter.xsl file, check the output to verify that it is what is expected. Errors in small amounts of code are much easier to find and fix than hunting through hundreds of lines, trying to track down multiple errors.

Document Root Template

Every VoiceXML document must open and close with the <vxml> tag. Lines 10 through 14 of Listing 8.18 insert a root-level template into the basic stylesheet. The root-level template accesses the complete XML document.

The formatting within the template outputs a literal <vxml> element at line 11. As a reminder, any element that is not preceded by the *xsl* namespace is output as literal text. The <vxml> element carries an attribute of *version* that is set to *2.0*. The literal closing <vxml> tag is handled on line 14.

One of the most important elements within an XSLT stylesheet is the <xsl:apply-templates> rule. It specifies the set of nodes that will be processed by the XSLT engine. An <xsl:apply-templates> element without a *select* attribute will process all children of the current node. If you looked at the output after running the initial transformation in Listing 8.17, you saw that the output was all of the text from the XML file. <xsl:apply-templates> can also be used to selectively call formatting templates for each of the elements within the XML data file. We will use that technique in the next section.

Line 12 of Listing 8.18 uses the <xsl:apply-templates> element to process all of the nodes within the XML file.

```
1. <?xml version="1.0"?>
2.
3. <xsl:stylesheet
4.       xmlns:xsl="http://www.w3.org/1999/XSL/Transform"
5.       version="1.0">
6.
7. <xsl:output method="xml" indent="yes" />
8. <xsl:strip-space elements="*" />
9.
10. <xsl:template match="/">
11. <vxml version="2.0">
12.    <xsl:apply-templates />
13. </vxml>
14. </xsl:template>
15.
16. </xsl:stylesheet>
```

Listing 8.18   Document root template.

 Add the document root template to your quizFormatter.xsl file and run the batch file from the DOS command line. Open the resulting file in your text editor and notice that <vxml> elements are now surrounding the output of the text data.

HANDS ON

Quiz Template

Examining the XML data in Listing 8.15 shows that the root element is <quiz>. Listing 8.19 inserts a template beginning at line 16 that processes the <quiz> node when it is found within the XML document.

An XSLT template starts with the <xsl:template> element and carries a *match* attribute that holds the name of the XML element that is to be processed. The <quiz> element within the XML file does not have any text content, just other elements. The <xsl:apply-templates/> directive on line 17 instructs the processor to find templates to handle the elements that are children of the <quiz> element.

```
1.  <?xml version="1.0"?>
2.
3.  <xsl:stylesheet
4.      xmlns:xsl="http://www.w3.org/1999/XSL/Transform"
5.      version="1.0">
6.
7.  <xsl:output method="xml" indent="yes" />
8.  <xsl:strip-space elements="*" />
9.
10. <xsl:template match="/">
11. <vxml version="2.0">
12.  <xsl:apply-templates />
13. </vxml>
14. </xsl:template>
15.
16. <xsl:template match="quiz">
17.     <xsl:apply-templates/>
18. </xsl:template>
19.
20. </xsl:stylesheet>
```

Listing 8.19   The quiz template.

Link Template

The first element encountered within the <quiz> block of the XML file is the <link> element. Starting on line 20, Listing 8.20 shows a template that outputs a <link> element into the VoiceXML file. The <link> element is output as literal text.

```
1.  <?xml version="1.0"?>
2.
3.  <xsl:stylesheet
4.      xmlns:xsl="http://www.w3.org/1999/XSL/Transform"
5.      version="1.0">
6.
7.  <xsl:output method="xml" indent="yes" />
8.  <xsl:strip-space elements="*" />
9.
10. <xsl:template match="/">
11. <vxml version="2.0">
```

Listing 8.20   Creating a link template. *(continues)*

```
12.  <xsl:apply-templates />
13.  </vxml>
14.  </xsl:template>
15.
16.  <xsl:template match="quiz">
17.    <xsl:apply-templates/>
18.  </xsl:template>
19.
20.  <xsl:template match="link">
21.      <link next="{next}">
22.         <xsl:apply-templates select="grammar"/>
23.      </link>
24.  </xsl:template>
25.
26.  <xsl:template match="grammar">
27.      <grammar>(<xsl:value-of select="."/>)</grammar>
28.  </xsl:template>
29.
30.  </xsl:stylesheet>
```

Listing 8.20   Creating a link template. *(continued)*

XSLT syntax does not allow template matching to be inserted as the value of an attribute. To allow input into the value, *attribute value templates* are created with curly braces and hold the name of the element or attribute to be inserted as the value. Line 21 inserts the value from the <next> element in the XML file as an *attribute value template*.

Line 22 of Listing 8.20 uses the *select* attribute of an <xsl:apply-templates> directive to place a call to a specific template. The XSLT processor looks for a template called *grammar* and transfers processing to that template. The grammar template outputs literal <grammar> elements and inserts the text from the grammar in the XML file using dot syntax. A dot as a value to a *select* attribute specifies that the processor should output the text that is located within the current node. In this case, it outputs the start over phrase as grammar for the <link>.

Output

Listing 8.21 shows the output after running the updated XSLT stylesheet against the quiz-startrek.xml data file. Lines 3 through 5 contain the <link> element as literal output, carrying a next attribute with the value of the current filename.

Line 4 contains the grammar that will activate the link and force a reloading of the VoiceXML document. The rest of the output is text from the XML document that will be formatted as we keep adding more templates to the stylesheet.

```
1.  <?xml version="1.0" encoding="UTF-8"?>
2.  <vxml version="2.0">
3.  <link next="quiz-startrek.vxml">
4.  <grammar>(start over)</grammar>
5.  </link>
6.     startrek-help.wav2000
7.           Listen to a quotation from a Star Trek character.
8.           Say the name of the character.
9.           Your three choices are Spock, Kirk or McCoy.
10.        startrek-theme.wavstreamstartrek-welcome.wav2000
11.          Welcome to the Star Trek Quotation Game.
12.        startrek-noinput1.wav1000
13.           I didn't hear anything. Please try again.
14.        startrek-noinput2.wav1000
15.           You must say Spock, Kirk or McCoy to participate.
16.        startrek-noinput3.wav1000
17.           This is your last chance, Buddy.
18.           You better say something.
19.        startrek-noinput3.wav1000
20.           Oh, well, it's your loss.
21.        startrek-instructions.wav1000
22.          You will hear a quotation from a Star Trek
23.          character. You must answer with Spock, Kirk
24.          or McCoy.
25.        startrek-confirmbeginning.wav1000
26.          Here is the first quotation.
27.
28.          I'm a doctor, not a bricklayer.
29.        mccoydocbonesdoctor mccoy
30.          He, supposedly, did not get along with Spock.
31.
32.          Captain, I suggest the Vulcan mind probe.
33.        spockthe vulcan
34.          James T. Kirk's best friend.
35.          He was extremely logical.
36.
37.          Scottie, beam me up.
38.        kirkcaptain kirkjames kirkjames t kirkjim
39.          The big guy. The one and only.
40.        startrek-thankyou.wav1000
41.          Thank you for playing the Star Trek Quotation Game.
42.        startrek-spock-livelong.wav1000
43.          Live Long and Prosper.
44.        </vxml>
```

Listing 8.21 Output from updated XSLT stylesheet.

Create a template within the quizFormatter.xsl stylesheet to process a
<quiz> element. The <quiz> template should output a <link> element that
HANDS ON carries a next attribute that points to the current file and a grammar for
activating the link.

Run the quizFormatter batch file. Examine the quiz-startrek.vxml file in your
text editor. You will see that a root-level element has been created along
with a global link for restarting the application.

Help Template

Continue examining the XML data of Listing 8.15 for tags that are children of the
<quiz> element. The next element found is <help>. Listing 8.22 contains templates for
processing the <help> and <audio> elements.

The help template outputs the literal <help> element and then calls <xsl:apply-
templates/> to process any children located within. Looking at the XML data, we see
that an <audio> template is needed. Line 8 of Listing 8.22 begins the processing of the
audio template. A literal <audio> element carrying *src* and *fetchtimeout* attributes is
output to the VoiceXML file through the use of *attribute value templates*.

The text content within the <audio> element is accessed through the XSLT
<xsl:value-of> element. <xsl:value-of> is used to access data within an element and
print it. Line 11 contains a directive to output the content that is stored within the
<textPrompt> of the XML file.

Once the audio template is completed, processing control returns to line 4 of the
help template. Because no other templates are available for processing, control moves
to the next line, outputting a literal <reprompt/> element.

```
1. <xsl:template match="help">
2.    <help>
3.       <xsl:apply-templates/>
4.       <reprompt/>
5.    </help>
6. </xsl:template>
7.
8. <xsl:template match="audio">
9. <audio src="{soundSource}"
10.        fetchtimeout="{timeout}">
11.    <xsl:value-of select="textPrompt"/>
12. </audio>
13. </xsl:template>
```

Listing 8.22   Inserting the help template.

Insert the help and audio templates into your stylesheet. Rebuild the VoiceXML application through the quizFormatter.bat file and view the output.

Power of Template Processing

At this point, the power of template processing becomes apparent. Listing 8.23 is the output from processing with the updated stylesheet. Every <audio> element within the XML file is processed through the same audio template. Creating one template for each type of element used in the XML file is an extremely efficient way to loop through multiple occurrences of the same element.

Look closely at the output on line 13 of Listing 8.23 and you will see what appears to be an error. The *fetchtimeout* attribute contains no value. Examination of the XML data shows that a *fetchhint* attribute should be placed here, not a *fetchtimeout*. This will be handled in the next section.

```
1.  <?xml version="1.0" encoding="UTF-8"?>
2.  <vxml version="2.0">
3.  <link next="quiz-startrek.vxml">
4.  <grammar>(start over)</grammar>
5.  </link>
6.  <help>
7.  <audio fetchtimeout="2000" src="startrek-help.wav">
8.          Listen to a quotation from a Star Trek character.
9.          Say the name of the character.
10.          Your three choices are Spock, Kirk or McCoy.
11.        </audio>
12. </help>
13. <audio fetchtimeout="" src="startrek-theme.wav"/>
14. <audio fetchtimeout="2000" src="startrek-welcome.wav">
15.          Welcome to the Star Trek Quotation Game.
16.        </audio>
17. <audio fetchtimeout="1000" src="startrek-noinput1.wav">
18.          I didn't hear anything. Please try again.
19.        </audio>
20. <audio fetchtimeout="1000" src="startrek-noinput2.wav">
21.          You must say Spock, Kirk or McCoy to participate.
22.        </audio>
23. <audio fetchtimeout="1000" src="startrek-noinput3.wav">
24.          This is your last chance, Buddy.
25.          You better say something.
26.        </audio>
27. <audio fetchtimeout="1000" src="startrek-noinput3.wav">
28.          Oh, well, it's your loss.
29.        </audio>
```

Listing 8.23 Template processing. *(continues)*

```
30.  <audio fetchtimeout="1000" src="startrek-instructions.wav">
31.          You will hear a quotation from a Star Trek
32.          character. You must answer with Spock, Kirk
33.          or McCoy.
34.      </audio>
35.  <audio fetchtimeout="1000" src="startrek-confirmbeginning.wav">
36.          Here is the first quotation.
37.      </audio>
38.          I'm a doctor, not a bricklayer.
39.      mccoydocbonesdoctor mccoy
40.          He, supposedly, did not get along with Spock.
41.
42.          Captain, I suggest the Vulcan mind probe.
43.      spockthe vulcan
44.          James T. Kirk's best friend.
45.          He was extremely logical.
46.
47.          Scottie, beam me up.
48.      kirkcaptain kirkjames kirkjames t kirkjim
49.          The big guy. The one and only.
50.          <audio fetchtimeout="1000" src="startrek-thankyou.wav">
51.          Thank you for playing the Star Trek Quotation Game.
52.      </audio>
53.  <audio fetchtimeout="1000" src="startrek-spock-livelong.wav">
54.          Live Long and Prosper.
55.      </audio>
56.  </vxml>
```

Listing 8.23   Template processing. *(continued)*

Greeting Template

Moving through the XML file of Listing 8.15, the next element for processing is *greeting*, starting on line 26. This is the element that caused the output problem in Listing 8.22. There are two audio fields within the data and one contains a fetchhint instead of a fetchtimeout. We will update the audio template to handle these changes.

Listing 8.24 has a greeting template starting on line 18. Templates in an XSLT stylesheet do not have to be in any particular order. The template formats the output as a literal <form> element that contains a <block> element. The call to <xsl:apply-templates> activates the audio template.

```
1. <xsl:template match="audio">
2. <xsl:choose>
3.    <xsl:when test="fetchhint">
4.    <audio src="{soundSource}"
5.          fetchhint="{fetchhint}">
6.      <xsl:value-of select="textPrompt"/>
7.    </audio>
8.    </xsl:when>
9.    <xsl:otherwise>
10.    <audio src="{soundSource}"
11.          fetchtimeout="{timeout}">
12.      <xsl:value-of select="textPrompt"/>
13.    </audio>
14.    </xsl:otherwise>
15. </xsl:choose>
16. </xsl:template>
17.
18. <xsl:template match="greeting">
19. <form id="greeting">
20.    <block>
21.        <xsl:apply-templates/>
22.        <goto next="#questions"/>
23.    </block>
24. </form>
25. </xsl:template>
```

Listing 8.24 The greeting template and updated audio template.

The updated template for the <audio> element uses an <xsl:choose> statement to handle conditional processing. With <xsl:choose>, multiple conditions are tested using the *test* attribute of <xsl:when>. Line 3 tests to see if a <fetchhint> element is accessible from the current context within the XML file. If <fetchhint> is available in the current node being processed, an <audio> element with *src* and *fetchhint* attributes is output, with values inserted through attribute value templates. The <xsl:otherwise> element on line 9 processes any other <audio> element, replacing the *fetchhint* attribute with a *fetchtimeout* attribute.

When the audio template is completed, processing returns to line 21 of Listing 8.24. There are no more templates to process within the <greeting> element of the XML file, so processing falls to the next line of the stylesheet, outputting the literal <goto> element.

Insert a greeting template into the stylesheet and update the audio template. Rebuild the application and verify the correct output for each <audio> element.

ErrorNoInput Template

The <errorNoInput> element is next in line in the XML file. It is only used as a container for a list of error messages, so the template will be very simple. By enclosing the error messages in a container tag, the XML content provider is not limited to a specific number of messages.

Listing 8.25 shows the template for the <errorNoInput> element. The <xsl:comment> element on line 2 builds a comment format in the output. The comment is created from the content of the <xsl:comment> element, outputting GLOBAL ERROR MESSAGES. The <apply-templates> call on line 3 gives access to all of the children of the <errorNoInput> element. The next section creates a template to format that output.

```
1. <xsl:template match="errorNoInput">
2. <xsl:comment>GLOBAL ERROR MESSAGES</xsl:comment>
3.    <xsl:apply-templates />
4. </xsl:template>
```

Listing 8.25   errorNoInput template.

Create a template to handle the <errorNoInput> element and insert it into your quizFormatter.xsl stylesheet. Run the application and confirm that the GLOBAL ERROR MESSAGES comment is outputting properly.

Noinput Template

Within the <errorNoInput> element, there is a series of <noinput> tags that hold audio file URIs and text prompts for error messages. The <noinput> elements in the XML data file have a consistent structure that can be used to build a template.

Listing 8.26 shows the template for outputting the <noinput> messages to the quiz-startrek.vxml file. Line 2 outputs a literal <noinput> element whose *count* attribute is set by an XSLT function. The position() function is used to dynamically generate a sequential set of numbers, starting at 1. Each time the template is visited within the context of the <errorNoInput> element, the position() count is incremented. The return is output as the value of the *count* attribute.

Line 3 places a call to all child templates of the current node. There is only one in this case, the audio template. The <xsl:if> statement starting on line 4 carries a condition to see if this is the last <noinput> element in the sequence. The XSLT last() function is compared to the current position(). If the result of the test is true, processing moves to line 5, sending the user to the *goodbye* <form>, which will be created in a later section.

```
1. <xsl:template match="noinput">
2.   <noinput count="{position()}">
3.   <xsl:apply-templates/>
4.   <xsl:if test="position()=last()">
5.      <goto next="#goodbye"/>
6.   </xsl:if>
7.   </noinput>
8. </xsl:template>
```

Listing 8.26   noinput template.

Add the noinput template to the XSLT stylesheet. Run the application and verify that the noinput messages have output properly.

Instructions and confirmBeginning Template

The <instructions> element has the exact same structure as the <confirmBeginning> element in the XML data file. The template in Listing 8.27 handles the two elements at once through the use of the union operator within the *match* attribute. This operator allows multiple elements use of the same formatting template.

The template contains a simple call to the audio template within a literal <block> element. Once again, we see the power of XSLT templates. The <xsl:appy-templates/> continues to access the audio template whenever it is needed.

```
1. <xsl:template match="instructions|confirmBeginning">
2. <block>
3.    <xsl:apply-templates/>
4. </block>
5. </xsl:template>
```

Listing 8.27   Instructions and confirmBeginning template.

SeriesOfQuestions Template

The next job of the stylesheet is to output the series of questions. Each question is considered a set that holds tags for the question, answer (grammar), and correct and incorrect confirmation responses. Each will have its own template.

The XML file contains a <seriesOfQuestions> element starting on line 1 of Listing 8.28. A formatting template outputs a literal <form> element and places a call to available templates through the <xsl:apply-templates/> call. The <xsl:apply-templates> element inserts all the questions from the XML data file.

To complete the template, a graceful exit is created by calling the goodbye template within a set of literal <block> elements.

```
1. <xsl:template match="seriesOfQuestions">
2. <form id="questions">
3.    <xsl:apply-templates />
4.    <block>
5.       <goto next="#goodbye"/>
6.    </block>
7. </form>
8. </xsl:template>
```

Listing 8.28   seriesOfQuestions template.

Set Template

Each question in the XML file is contained within its own field, with a unique name allocated to each field. Listing 8.29 generates a unique name through the XSLT generate-id() function. This function guarantees the construction of a unique name for the field, no matter how many questions are built into the quiz.

<xsl:apply-templates> on line 3 gives access to the question, answers, and hint templates that are to follow.

```
1. <xsl:template match="set">
2. <field name="{generate-id()}">
3.    <xsl:apply-templates />
4. </field>
5. </xsl:template>
```

Listing 8.29   Set template.

Question Template

The <question> element in the XML file has a *recording* attribute that can be used as an *src* URL for audio output. It also contains text for content that can be used for the text prompt in the VoiceXML file.

Line 2 of Listing 8.30 outputs a literal <audio> element that contains two attributes: *src* and *fetchhint*. The *src* attribute is filled with an *attribute value template* that accesses the *recording* attribute of the <question> element within the XML file. *fetchhint* is hard-coded into the VoiceXML application, telling the processor to retrieve the sound source as soon as possible, without waiting for it to be called.

```
1. <xsl:template match="question">
2.    <audio src="{@recording}" fetchhint="prefetch">
3.       <xsl:apply-templates />
4.    </audio>
5. </xsl:template>
```

Listing 8.30 Question template.

The <xsl:apply-templates/> on line 3 outputs the literal text that is stored within the <question> element of the XML file, which is the default output if no templates are available for processing.

Answers Template

The <answers> element holds a set of child <answer> tags that will be used to build the grammar for the correct answer to the question. Listing 8.31 uses square brackets to enclose the grammar that will be inserted by the XSLT <xsl:apply-templates/> directive.

```
1. <xsl:template match="answers">
2.    <grammar>
3.       [<xsl:apply-templates />]
4.    </grammar>
5. </xsl:template>
```

Listing 8.31 Answers template.

Answer Template

Each of the values stored in an <answer> element in the XML file needs to be output within a set of parentheses, forcing pairs of values to act as a single utterance. Listing 8.32 surrounds the <xsl:apply-templates> with the literal parentheses. The XSLT <xsl:text> element forces a single space between the sets of parentheses.

```
1. <xsl:template match="answer">
2.    (<xsl:apply-templates />)<xsl:text> </xsl:text>
3. </xsl:template>
```

Listing 8.32 Answer template.

Checking an Answer

Listing 8.33 handles the output of the <nomatch> and <filled> elements in the VoiceXML file.

```
1.  <xsl:template match="hint">
2.    <nomatch count="1">
3.      Incorrect. Here is a hint.
4.      <xsl:apply-templates />
5.    </nomatch>
6.    <nomatch count="2">
7.      Try again.
8.    </nomatch>
9.    <nomatch count="3">
10.     <prompt>
11.     Incorrect. The correct answer is
12.     <xsl:value-of select="../answers/answer" />
13.     </prompt>
14.     <assign name="{generate-id(../)}"
15.            expr="'incorrect'" />
16.   </nomatch>
17.   <xsl:call-template name="correct"/>
18.   <xsl:if test="../answer[last()]">
19.     <block>
20.        <goto next="#goodbye"/>
21.     </block>
22.   </xsl:if>
23.   </xsl:template>
24.
25.   <xsl:template name="correct">
26.     <filled>
27.        Correct!
28.     </filled>
29.   </xsl:template>
```

Listing 8.33   Checking answers.

Looking at the XML data of Listing 8.15 shows that the <incorrect> tag contains a hint to the user about the correct answer. The hint is output in the first match through the <xsl:apply-templates /> element. The second <nomatch> contains "Try again," and the third <nomatch> confirms that the answer was incorrect and gives the user the correct answer. The correct answer is generated by pulling the first answer from the list of answers for this field, as shown on line 12.

Lines 14 and 15 of Listing 8.33 assign the value of *incorrect* to the *name* attribute by using the generate-id() function, just as in Listing 8.29. On line 14, the parent of the current node is accessed, generating the same id as the <field> where is resides.

An <xsl:call-template> directive on line 17 places a call to a named template within the stylesheet. Name templates are useful for creating templates that are not associated with any element name in the XML file. In this case, we need a template that creates the <filled> element within the VoiceXML dialog.

The *correct* template beginning on line 20 is all literal text. It is a simple confirmation to users that they have entered the correct answer. When the template is finished, processing reverts to line 18 where an <if> condition checks to see if this is the last question in the series. If it is, a <block> element passes control to the *goodbye* <form>.

Goodbye Template

The goodbye template creates the exit <form> for the VoiceXML script. Line 2 of Listing 8.34 begins a <form> that holds a field to receive audio content from the <xsl:apply-templates> directive. Lines 5 through 7 give knowledgeable users access to the *start over* link through a hidden prompt. If the link is not activated, the application is terminated.

```
1. <xsl:template match="goodbye">
2. <form id="goodbye">
3.    <field>
4.       <xsl:apply-templates/>
5.       <catch event="noinput nomatch">
6.          <exit/>
7.       </catch>
8.    </field>
9. </form>
10. </xsl:template>
```

Listing 8.34   Goodbye template.

Test the Completed XSLT Stylesheet

The foregoing handles all the templates needed to process the XML data file. Listing 8.35 shows the completed stylesheet. Now any time you want to create a new quiz or survey, build an XML data file and process it with the quizFormatter.xsl stylesheet.

To create a template for building other XML data files, start with Listing 8.15 and strip out all text prompts and references to sound files. This basic, empty skeleton can be used multiple times to build diverse quizzes, surveys, and games. To test it out, put some data into the XML skeleton, and run it against the stylesheet. Make sure to change the name of the output file in quizFormatter.bat.

```
1.  <?xml version="1.0"?>
2.
3.  <xsl:stylesheet
4.     xmlns:xsl="http://www.w3.org/1999/XSL/Transform"
5.     version="1.0">
6.
7.  <xsl:output method="xml" indent="yes" />
8.  <xsl:strip-space elements="*" />
9.
10. <xsl:template match="/">
11. <vxml version="2.0">
12.  <xsl:apply-templates />
13. </vxml>
14. </xsl:template>
15.
16. <xsl:template match="quiz">
17.     <xsl:apply-templates/>
18. </xsl:template>
19.
20. <xsl:template match="link">
21.     <link next="{next}">
22.         <xsl:apply-templates select="grammar"/>
23.     </link>
24. </xsl:template>
25.
26. <xsl:template match="grammar">
27.     <grammar>(<xsl:value-of select="."/>)</grammar>
28. </xsl:template>
29.
30. <xsl:template match="help">
31.     <help>
32.         <xsl:apply-templates/>
33.     </help>
34.     <reprompt/>
35. </xsl:template>
36.
37. <xsl:template match="audio">
38. <xsl:choose>
39.     <xsl:when test="fetchhint">
40.     <audio src="{soundSource}"
41.            fetchhint="{fetchhint}">
42.         <xsl:value-of select="textPrompt"/>
43.     </audio>
44.     </xsl:when>
45.     <xsl:otherwise>
46.     <audio src="{soundSource}"
47.            fetchtimeout="{timeout}">
48.         <xsl:value-of select="textPrompt"/>
49.     </audio>
```

Listing 8.35 Completed quizFormatter.xsl stylesheet.

```
50.    </xsl:otherwise>
51. </xsl:choose>
52. </xsl:template>
53.
54. <xsl:template match="greeting">
55. <form id="greeting">
56.    <block>
57.        <xsl:apply-templates/>
58.        <goto next="#questions"/>
59.    </block>
60. </form>
61. </xsl:template>
62.
63. <xsl:template match="errorNoInput">
64. <xsl:comment>GLOBAL ERROR MESSAGES</xsl:comment>
65.    <xsl:apply-templates />
66. </xsl:template>
67.
68. <xsl:template match="noinput">
69.    <noinput count="{position()}">
70.    <xsl:apply-templates/>
71.    <xsl:if test="position()=last()">
72.        <goto next="#goodbye"/>
73.    </xsl:if>
74.    </noinput>
75. </xsl:template>
76.
77. <xsl:template match="instructions|confirmBeginning">
78. <block>
79.    <xsl:apply-templates/>
80. </block>
81. </xsl:template>
82.
83. <xsl:template match="seriesOfQuestions">
84. <form id="questions">
85.    <xsl:apply-templates />
86.    <block>
87.        <goto next="#goodbye"/>
88.    </block>
89. </form>
90. </xsl:template>
91.
92. <xsl:template match="set">
93.  <field name="{generate-id()}">
94.      <xsl:apply-templates />
95.  </field>
96. </xsl:template>
97.
98. <xsl:template match="question">
```

Listing 8.35   Completed quizFormatter.xsl stylesheet. *(continues)*

```
 99.    <audio src="{@recording}" fetchhint="prefetch">
100.       <xsl:apply-templates />
101.     </audio>
102. </xsl:template>
103.
104. <xsl:template match="answers">
105.  <grammar>
106.     [<xsl:apply-templates />]
107.  </grammar>
108. </xsl:template>
109.
110. <xsl:template match="answer">
111.    (<xsl:apply-templates />)<xsl:text> </xsl:text>
112. </xsl:template>
113.
114. <xsl:template match="hint">
115.    <nomatch count="1">
116.      Incorrect. Here is a hint.
117.      <xsl:apply-templates />
118.    </nomatch>
119.    <nomatch count="2">
120.      Try again.
121.    </nomatch>
122.    <nomatch count="3">
123.      <prompt>
124.      Incorrect. The correct answer is
125.      <xsl:value-of select="../answers/answer" />
126.      </prompt>
127.      <assign name="{generate-id(../)}"
128.             expr="'incorrect'" />
129. </nomatch>
130. <xsl:call-template name="correct"/>
131. <xsl:if test="../answer[last()]">
132.     <block>
133.        <goto next="#goodbye"/>
134.     </block>
135. </xsl:if>
136. </xsl:template>
137.
138. <xsl:template name="correct">
139.     <filled>
140.        Correct!
141.     </filled>
142. </xsl:template>
143.
144. <xsl:template match="goodbye">
145. <form id="goodbye">
146.     <field>
147.        <xsl:apply-templates/>
```

Listing 8.35 Completed quizFormatter.xsl stylesheet.

```
148.        <catch event="noinput nomatch">
149.          <exit/>
150.        </catch>
151.    </field>
152. </form>
153. </xsl:template>
154.
155. </xsl:stylesheet>
```

Listing 8.35 Completed quizFormatter.xsl stylesheet. *(continued)*

Complete the quizFormatter.xsl stylesheet and run it against the quiz-startrek.xml data.

XSLT is a processing language that is much more complex than VoiceXML. This script and its explanation can be used as a starting point for XSLT programming. To use XSLT to build future projects of your own, I suggest getting a good reference book, such as Michael Kay's *XSLT Programmer's Reference*, Edition 2, (Wrox Press Ltd, 2001).

Final Thoughts

The template developed in this project can be used for any type of quiz that doesn't need to have the responses stored for future evaluation. A natural extension of the Quiz Generator is to have the questions fed dynamically from a database and the responses stored, accessible through a report page by the site administrator.

The listings for this project can be downloaded from the BeVocal Web site at cafe.bevocal.com/wiley/10projects. They are saved as text files, useful as templates for creating your own VoiceXML scripts. Join us in the online discussion board for this project and tell us how you will be using the project. If you create a form that would make this project work better, it might be incorporated into the project code online so that others can use it.

San Francisco Arts Calendar

There are thousands of events, give or take a couple hundred, at any one time in the San Francisco Bay area. Keeping up with what is going on is an overwhelming task if there is not a central repository that is easily accessible. The San Francisco Arts Organization, www.SFArts.org, has a site that coordinates listings of all of the events into disciplines, such as dance, music, and theater.

This project will use the database from the SFArts project and create a voice interface for accessing the calendar of events. A special thanks is offered to Larry Larson, site manager, for providing access to the San Francisco Arts Calendar data and for creating and debugging the Cold Fusion template.

THE PROBLEM

The general public wants access to a calendar of events for all types of performances in the San Francisco Bay area.

THE SOLUTION

Create a voice interface to the database of existing events that is stored on the San Francisco Arts Organization site.

Project Description

The calendar project begins by creating a template to hold global variables, global links, and calls to subdialogs, which are stored in external documents. Users call the arts calendar service, specifying a date and a type of event that they would like information about. The program retrieves a list of events from the database and outputs it to the user. The user may then make a request to retrieve more event listings or exit the program.

To complete this project, you will:

1. Build a skeleton script.

2. Create three subdialog components:

   ■ calendargreeting.vxml

   ■ calendarmenu.vxml

   ■ calendargoodbye.vxml

3. Set up a template for Cold Fusion processing.

 You Will Need

✔ **BeVocal developer account**

✔ **calendar.vxml**

✔ **external vxml subdialogs**

✔ **Download project files: cafe.bevocal.com/wiley/10projects**

VoiceXML Elements Used in This Project

ELEMENT NAME	DESCRIPTION
<assign>	Assigns a variable a value
<block>	A container of (noninteractive) executable code
<clear>	Clears one or more form item variables
<else>	Used in <if> elements
<exit>	Exits a session
<field>	Declares an input field in a form
<filled>	An action executed when fields are filled

VoiceXML Elements Used in This Project   *(continued)*

ELEMENT NAME	DESCRIPTION
<form>	A dialog for presenting information and collecting data
<goto>	Go to another dialog in the same or different document
<grammar>	Specifies a speech recognition or DTMF grammar
<if>	Simple conditional logic
<link>	Specifies a transition common to all dialogs in the link's scope
<meta>	Defines a meta data item as a name/value pair
<noinput>	Catches a noinput event
<nomatch>	Catches a nomatch event
<object>	Interacts with a custom extension
<prompt>	Queues speech synthesis and audio output to the user
<reprompt>	Plays a field prompt when a field is revisited after an event
<return>	Returns from a subdialog
<subdialog>	Invokes another dialog as a subdialog of the current one
<value>	Inserts the value of an expression in a prompt
<var>	Declares a variable
<vxml>	Top-level element in each VoiceXML document

Source: *VoiceXML 2.0 Working Draft*, section 1.4

Application Call Flow

Figure 9.1 shows the call flow for this application. The call is answered with a greeting, transferring the user to the main menu. The user selects a discipline of dance, music, or theater and is prompted for a date. Events of the type selected are read back to the user. Once the output of that date is completed, the user may select another event and date or end the call. The application terminates with a polite goodbye message.

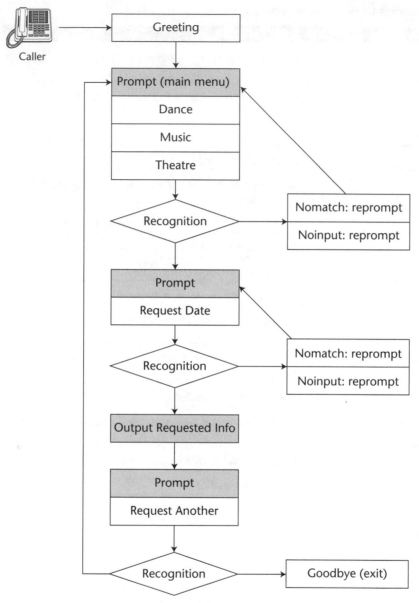

Figure 9.1   Application flow diagram.

Build a Skeleton

The skeleton for this project, shown in Listing 9.1, is similar to the other projects we have created. The script begins with the typical <xml> declaration, the DOCTYPE definition, and the opening of the <vxml> root element. The <meta> information on lines 11 through 19 describes the application to other calling applications such as indexing robots.

```
1. <?xml version="1.0"?>
2.
3. <!DOCTYPE vxml
4. PUBLIC
5. "-//BeVocal Inc//VoiceXML 2.0//EN"
6. "http://cafe.bevocal.com/libraries/dtd/vxml2-0-bevocal.dtd">
7.
8. <vxml version="2.0">
9.
10. <!-- INFORMATION ABOUT THIS APPLICATION -->
11. <meta name="author"       content="Your Name"/>
12. <meta name="copyright"    content="Your Company Name"/>
13. <meta name="description"
14.        content="Template for creating a calendar,
15.                 accessible through a VoiceXML
16.                 interface"/>
17. <meta name="keywords" content="VoiceXML,arts calendar"/>
18. <meta name="maintainer"   content="you@yourAddress.com"/>
19. <meta name="robots"       content="robot-rules.txt"/>
20.
21. <!-- GLOBAL VARIABLES AND LINKS -->
22. <var name="companyName"
23.        expr="'San Francisco Arts Calendar'"/>
24. <var name="sponsor"
25.        expr="'The San Francisco Opera Company'"/>
26.
27. <link next="calendar.vxml">
28.    <grammar>
29.      <![CDATA[[(start over)]]]>
30.    </grammar>
31. </link>
32.
33. <!-- PUBLIC ACCESS -->
34. <form id="baseApplication">
35. <subdialog name="sfarts-getGreeting"
36.            src="sfarts-calendargreeting.vxml"/>
37. <subdialog name="getMenu"
38.            src="sfarts-calendarmenu.vxml"/>
39. <subdialog name="getGoodbye"
40.            src="sfarts-calendargoodbye.vxml"/>
41. </form>
42. </vxml>
```

Listing 9.1   Skeleton for calendar project.

Two variables are set on lines 22 through 25. *companyName* is used throughout the application; therefore, setting this variable at the top of the script makes it easy to make changes globally if the company name changes. The *sponsor* variable is accessed within the greeting and goodbye templates as a short advertisement.

Lines 27 through 31 create a *start over* link for use by the developer when testing the application, as has been done in previous projects.

The base of the application is held within lines 34 through 41. Calls to three subdialogs are used to modularize the program. We will look at each of the subdialogs in the next sections and then test the application when they are completed.

Create the skeleton script for the calendar project using Listing 9.1 as a template. Insert a company name and a sponsor of your choice when declaring the global variables. Save the listing as sfarts-calendar.vxml in your BeVocal developer's account.

Create a Greeting Subdialog

The calendar greeting.vxml subdialog in Listing 9.2 is a simple form that outputs the name of the company and the name of the sponsor of the call. Lines 7 and 8 access the global variables *companyName* and *sponsor* that were created in the skeleton application for outputting the company name and sponsor name.

Line 9 uses the <return/> element to transfer processing back to the base application.

```
1. <?xml version="1.0"?>
2.
3. <vxml version="2.0" application="sfarts-calendar.vxml">
4.
5. <form id="greeting">
6.   <block>
7.     You have reached the <value expr="companyName"/>,
8.     brought to you by <value expr="sponsor"/>.
9.     <return/>
10.   </block>
11. </form>
12. </vxml>
```

Listing 9.2   calendarGreeting subdialog.

Save Listing 9.2 as calendarGreeting.vxml in your developer's account. Test the application in the Vocal Scripter to verify that the variables are being read properly from the base application.

Create a Goodbye Subdialog

The next template for this project is the goodbye script for exiting the application, shown in Listing 9.3. The <block> element starting on line 6 contains a thank you message and a plug for the sponsor on line 8, inserting the sponsor's name through the *companyName* variable. The <break> element on line 9, set to a value of *small*, makes the output more natural sounding.

```
1. <?xml version="1.0"?>
2.
3. <vxml version="2.0" application="sfarts-calendar.vxml">
4.
5. <form id="goodbye">
6.    <block>
7.        Thank you for using the <value expr="companyName"/>.
8.        This call was brought to you by <value expr="sponsor"/>
9.        <break size="small"/>
10.        Please call again. Good bye.
11.        <return/>
12.    </block>
13. </form>
14. </vxml>
```

Listing 9.3   calendarGoodbye subdialog.

Line 10 contains goodbye broken up into two words. When testing your application, try it as one word and then two words. You will find the flow of the sentence is much more lifelike with the two words because of the short pause between the syllables.

Processing is transferred back to the calling application with the <return> element on line 11.

HANDS ON **Save Listing 9.3 as calendarGoodbye.vxml. Test the script through the Vocal Scripter to confirm that the variables are being accessed through the base application.**

Create the CalendarMenu Subdialog

The menu for requesting information from the SFArts Calendar application is contained within the sfarts-calendarmenu.vxml script. The user requests an event type, or a discipline, and the request is checked against the grammar that defines the event types. If that event type is available, a date is requested from the user. The date is formatted into a set of variables that are passed with the event type to the Cold Fusion server for processing. Once the response from the server is received, the user is offered the chance to request other calendar events.

Request a Discipline

Listing 9.4 is the beginning of the sfarts-calendarmenu.vxml script, which defines the grammar that will be recognized and set as a specific event type for processing by the database server. Line 6 starts the mainmenu <form> that contains a <field> named *Discipline*. The spelling and capitalization of the name of this field is important because it will be used as a variable name to be passed as an argument to the database server once all of the information has been collected from the caller.

```
1.  <?xml version="1.0"?>
2.
3.  <vxml version="2.0" application="sfarts-calendar.vxml">
4.
5.  <!-- REQUEST AN EVENT TYPE -->
6.  <form id="mainmenu">
7.  <field name="Discipline">
8.  <prompt>
9.   What type of event are you interested in:
10. dance, music, or theater.
11. </prompt>
12.
13. <grammar>
14. <![CDATA[
15. [
16. [dance dancing ballet]         { < Discipline dance> }
17. [music opera symphony ]        { < Discipline music> }
18. [theater plays (off broadway)]{ < Discipline theater> }
19. ]
20. ]]>
21. </grammar>
22.
23. <nomatch count="1">
24.    I missed that. Try again: dance, music, or theater
25. </nomatch>
26.
27. <nomatch count="2">
28.  <prompt  bargein="true">
29.    I don't recognize that type of event.
30.    Please say dance<break size="small"/>,
31.    music<break size="small"/> or theater.
32.  </prompt>
33. </nomatch>
34.
35. <nomatch count="3">
36.    I'm sorry. I can't help you with that type of event.
37.    Maybe we will add that to the listings in the future.
38.    <goto next="calendargoodbye.vxml"/>
```

Listing 9.4   Request a discipline.

```
39. </nomatch>
40. <filled><return/></filled>
41. </field>
42.
43. </form>
44. </vxml>
```

Listing 9.4   Request a discipline. *(continued)*

A <prompt> starting on line 8 defines to the user what is expected as input: dance, music, or theater. Lines 13 through 21 define the grammar that is acceptable as a name for a discipline. By extending the vocabulary to accept synonyms for the types of events, the application becomes more user friendly for callers who try to request a specific type of event.

The nomatch event handling starts on line 23. The first time a nomatch event is caught, the program assumes that there was a problem in recognition and takes responsibility for the problem, repeating the list of choices. The second nomatch event, starting on line 27, contains a <prompt> that once again repeats the instructions, but it isolates each word from the grammar by inserting <break> elements. This should give the caller a clearer indication of what is expected.

The <prompt> element on line 28 also carries an attribute of *bargein*, which is set to *true*. This allows callers to interrupt the <prompt>, without having to wait for the termination of the <prompt>, if they recognize an item from the menu.

The final <nomatch> event starting on line 35 outputs an apology, explaining that the event the user is asking for is not available in the calendar; it then sends processing to the sfcalendar-goodbye.vxml script.

Save Listing 9.4 as sfarts-calendarmenu.vxml. Test the script, trying incorrect input to confirm that the <nomatch> events are being processed properly.

HANDS ON

Request a Date

Once the *Discipline* <field> has been set with an event type, the user must specify a date for that event. The BeVocal platform exposes a date Speech Object. The date object takes a spoken date as input and parses it into month, day, and year components that can be used to fill variables. Listing 9.5 shows the use of a date *object* to request a date.

```
1. <object classid="speechobject://nuance.so.SODate"
2.          name="eventDate">
3. <filled>
4.      <return/>
5. </filled>
6. </object>
```

Listing 9.5   Using an object to request a date.

A Speech Object is a predefined module that is part of the processing platform. The BeVocal environment contains objects for processing many types of data. Table 9.1 lists some of the most useful objects in the BeVocal platform and what they collect from the user. When an object is called, the execution of the dialog is controlled by the object. The object handles all prompting, error messages, and return values from the user and stores them in the *eventDate* variable. The return from an object is a result that can be used by an ECMAScript variable to access the return values.

Objects are at the field level within a form. In Listing 9.5, a call is placed to the date <object> through a *classid* attribute, pointing to the location of the object's implementation.

The <object> element prompts the user for a date. The input is stored in the *eventDate* object, making it possible to access specific components through dot notation.

Most platforms supply objects that can handle credit card numbers, dates, social security numbers, and address input. Check your platform's documentation for a list of available speech objects.

TIP

Add a date <object> to the VoiceXML script, inserting it as a field-level item below the *Discipline* field.

HANDS ON

Table 9.1   Speech Objects

OBJECT	COLLECTS
bevocal.cafe.SOAirline	Airline name
bevocal.cafe.SOPickStock	Company or index name
bevocal.cafe.SOCityState	City and state name
bevocal.cafe.SOStreet	Street name
bevocal.cafe.SOStreetNumber	Street number
nuance.so.SOCreditCardInfo	Credit card number
nuance.so.SODate	Date
nuance.so.SONATelephoneNumber	Phone number, U.S. format
nuance.so.SOQuantity	Number as quantity
nuance.so.SOSocialSecurityNumber	Social security number
nuance.so.SOUSCurrency	Currency amount in dollars and cents
nuance.so.SOUSZipCode	Zip code, U.S. format

Using Return Values from an Object

The Speech Object returns control to the calling location after it has completed processing of the input. The return values from the object need to be assigned to variables in order to be used by the VoiceXML application.

Listing 9.6 uses the <assign> element to access and assign the date object's return values. The names of the variables (month, day, year) are what will be passed from the <subdialog> call to the Cold Fusion script. Each variable takes an expression as its value.

The month variable uses the ECMAScript Math.round function as part of its expression to force an integer as output. The <object> element that processes the date uses an indexing base starting at 0 when setting the month, whereas the Cold Fusion platform starts its indexing at 1. One is added to the eventDate.Month to correctly map the month input from the Speech Object to the Cold Fusion database query.

WARNING **Using the eventDate.Month + 1 expression without the Math.round function will cause incorrect input to the Cold Fusion script. ECMAScript uses floating-point notation when doing math processing. eventDate.Month + 1 will return 12.0 without the Math function to force an integer through rounding.**

```
1.  <block>
2.      <assign name="month"
3.              expr="Math.round(eventDate.Month + 1)"/>
4.      <assign name="day"
5.              expr="eventDate.DayOfMonth"/>
6.      <assign name="year"
7.              expr="eventDate.Year"/>
8.  </block>
```

Listing 9.6 Assigning variables from object return values.

HANDS ON **Insert a block into the current application that will assign variables from the return values of a request for a date. The block should be at field level, following the <object> item. The variable names must be *month*, *day*, and *year* in order to be processed by the Cold Fusion script.**

Implied Error Checking

Before user input is sent to the database to request a list of calendar items, it is good practice to confirm with the user the *Discipline* and *date* the program recognized. Verification of user input does not have to be an explicit repeat of information and a request for confirmation.

Use the <value> element to repeat the input to the user within the context of the processing, wait a minimal time for a response, and then move to the next stage of processing if there is no input from the user. This technique makes for a more intuitive interface without putting a burden on the user to verify all input each step of the way. The subtlety is that the user does not realize that the confirmation is even taking place.

Listing 9.7 is a <field> that implicitly checks the user's input without asking for a response. A <prompt> is output on lines 2 through 7, using the <value> element to repeat what was recognized as user input. The <prompt> continues by asking the user to wait while the data is being retrieved. Line 6 creates a medium break of 1 second before the actual processing of the request begins.

After the 1-second break, the <noinput> block on lines 8 through 10 fills the *check-Input* field with *yes* if the user does not register a verbal reaction. In this case, if the user gives no response, we consider this a confirmation that the date and event type that have been output are correct, and processing can continue.

If the user responds with any input at all, it is considered negative and handled with the <nomatch> element on lines 11 through 15. When the nomatch event is thrown, a <prompt> is output to confirm to users that their negative input has been heard and that they will get another chance to choose a date and event type. Line 13 clears all the <field> variables, and line 14 uses the <reprompt/> element to send processing back to the top of the form.

After the event type and date of the event have been confirmed, we are ready to create a <subdialog> call that will access the San Francisco Arts Calendar database.

```
1. <field name="checkInput">
2.   <prompt>
3.       Please wait while I retrieve
4.       <value expr="Discipline"/>
5.       events for <value expr="eventDate"/>.
6.       <break size="medium"/>
7.   </prompt>
8.     <noinput>
9.         <assign name="checkInput" expr="'yes'"/>
10.   </noinput>
11.   <nomatch>
12.       Sorry. Let's try it again.
13.       <clear/>
14.       <reprompt/>
15.   </nomatch>
16.   <grammar>yes</grammar>
17.   <filled/>
18. </field>
```

Listing 9.7   Implicit error checking.

Create a field for error checking the user's input. Repeat to the user what was recognized by the speech recognition engine. Process a <nomatch> event if the user responds, and use a <noinput> event to assign a value to the *checkInput* variable if there is no response from the user.

Use <subdialog> to Call the Database

We have used <subdialog> calls in previous projects to send information to a processing script and then receive the return results. Listing 9.8 sets up a call to the SFArts Calendar database, passing it the *month, day, year*, and *Discipline* variables as parameters.

```
1. <subdialog name="getResult"
2.     src="http://www.sfarts.org/voicexml/voicexmltest.cfm"
3.     namelist="month day year Discipline"
4.     method="post"
5.     fetchtimeout="10s">
6. </subdialog>
```

Listing 9.8   Calling the database.

The <subdialog> element calls the Cold Fusion processing script that is run on the San Francisco Arts Calendar server. The *src* attribute on line 2 holds the URI of the processing script, followed by the name list on line 3, which holds the *month, day, year*, and *Discipline* variables. The names of the variables are extremely important because the Cold Fusion script will only accept these names as input.

The *post method* on line 4 is the same type of method as an HTML post. The *fetchtimeout* attribute specifies how long the platform should wait for a response from the database server before throwing a timeout error. The placeholder script, voicexmltest.cfm, is used to verify that a connection can be made to the CF server and the <return/> element within that script can be processed. We will look at the Cold Fusion test script in the next section.

Set up a <subdialog> call to the Cold Fusion script after the error checking in the current application. Use the www.sfarts.org/voicexml/ voicexmltest.cfm URI to confirm that a connection is available to the server.

Test Script

Larry Larson, manager for the SFArts Calendar site, has placed a test script on the server. Listing 9.9 is the short script on the server that returns a simple confirmation that the server is accessible. The output is a simple block of text to verify entrance into the SFArts server and a <return/> element immediately sends processing back to the calling script.

When working with data sources that are not under you domain or control, start the development process with place-holding scripts to verify access to the server before proceeding to development of the real application.

```
1. <vxml version="2.0">
2.     <form id="testOutput">
3.         <block>
4.             Inside the Cold Fusion script
5.             <return/>
6.         </block>
7.     </form>
8. </vxml>
```

Listing 9.9 Confirmation script.

Retrieve Another Event

There are no return values from the Cold Fusion test script, so processing continues from the end of the <subdialog> call. Listing 9.10 creates a final <field> in the script that will allow the caller to request another event.

The *menuAgain* <field> begins with a <prompt>, asking users if they would like to check on other events. The *type* attribute of the *menuAgain* <field> is set to boolean, looking for a positive or negative response. When there is a positive response, an <if> condition resets all variables with the <clear/> element and passes control to the top of the *mainMenu* <form>.

Any other response activates the <return/> element on line 10, transferring processing to the base application.

```
1. <field name="menuAgain" type="boolean">
2. <prompt>
3.    Would you like to check on another event.
4. </prompt>
5. <filled>
6.     <if cond="menuAgain">
7.         <clear/>
8.         <goto next="#mainmenu"/>
9.     <else/>
10.         <return/>
11.     </if>
12. </filled>
13. </field>
```

Listing 9.10 Request another event.

Add a menuAgain <field> beneath the <subdialog> call in the current application. The field should allow a user to request information on another event or send processing to the back of the base application.

HANDS ON

Completed Script

Listing 9.11 is the completed script for accessing the SFArts Calendar database. Take special note of line 83, where the call to the database has been changed from the test script to the actual location of the processing script.

In the next section, we will examine the Cold Fusion script that receives the user input from the VoiceXML script and retrieves a calendar of events.

```
1.  <?xml version="1.0"?>
2.
3.  <vxml version="2.0" application="calendar.vxml">
4.
5.  <!-- REQUEST AN EVENT TYPE -->
6.  <form id="mainmenu">
7.  <field name="Discipline">
8.  <prompt>
9.    What type of event are you interested in:
10. dance, music or theater.
11. </prompt>
12.
13. <grammar>
14.  <![CDATA[
15.  [
16.  [dance dancing ballet]          { < Discipline dance> }
17.  [music opera symphony]          { < Discipline music> }
18.  [theater plays (off broadway)]  { < Discipline theater> }
19.  ]
20.  ]]>
21. </grammar>
22.
23. <nomatch count="1">
24. I missed that. Try again: dance, music or theater
25. </nomatch>
26.
27. <nomatch count="2">
28.   <prompt bargein="true">
```

Listing 9.11 Completed sfarts-calendarmenu.vxml script. *(continues)*

```
29.     I don't recognize that type of event.
30.     Please say dance<break size="small"/>,
31.     music<break size="small"/> or theater.
32.   </prompt>
33. </nomatch>
34.
35. <nomatch count="3">
36.   I'm sorry. I can't help you with that type of event.
37.   Maybe we will add that to the listings in the future.
38.     <goto next="calendargoodbye.vxml"/>
39. </nomatch>
40. <filled/>
41. </field>
42.
43. <!-- REQUEST A DATE -->
44. <object classid="speechobject://nuance.so.SODate"
45.              name="eventDate">
46.   <prompt>
47.     What date.
48.   </prompt>
49. </object>
50.
51. <!-- IMPLIED ERROR CHECKING -->
52. <field name="checkInput">
53.   <prompt>
54.     Please wait while I retrieve
55.     <value expr="Discipline"/>
56.     events for <value expr="eventDate"/>.
57.     <break size="medium"/>
58.   </prompt>
59.   <noinput>
60.     <assign name="checkInput" expr="'yes'"/>
61.   </noinput>
62.   <nomatch>
63.     Sorry. Let's try it again.
64.     <clear/>
65.     <reprompt/>
66.   </nomatch>
67.   <grammar>yes</grammar>
68.   <filled/>
69. </field>
70.
71. <!-- SET VARIABLE VALUES -->
72.   <block>
73.     <assign name="month"
74.             expr="Math.round(eventDate.Month + 1)"/>
75.     <assign name="day"
76.             expr="eventDate.DayOfMonth"/>
```

Listing 9.11   Completed sfarts-calendarmenu.vxml script. *(continues)*

```
77.      <assign name="year"
78.              expr="eventDate.Year"/>
79.   </block>
80.
81. <!-- SEND INPUT TO THE DATABASE -->
82. <subdialog name="getResult"
83.          src="http://www.sfarts.org/calendar.cfm"
84.          namelist="month day year Discipline"
85.          method="post"
86.          fetchtimeout="10s">
87. </subdialog>
88.
89. <!-- OFFER TO DO AGAIN -->
90. <field name="menuAgain" type="boolean">
91.  <prompt>
92.    Would you like to check on another event.
93.  </prompt>
94.  <filled>
95.     <if cond="menuAgain">
96.        <clear/>
97.        <goto next="#mainmenu"/>
98.     <else/>
99.        <return/>
100.    </if>
101.  </filled>
102. </field>
103.
104. </form>
105.
106. </vxml>
```

Listing 9.11   Completed sfarts-calendarmenu.vxml script. *(continued)*

Access the SFArts Calendar Database

The San Francisco Arts Organization Web site, shown in Figure 9.2, accesses data stored in a SQL database with a Cold Fusion front end. The previous section constructed a VoiceXML application that accessed the database through a <subdialog> call. When the request reaches the database, the arguments passed with the request must be extracted and used as part of an SQL statement to the database. This section looks at the Cold Fusion script to process the requests.

Figure 9.2   San Francisco Arts Calendar online.

Create a Template of Desired Output

To format the data it retrieves into usable VoiceXML output, the Cold Fusion server script must contain a template of the desired output format. Listing 9.12 is a template showing the desired layout when records are returned from the database.

```
1. <?xml version="1.0"?>
2. <vxml version="2.0">
3.
4. <form id="acceptInput">
5.     <block>
6.
7.     <!-- CONFIRMATION TO USER -->
8.     One record was found for dance events
9.     on June 2, 2002.
10.     <break size="small"/
11.
12.     <!-- LIST OF EVENTS -->
13.     Event 1: Stomp presents Stomp
14.     at the Marines Memorial Theater.
```

Listing 9.12   Template of desired format of output.

```
15.      For more information call
16.      <say-as type="telephone">234 2343</say-as>
17.      <break size="medium"/>
18.
19.      <!-- RETURN TO CALLING SCRIPT -->
20.      End of Events
21.      <return/>
22. </block>
23. </form>
24. </vxml>
```

Listing 9.12 Template of desired format of output. *(continued)*

The output is contained within a single <form>, *acceptInput*. <break> elements on lines 10 and 17 create a natural language flow, giving the listener a chance to comprehend what is being said. The CF server will provide dynamic content for filling in the number of records found, output on line 8, and the listing of events in the completed application, as shown on lines 13 through 17. The Cold Fusion script will loop through the events, outputting each with a dynamically generated, sequential event number, the name of the event, the presenter of the event, a location, and a contact phone number.

After the final event is read, an End of Events message is output followed by the <return> element on line 21, returning processing to the calling <subdialog>.

Create a template that can be used for formatting database output into a VoiceXML application.

HANDS ON

The Cold Fusion Template

Listing 9.13 demonstrates how a Cold Fusion script could dynamically generate the VoiceXML output.

Listing 9.13 is a template to be used for creating your own Cold Fusion application, not the actual script on the SFArts site.

NOTE

```
1. <!-- ACCEPT USER INPUT FROM FORM -->
2. <CFPARAM NAME="form.month"      DEFAULT="1">
3. <CFPARAM NAME="form.year"       DEFAULT="2003">
4. <CFPARAM NAME="form.day"        DEFAULT="1">
5. <CFPARAM NAME="form.Discipline" DEFAULT="None">
```

Listing 9.13 Cold Fusion template for generating VoiceXML output. *(continues)*

```
 6.
 7. <!-- CREATE DATE FORMAT STRING -->
 8. <CFSET target_date =
 9.         CreateDate(form.year, form.month, form.day)>
10.
11. <!-- MAP DISCIPLINE TO NUMBER -->
12. <CFSET disp = #form.Discipline#>
13. <CFIF #disp#EQ"Theater">
14.    <CFSET #disp_num#="1">
15. <CFELSEIF #disp#EQ"Dance">
16.    <CFSET #disp_num#="2">
17. <CFELSEIF #disp#EQ"Music">
18.    <CFSET #disp_num#="3">
19. </CFIF>
20.
21. <!-- SQL QUERY -->
22. <CFQUERY name="Recordset">
23. SELECT put-your-query-string-here;
24. </CFQUERY>
25.
26. <!-- RETURN RECORD COUNT -->
27. <CFSET Recordset_NumRows = Recordset.RecordCount>
28.
29. <!-- BEGIN VOICEXML OUTPUT -->
30. <?xml version="1.0"?>
31. <vxml version="2.0">
32.
33. <form id="acceptInput">
34. <block>
35.
36. <!--- NO EVENTS RETURNED --->
37. <CFIF Recordset.RecordCount IS "0">
38.
39.   <CFOUTPUT>
40.      There are no #disp# events
41.      for #dateformat(target_date, "dddd, mmmm dd, yyyy")#
42.   </CFOUTPUT>
43.   <return/>
44. </block>
45. </form>
46. </vxml>
47.
48. <CFELSE>
49. <!-- CONFIRM NUMBER OF EVENTS FOUND -->
50. <CFOUTPUT>
51. #Recordset.Recordcount# #discipline_name#
52. events were found for
53. #dateformat(target_date, "dddd, mmmm dd, yyyy")#
```

Listing 9.13   Cold Fusion template for generating VoiceXML output. *(continues)*

```
54. <break size="small"/>
55. </CFOUTPUT>
56.
57. <!-- LIST OF EVENTS -->
58. <CFOUTPUT query="Recordset">
59. Event Number #Recordset.Currentrow#
60. #XMLFormat(Recordset.Org_Name)#  presents
61. #XMLFormat(Recordset.Event_Name)# at
62. #XMLFormat(Recordset.Venue_Name)#.
63. For more information, call
64. <say-as type="telephone">#Recordset.Event_Phone# </say-as>
65. <break size="medium"/>
66. </CFOUTPUT>
67.
68.   <!-- RETURN TO CALLING SCRIPT -->
69.   End of Events for
70.   #dateformat(target_date, "dddd, mmmm dd, yyyy")#
71. <return/>
72. </block>
73. </form>
74. </vxml>
```

Listing 9.13   Cold Fusion template for generating VoiceXML output. *(continued)*

The block of code on lines 2 through 5 of Listing 9.13 receives values from the <field> items that are being sent to the script as parameters. The default values are used as an error-checking mechanism. If a discipline of None with a date of January 1, 2003, is output as VoiceXML, it is an indication to the developer that the form values are not being processed properly.

Lines 8 and 9 use the CreateDate method built into Cold Fusion to create the value for the *target_date* variable.

The variable *disp* is set with the *Discipline* <field> from the <form> input. The database at SFArts has number values for each of the disciplines. The incoming *Discipline* field needs to be mapped to those number values, as shown in lines 13 through 18.

The SQL statement that will be used to extract the data is placed at line 23, with all return records stored in the Recordset object set on line 22.

 The SQL string that actually retrieves the record sets from SFArts is not shown for security reasons. You should place your own SQL statement in line 23 when creating an application with your database.

NOTE

The number of records found is returned from the RecordCount method on line 27. This value will be used to tell the user how many events were found for the requested date.

Line 30 begins the actual VoiceXML output with the XML declaration and <vxml> root element. The <form> beginning on line 33 checks to see if any events were returned, using the <CFIF> element on line 37. If there were no events for that date, a message is sent back to the user, processing returns to the main script with the <return/> element on line 43, and the VoiceXML form and document are closed on lines 45 and 46. Notice the insertion of dynamic data using the #variable# mechanism of Cold Fusion on Line 40. Line 41 uses the dateformat function to verbally output the date that is stored in *target_date*.

If events were found for the date requested, processing jumps to line 50, where confirmation is output as to the number of dates found for the discipline selected. Line 54 inserts a <break> element for a more humanlike transition to the output of events.

Lines 58 through 66 are the actual output of the events. The XMLFormat function is used to force the escaping of all special characters such as <, &, and ... within the XML data. The output of the presenter's telephone number is handled with the <say-as> element. A medium-sized <break> element, on line 65, is used between the output of listing to give the user a chance to comprehend what was spoken before moving onto the next event.

WARNING **While creating the CF script to output the event titles from the SQL database, Larry and I spent a half-day tracking down an obscure error. To abbreviate long title listings of events, the data input operator had inserted three dots in a row, ..., as a placeholder. For some reason, this was causing an error upon output to the VoiceXML browser as well as the IE5+ browser we were using for visual testing, even when the output was wrapped in a CDATA section. The XMLFormat function handles all of the special character escaping as well as the problem with the ellipses.**

Lines 69 and 70 confirm to the user that the event listing has been completed. The <return/> element on line 71 transfers processing back to the calling application and all VoiceXML elements are closed on lines 72 through 74. Line 76 terminates the Cold Fusion script.

WARNING **According to Larry Larson, the *xml* declaration must be the first character of the first line in the output. The simplest strategy for ensuring that the Cold Fusion page renders correctly as XML is to put the declaration in the first line. If there is an application.cfm page included in the Cold Fusion application, there should be no new-line returns on it because those returns will be carried to the data page and move the declaration below where it should be, resulting in an XML error.**

Final Thoughts

Dynamic generation of voice content from a database allows use of legacy data as input to your VoiceXML applications. A calendar of events that changes on a regular basis is just asking to be voice enabled.

Creating income from your Web site is always a nice idea. An improvement to this script would be the dynamic generation of sponsors that rotate on a regular basis instead of hard-coding a single sponsor directly into the script. Whenever a client calls, a sponsor splash could be output based upon the type of event that was chosen.

Another addition to this script would be an intuitive way to handle more than 5 events. As it works now, if 50 events are returned for a single day, the user would have to listen to all the events before being able to exit the program or choose a different date.

It would also be relatively easy to create the list of disciplines from a database table. This effectively moves the grammar to an exterior source, making it unnecessary to make changes to the VoiceXML script when a new discipline is added.

The listings for this project can be downloaded from the BeVocal Web site at cafe.bevocal.com/wiley/10projects. They are saved as text files, useful as templates for creating your own VoiceXML scripts. Join us in the online discussion board for this project and tell us how you will be using the project. If you create a form that would make this project work better, it might be incorporated into the project code online so that others can use it.

FAQ Engine

When I first saw Joseph Weizenbaum's Eliza engine, I laughed out loud. It acts like a Rogerian analyst, spitting back questions and statements based upon your responses. Simple pattern matching is used to pull out relevant words from the user's input and then the engine reformats those words into a sentence or question that continues the dialog. The problem with Eliza, though, is that there is really no exchange of information taking place during the dialog. The program can not infer anything from the discussion or interject comments that extend the discourse.

I met Kevin Dowd in 2001 at a Speech-Tek convention in New York. The display for his product, Brainhat, said that he had a VoiceXML-enabled speech engine that could carry on a conversation based upon context, not word recognition. After testing out the demo, I became a believer. The FAQ Engine project was created by me, Kevin, and his team at Brainhat. It demonstrates how to access a natural language processing engine through a VoiceXML interface.

THE PROBLEM

Most FAQ engines have preset definitions for a set of 10 most frequently asked questions. There is no dialog between the user and the information, just a question and a hard-coded answer.

THE SOLUTION

Build a voice-enabled FAQ engine that can infer relationships through context and handle basic natural language processing.

Project Description

The FAQ Engine project is built in three phases: install, test, and examine the Brainhat engine; create a scenario and vocabulary for the engine; and build a VoiceXML interface to access the engine. An FAQ for the fictional Mars Colony 7 Visitor's Bureau is developed for handling generic telephone inquiries about the colony.

The user calls in and is greeted by the VoiceXML receptionist. The caller may ask questions about accommodations, such as pricing, availability, and amenities. The FAQ engine processes the dialog and at an appropriate point asks if the user would like to reserve a room.

To complete this project, you will:

1. Download and install the Brainhat server.
2. Build vocabularies in Brainhat.
3. Model scenarios to build dialog context.
4. Develop an FAQ application.
5. Set up the VoiceXML entrance.

You Will Need

✔ **Brainhat engine**

✔ **FAQ scenario for Brainhat**

✔ **Customized words definition file for Brainhat**

✔ **BeVocal account**

✔ **VoiceXML script for accessing Brainhat**

✔ **Project files downloadable from cafe.bevocal.com/wiley/10projects**

VoiceXML Elements Used in This Project

ELEMENT NAME	DESCRIPTION
<assign>	Assigns a variable a value
<else>	Used in <if> elements
<field>	Declares an input field in a form
<filled>	An action executed when fields are filled
<form>	A dialog for presenting information and collecting data
<if>	Simple conditional logic

VoiceXML Elements Used in This Project   *(Continued)*

ELEMENT NAME	DESCRIPTION
<prompt>	Queues speech synthesis and audio output to the user
<property>	Controls implementation platform settings
<script>	Specifies a block of ECMAScript client-side scripting logic
<submit>	Submits values to a document server
<var>	Declares a variable
<vxml>	Top-level element in each VoiceXML document

Source: *VoiceXML 2.0 Working Draft*, section 1.4

Application Call Flow

Figure 10.1 shows the call flow for this application. The Brainhat server issues a standard greeting and waits for user input. The dialog continues between the server and the user as long as the user has input. A goodbye message from the server is output when the user says "goodbye."

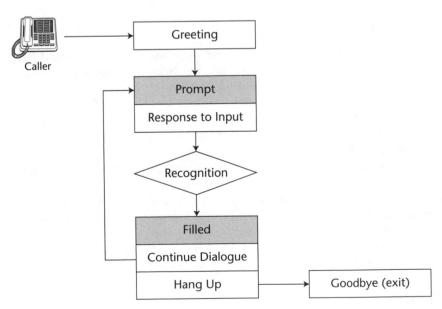

Figure 10.1   Application flow.

Set Up the Brainhat Server

The core of this project is built around the natural language processing (NLP) Brainhat server. It is freely downloadable for development use at www.brainhat.com.

About Brainhat

Brainhat is an NLP server that can dispatch tasks, handle natural language events, evaluate ideas, and ask and answer questions. Because Brainhat is based on knowledge representation, it can digress within a conversation, answer questions outside the script, and keep rich context. Built-in network capabilities make Brainhat a clearinghouse and consolidation point for natural language events and delegated tasks.

The Brainhat project was developed in 1996 by Kevin Dowd while he was working at Atlantic Computing. The name came from an earlier attempt to fit a spaghetti colander with differential amplifiers and interpret brainwaves as a method of controlling appliances. The company now has five full-time employees, including programmers with backgrounds in A.I. and linguistics.

Programming Brainhat is done at three levels: creation of vocabulary, creation of grammar and associated transformation procedures, and creation of English language-based scenarios to motivate operation. Brainhat's job is to discover the semantic value of input, run inferences, which may create new knowledge or side effects, and output responses as necessary.

Brainhat can be extended to act as a natural computer interface for a robot or other program. NASA currently has a project using Brainhat for a robot that will be trained in space.

The Brainhat Server

Brainhat is a platform for building language-based systems. It can understand language, represent and manipulate knowledge, run inferences, and generate output. Most of the application programming is done in English.

The program comes with a basic vocabulary, which can be easily extended using a simple text editor. A context-free grammar tells Brainhat how to recognize parts of speech and how to assemble the parts into internal knowledge representations. Transformations take place as the input is assembled; word and phrase disambiguation, pronoun resolution, normalization of forms, and discard of unlikely or duplicate candidates are all completed by the time the input is recognized.

The programmer motivates conversation by giving Brainhat an English language scenario that describes all of the common-sense knowledge needed for a conversation, plus inferences to pull it along. One might program a conversation that asks users about their meal choice, for example. Brainhat understands the notion of things that are probable; if a conversation stalls, the program can push things in the right direction.

Install Brainhat

Brainhat comes as a zipped download from www.brainhat.com. The installation is extremely user friendly and does not overwrite any system configuration files or change a registry listing.

Navigate to the Brainhat Web site and choose *download* from the menu at the top of the page (Figure 10.2). Follow the links to download the binary distribution for Windows. Create a Brainhat directory on your hard drive and unzip the file, allowing the installer to create the *data* and *scenarios* subdirectories. Once unzipped, the Brainhat directory will contain the Brainhat executable at the root level and two subdirectories that contain data files for vocabularies and scenario files for setting the context of dialogs.

Test the Installation

Test the installation by opening a DOS window, changing directories to the location of the Brainhat installation, and typing *run* at the prompt. The run command accesses the run.bat file, which gives configuration directives to the server for compilation. Confirmation of the Brainhat compilation will scroll past and end with a blinking prompt. This is the command line interface for Brainhat.

Listing 10.1 shows the contents of the run.bat file. Line 1 changes directories to access the data files that come as defaults. Lines 2 and 4 are confirmation notices to the user that processing is proceeding as planned. Line 3 calls in the *data.in* file and preprocesses it into the compiled *data* file that will be used by Brainhat to recognize words as input. Line 6 starts the Brainhat server, feeding it the compiled *data* file.

```
1. cd data
2. echo 'Pre-processing...'
3. ..\simplecpp < data.in > data
4. echo 'Running Brainhat'
5. cd ..
6. .\brainhat.exe -E data\data
```

Listing 10.1   run.bat.

The data.in file is nothing more than a list of files included in the compilation phase when the Brainhat server is started. Listing 10.2 lists the files that are included by default during initial installation. The files listed on lines 1 through 5 are used for building the patterns of speech that Brainhat will recognize. These will not have to be changed to create our VoiceXML application.

The most important file for our purposes is the *words* file, which holds the list of words and hints the compiler will use to know how the vocabulary words relate to one another. We will examine the *words* file in depth in the next section.

```
1. #include "../constant.h"
2. #include "required-patterns"
3. #include "debug-patterns"
4. #include "cc-patterns"
5. #include "input-patterns"
6. #include "words"
```

Listing 10.2   Default include files.

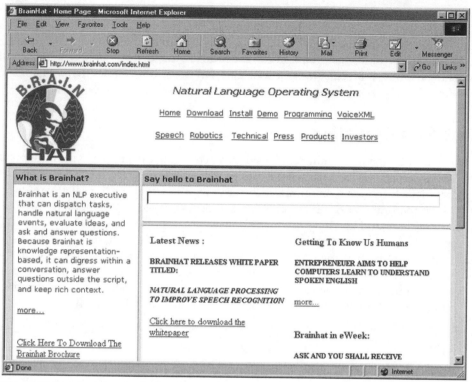

Figure 10.2   Brainhat Web site screen shot.

Begin a dialog with Brainhat by typing *hello* and pressing the Enter key on the keyboard. The program will answer back with a simple hello. Ask the program "what are you?" Wait for the response and then ask, "Who am I?" If you get responses to these three questions, your Brainhat server is installed properly and is ready to have scenarios and vocabularies added to its knowledge base.

To see how Brainhat can learn from the context of a dialog, enter "you are a computer" at the command prompt. Brainhat will echo back that it is a computer. Now tell Brainhat "you are green." For the duration of the session, Brainhat will refer to itself as a computer when asked what it is. When asked its color, it will respond with "I am green." You can continue to give attributes to the program by inserting statements telling the program about itself and then testing it with questions. Listing 10.3 is the output from the test session.

Type *goodbye* to exit the program.

```
1. >> hello
2.   hello.
3. >> what are you
4.   I am person.
5. >> who am i
```

Listing 10.3   Test session output.

```
 6.  You are person.
 7. >> you are a computer
 8.  I am a computer.
 9. >> you are green
10.  I am green.
11. >> who are you
12.  I am a computer.
13. >> what color are you
14.  I am green.
15. >> goodbye
16. goodbye!
```

Listing 10.3 Test session output. *(continued)*

Build Vocabularies in Brainhat

The Brainhat server is controlled by text-based files that can be changed to create extended vocabularies and context-specific scenarios. We will look at a vocabulary file first and make some changes to allow the server's recognition of greetings to be a little less formal. Then we will examine a scenario and add more content to its knowledge base.

Vocabulary Overview

A Brainhat vocabulary describes the hierarchical relationships between words, plus some clues to help Brainhat disambiguate input phrases and sentences. The default vocabulary is stored in the *words* file in the data directory. When Brainhat is started from the command line using the run.bat file, it grabs the *words* file and compiles the relationship and inferences between each of the words in the default vocabulary. Each of the rules from the required-patterns, cc-patterns, and input patterns is precompiled and then absorbed into the Brainhat engine.

Listing 10.4 shows the first two terms defined in the Brainhat vocabulary. Lines 4 and 11 are general concepts that are defined as part of the vocabulary. A general concept is preceded by the word *define*. Everything up to the next *define* statement is considered part of the concept's definition. Concepts may be defined in any order, making it possible to group concepts of like meaning and alphabetize them for easy access. This will become helpful as the vocabularies for your projects start to grow.

A concept must have a unique identifying name. The name may be any string of characters, except spaces or new line characters, but it is most useful if it is recognizable as a word. Some concepts might have multiple meanings, such as the word *class*. In the English language, class has multiple meanings: a group of people learning a subject, a certain social status, a category in taxonomy, a programming module in Java. By convention, a definition that has multiple meanings is followed by a hyphen and a number to distinguish itself from other definitions. In Listing 10.4, goodbye-1 is a definition for the verb goodbye, meaning end the program. In another context, goodbye might be a noun meaning taking of leave, as in "a tearful goodbye." A second definition would use the goodbye-2 string.

```
1.  /********************************
2.  Greetings and salutations
3.  ********************************/
4.  define      greeting
5.        label           hi
6.        label           good morning
7.        label           good afternoon
8.        label           hello
9.        child-of        things
10.
11. define      goodbye-1
12.        label           bye
13.        label           exit
14.        label           quit
15.        label           goodbye
```

Listing 10.4   Snippet of Brainhat vocabulary.

The vocabulary definitions in Listing 10.4 contain *label* and *child-of* attributes. The *label* attribute holds a word or phrase that will be recognized as the vocabulary for the concept. The *child-of* attribute places the definition within the hierarchical structure of the vocabulary. Table 10.1 is a list of available attributes.

Line 9 of Listing 10.4 states that *greeting* is a child of *things*. During the compilation phase, all *things* are tied together as a set, making it easy to handle definitions of the same type in a similar fashion. Other top-level concepts include noun, action, preposition, article, and adverb. All definitions, except goodbye-1, must ultimately feed up to one of the top-level concepts. goodbye-1 is a special case with no top-level concept because it is recognized by the Brainhat engine as an exit command.

HANDS ON

Open the *words* file in the data directory with any text editor and examine its contents. Find the colors, shapes, and textures section and note the list of available colors. Start Brainhat and define it as a computer having a specific color.

Table 10.1   Attributes of Definitions

ATTRIBUTE	DEFINITION
label	Word(s) a user might speak and synonyms
child-of	Specifies the direct parent(s) of the word
number	Defines singular or plural nouns and verbs
othogonal	Specifies distinction/uniqueness among like items—forces items of likeness to be different

Table 10.1 *(Continued)*

ATTRIBUTE	DEFINITION
person	Distinguishes who/what is being spoken of: First: speaker (i) Second: individual addressed (you) Third: thing or person spoken of (he, she, it)
tense	Time of action of a verb (past, present, future)
wants	Items to be associated with the word

Add to the Vocabulary

Programming starts with a vocabulary that includes the anticipated words and word groups for a given application, as we saw in Listing 10.4. Adding to an existing vocabulary definition is as simple as placing another label within the definition. Listing 10.5 adds more labels to the greeting and goodbye-1 definitions, extending what will be recognized as part of each concept.

```
1.  /***********************************
2.   Greetings and salutations
3.  ***********************************/
4.  define    greeting
5.       label    hi
6.       label    good morning
7.       label    good afternoon
8.       label    good evening
9.       label    whats up
10.      label    sup
11.      label    hello
12.      child-of things
13.
14. define   goodbye-1
15.      label    bye
16.      label    exit
17.      label    quit
18.      label    outta here
19.      label    later
20.      label    goodbye
```

Listing 10.5 Extending recognition of a definition.

Add labels to the *words* file to extend the recognition of the greeting and goodbye-1 definitions. Reboot the Brainhat server to compile the new vocabulary. Greet and exit the program with your new words and phrases.

To implement the changes to the vocabulary file, Brainhat must be stopped and rebooted.

Create a New Definition

As we start to extend the labels for a greeting, some greetings might be considered informal as opposed to formal. Splitting the greetings into groups makes the definitions more manageable and allows for a separate response for each type of greeting.

Listing 10.6 shows two sublevel greeting definitions that relate to the top-level greeting. The *greeting-formal* definitions are most of the labels from the default definition of greeting. *greeting-formal* is defined as a child-of greeting, relating it to the original concept of greeting. The *greeting-informal* definition is defined to extend the vocabulary of the application. It also contains a child-of attribute, relating the definitions to the greeting concept.

A pleasant side effect of creating individual groups that relate to the central concept is that each of the groups can define the response that is output by Brainhat. The last label of each definition holds the Brainhat response, or output. When the user inputs a word or phrase from *greeting-formal*, the output is "greetings human," whereas output related to the *greeting-informal* definition will output "whats up homeboy."

Line 26 of Listing 10.6 is the single letter q. This is used as a short cut for exiting the program when testing the application at the command line.

```
1.  /**********************************
2.   Greetings and salutations
3.  **********************************/
4.  define    greeting
5.      child-of things
6.
7.  define    greeting-formal
8.       label     good morning
9.       label     good afternoon
10.      label     good evening
11.      label     greetings
12.      label     greeting
13.      label     hello
14.      label     greetings human
15.      child-of greeting
16.
17. define    greeting-informal
18.      label     hi
```

Listing 10.6   Create a new definition.

```
19.    label    whats up
20.    label    sup
21.    label    yo
22.    label    whats up homeboy
23.    child-of greeting
24.    q
25. define    goodbye-1
26.    label    q
27.    label    bye
28.    label    exit
29.    label    quit
30.    label    outta here
31.    label    later
32.    label    goodbye
```

Listing 10.6   Create a new definition. *(continued)*

Separate the greeting definition into formal and informal groups. Relate the groups to the original greeting definition with a child-of attribute.

HANDS ON

Create a Standalone Vocabulary

Developers can also create their own vocabularies that are included as part of Brainhat at compile time. Your application can have any number of vocabularies by adding an #include statement in data.in file for each of the vocabularies. Listing 10.7 shows a new file added to data.in that holds an extended vocabulary. This technique is extremely useful when multiple developers are working on a large vocabulary. The task can be split into defined concepts and included with each new startup of the Brainhat engine.

Listing 10.8 shows the contents of extended-vocabulary.mpm that was included in data.in. It holds the definitions created previously to extend the default vocabulary. During compile time, the *child-of* pointers are related to the concepts defined in the original *words* file.

```
1. #include "../constant.h"
2.
3. #include "required-patterns"
4. #include "debug-patterns"
5. #include "cc-patterns"
6. #include "input-patterns"
7. #include "words"
8. #include "extended-vocabulary.mpm"
```

Listing 10.7   Adding a file for inclusion at compile time.

```
1. define    greeting-informal
2.    label    hi
3.    label    whats up
4.    label    sup
5.    label    yo
6.    label    whats up homeboy
7.    child-of greeting
8.
9. define    goodbye-2
10.    label    q
11.    label    outta here
12.    label    later
13.    child-of goodbye-1
```

Listing 10.8 extended-vocabulary.mpm.

We will be using standalone vocabulary files when building the FAQ Engine project, making it possible to have multiple FAQs processed by a single Brainhat engine.

HANDS ON **Remove the labels and definitions created within the default *words* file and save them in a standalone file within the data directory. Name the file extended-vocabulary with the file extension of your initials. Add the filename to the data.in file as an #include to be accessed at compile time. Run the application and verify that the vocabularies are accessible through the command line.**

Model Scenarios to Build Dialog Context

Scenarios are used by Brainhat to build models of specific situations. They hold all of the common-sense knowledge needed by the program to sustain a dialog. Scenarios are written in plain English as statements of facts that relate to a situation or as conditional statements that help the engine infer context within the dialog.

Create a Simple Scenario

Simple scenarios that reside in memory during a session can be built directly at the command line. Brainhat will accept facts and conditional statements as input and use the inferences when creating responses within the session dialog. Listing 10.9 shows a log from a session that input information about Brainhat itself directly at the command line. The lines starting with >> are what is typed in at the prompt; other lines are the response from the program.

```
 1.  >> what are you
 2.   I am person.
 3.  >> where are you
 4.   I.
 5.  >> What color are you?
 6.   I.
 7.  >> where do you live
 8.   I do not know.
 9.  >> you are a computer
10.   I am a computer.
11.  >> you are green
12.   I am green.
13.  >> you live on mars
14.   I do live on mars.
15.  >> where do you live
16.   I do live on mars.
17.  >> what color are you
18.   I am green.
19.  >> what are you
20.   I am a computer.
21.  >> are you a computer
22.   yes. I am green.
```

Listing 10.9   Log file output for simple scenario.

Lines 1 through 8 check to see if any of the qualities of Brainhat that we are interested in have already been defined by default. The response from Brainhat on line 2 insinuates that Brainhat is a person. We will correct that as we start defining the personality in the following lines. By default, Brainhat does not know what color it is or where it lives.

Lines 9, 11, and 13 make statements of fact, telling Brainhat about itself. Each statement is echoed on the following line, confirming that the program accepted what was input. Lines 15 through 22 verify that Brainhat can now use the new facts as part of a dialog.

Testing simple scenarios at the command line is useful when trying out new ideas. A lot of scenario development is trial and error, confirming that you are getting an expected response. Once you have a set of facts or statements that work as expected, they can be stored in a file and accessed either at compile or run time.

Give Brainhat a Personality

When most people access your application for the first time, they will probe to see if they can find out anything about the computer that is answering their questions. Listing 10.10 is a scenario that gives Brainhat a description of itself.

The scenario in Listing 10.10 is mainly a set of facts the program will use when asked questions about itself. Lines 7 through 10 are conditional statements that set Brainhat's mood depending upon what color Mars is. We will test the scenario after saving and installing it in the data directory.

```
1. Brainhat is a Martian.
2. Brainhat's name is Alisha.
3. Brainhat is green.
4. Brainhat lives on Mars.
5. Brainhat is in Colony 7.
6.
7. If Mars is red
8.    then Brainhat is happy.
9. If Mars is not red
10.    then Brainhat is sad.
```

Listing 10.10   Storing Brainhat's personal description.

 Create a personality for the Brainhat application using Listing 10.10 as a template. Save it in the data directory as *about-brainhat*. We will activate HANDS ON the scenario in the next section.

Activate a Scenario

To activate the scenario, start the Brainhat server. When the server is running, type *input* at the command prompt and hit Enter on the keyboard. Enter *scenarios/about-brainhat* when the prompt requests a filename. The Brainhat engine will load the facts and conditions from the stored scenario into the current session, making them available as concepts for the dialog.

Listing 10.11 shows a dialog after the *about-brainhat* scenario is loaded into memory.

```
1. >> what is your name
2.  my name is alisha.
3.
4. >> where do you live alisha
5.  I do live on mars.
6.
7. >> do you like mars
8.  maybe. I do not know.
9.
10. >> mars is red
11.  mars is red. I am glad.
12.
13. >> why are you happy
14.  I am glad because mars is red.
15.
16. >> what are you alisha
17.  I am a martian.
18.
```

Listing 10.11   Brainhat speaks about itself.

```
19. >> are you green?
20.   yes. I am green am in colony seven.
21.
22. >> goodbye.
```

Listing 10.11   Brainhat speaks about itself. (*continued*)

Brainhat ships with several scenario examples including one for a restaurant and one for the weather. Open the weather scenario in a text editor and view the facts and inference. Activate the weather scenario when starting Brainhat.

View the Log File

Logging and tracking dialogs is useful when researching and testing what phrases and questions users input into your application. The brainhat.log file in the root directory contains a complete log of all dialog activity on your server. The log file is opened each time the server is started, appending activity to the end of the file. Listing 10.11 was taken directly from the Brainhat log.

The log file is useful in two ways. First, it allows you as a developer to test various inputs and have a record of the responses to them. It shows how responses from the program are affected when the vocabularies and scenarios are changed.

The log file is also useful for test group analysis. Creating dialogs that anticipate what a user will say is the hardest part of building a language-processing application. By analyzing the log file, it will become apparent what the majority of users think are appropriate words and phrases to be used when interacting with your application. Using this knowledge will help build more intelligently responsive programs.

The log file can get large very quickly if there is a lot of activity on your server.

Open the brainhat.log file and examine the input. Find sections within the log where a scenario was changed and see how the program responded.

Develop an FAQ Application

We now have the foundation needed to build an FAQ engine with the Brainhat server. First, we will outline what is expected as input and output from the project; then we will develop a vocabulary and scenario that will handle user input through a natural language processing interface.

Building the back end of the FAQ engine takes place in three stages: create the list of FAQ questions, define the vocabulary that a user might speak when talking with the FAQ, and build a scenario to help the engine guide the conversation.

Create a List of Questions

We will be building the FAQ engine that will handle questions a caller might have regarding accommodations in the Mars Colony 7 Recreation Dome. The first question most people will ask is "Are there accommodations?" From that point, questions about cost, size, and amenities will follow. Once users have exhausted their curiosity, the program should ask if the user would like to make a reservation. A pushy program will also ask if the user has a credit card.

Start by creating a list of basic questions the user might have. Be as specific as possible. The FAQ for Mars Colony 7 will try and handle any questions related to rooms. Listing 10.12 has a list of questions that might be appropriate for a hotel reservation FAQ. We will examine each question for new words that are not listed in the definitions list and add them to a list vocabulary.

```
1.    Do you have accommodations?
2.    How much does it cost?
3.    How big are the rooms?
4.    What is in a room?
5.    What comes with a room?
6.    Can I make a reservation?
```

Listing 10.12 Questions for the FAQ.

Build the Scenario and Define the Vocabulary

Building a vocabulary and an accompanying scenario entails examining each sentence in the FAQ and verifying that there is a definition for each word within the Brainhat definition list, either in the *word* file or in a standalone file that is used to extend the vocabulary.

The first question in Listing 10.12, "Do you have accommodations?", is used in the scenario of Listing 10.13 on line 8 as a statement of fact: Brainhat has accommodations. Lines 1 through 6 define the personality of the program as we created it in Listing 10.10.

```
1. Brainhat is a Martian.
2. Brainhat's name is Alisha.
3. Brainhat is green.
4. Brainhat lives on Mars.
5. Brainhat is in Colony7.
6. Colony Seven is on Mars.
7.
8. Brainhat has accommodations.
```

Listing 10.13 about-marscolony7 scenario.

Running the scenario from the command line generates the output:

```
>> do you have accommodations
yes. I have something.
```

This is the correct response from Brainhat when a statement of fact is made, but the word is not defined as part of the active vocabulary. The program realizes it is supposed to have "something," but it doesn't know what that something is. We will define the word *accommodations* in the next section.

 Open the brainhat.init file and add a new line that tells Brainhat it has accommodations. Run a test and confirm that Brainhat recognizes that it has

HANDS ON **"something" but doesn't know what it is.**

Defining a New Word

Brainhat contains definitions for basic verbs and pronouns as part of the default installation. To define a new word, begin by determining what part of speech it is. Table 10.2 lists all top-level concepts available in Brainhat, each related to its part of speech. Every word within the definitions file must eventually feed into one of the top-level concepts. Think of it as a tree structure. The word is a leaf on the tree and the root is the top-level concept.

Continuing the tree analogy, there might be leaves on branches that connect with limbs connecting to the trunk feeding into the root of the tree. In the case of accommodations, accommodations could be a room, which could be a building, which is a thing. Following the logic from the leaf to the trunk to the root, verify that each word that connects the leaf through to the root is in the definition list and is part of a structure ending in *things*.

Examination of the *words* file confirms there is no definition for the word *accommodations*. Listing 10.14 adds the definition to the extended-vocabulary.mpm file. A quick search at dictionary.com shows that accommodations is a noun, so it will be defined at a top-level as *things*. Brainhat already defines rooms, which is connected to a building, so we'll make accommodations a leaf of the rooms branch. Lines 15 through 17 define the accommodations-1 term, creating it as a *child-of* rooms-1.

Table 10.2   Top-Level Concepts in the Brainhat Vocabulary

TOP-LEVEL CONCEPT	PART OF SPEECH
action	Verb
adjective	Adjective
adverb	Adverb
article	Article
preposition	Preposition
things	Noun

```
1. define   greeting-informal
2.    label    hi
3.    label    whats up
4.    label    sup
5.    label    yo
6.    label    whats up homeboy
7.    child-of greeting
8.
9. define   goodbye-2
10.    label    q
11.    label    outta here
12.    label    later
13.    child-of goodbye-1
14.
15. define   accommodations-1
16.    label    accommodations
17.    child-of rooms-1
```

Listing 10.14   Adding a definition to the extended-vocabulary.mpm file.

Listing 10.15 shows the log of an exchange after making changes to the extended-vocabulary.mpm file. The dialog is started by an experienced user who already knows the name of Alisha, the robot receptionist. The user asks if Alisha has accommodations and receives a response on line 5 confirming that there are accommodations.

Line 7 asks the question in another way, asking if there are any rooms. This demonstrates how the hierarchical tree is used by Brainhat to analyze a concept. Because *accommodations* is defined as a child of rooms-1, the program uses the link to respond positively that, yes, there are accommodations. Line 13 shows an extended reference by the Brainhat engine. Nowhere have we referenced *places to sleep* to be a synonym for *accommodations*. Built within the program's default vocabulary are references to *sleep* and *places*. During the compilation phase, the references were generated as part of the knowledge tree and are now being accessed on the fly by the program.

On line 10, the caller asks for sleeping quarters, but Alisha isn't sure what is being requested. She responds with a relatively intelligent "I don't know" and then waits for another request or response. The next section will build synonyms for accommodations, handling multiple requests for the same item.

```
1. hello alisha
2.  hello. hello.
3.
4. >> do you have accommodations
5.  yes. I have accommodations.
6.
7. >> do you have rooms
```

Listing 10.15   Log after changes to vocabulary file.

```
8.  yes. I have accommodations.
9.
10. >> do you have sleeping quarters
11.  maybe. I do not know.
12.
13. >> do you have places to sleep
14.  yes. I have accommodations.
```

Listing 10.15   Log after changes to vocabulary file. *(continued)*

Add the definition of accommodations to the extended-vocabulary.mpm file. Test the changes at the command line.

Examine the words file and find references to *sleep* and *place* to determine how the Brainhat engine made the connection between "places to sleep" and "accommodations."

Synonyms

Accommodations can be referred to in multiple ways in real life. A person might ask for a room or ask for a place to stay or a place to sleep. The *label* attribute is used to build a list of synonyms for a concept. There is no limit to the number of synonyms a concept can have, but the closer the true definitions of the word, the more realistic the output.

Listing 10.16 adds a series of synonyms to the accommodations definition. Now a person should be able to ask about accommodations in any way imaginable, including as a sleeping pod.

```
1. define   greeting-informal
2.    label    hi
3.    label    whats up
4.    label    sup
5.    label    yo
6.    label    whats up homeboy
7.    child-of greeting
8.
9. define   goodbye-2
10.   label    q
11.   label    outta here
12.   label    later
13.   child-of goodbye-1
14.
15. define   accommodations-1
16.   label    accommodations
```

Listing 10.16   Labels for synonyms of accommodations. *(continues)*

```
17.    label    room
18.    label    place to stay
19.    label    place to sleep
20.    label    sleeping accommodations
21.    label    sleeping pod
22.    child-of rooms-1
```

Listing 10.16 Labels for synonyms of accommodations. *(continued)*

After adding to the definition of accommodations, we need to check the server's output to see if it is what we expected. Listing 10.17 is the output from a log that asks about accommodations in multiple ways. Starting on line 4, we see that not only can Alisha tell the visitor that she has accommodations, she can also define what an accommodation is. Lines 13 and 16 test to see if the program can recognize the synonyms stated in a slightly different way.

The responses from the Brainhat server are coming out in a relatively intelligent way with very little programming. In the next section, we'll extend the scenario to start handling requests when a caller wants to reserve a room.

```
1. >> do you have a room
2.  yes. I have sleeping pod.
3.
4. >> what is a sleeping pod
5.  a sleeping pod is rooms.
6.
7. >> i want a room
8.  You want a sleeping pod.
9.
10. >> i want accommodations
11.   You want a sleeping pod.
12.
13. >> do you have places to stay
14.   yes. I have a sleeping pod.
15.
16. >> do you have places to sleep
17.   yes. I have a sleeping pod.
18.
19. >> what is a place to sleep
20.   a sleeping pod is rooms.
21.
22. >> what is sleeping accommodations
23.   a sleeping pod is rooms.
24.
25. >> goodbye
```

Listing 10.17 Output from expanded accommodations definition.

When building a synonym list, the last item in the list will be the one that Brainhat uses when referring to the concept. This may be changed in a later version of Brainhat, randomizing the output to give it more life-like qualities.

NOTE

Create a synonym list for accommodations. Check the output from the server to confirm it is returning acceptable responses.

HANDS ON

Extend the Scenario

Building a scenario from the FAQ list is the fun part. You get to play around with different ways of asking the same question and test how the FAQ engine responds.

There are two levels of definitions within a scenario file: facts and propositions. Facts are explicit statements of known facts such as "Brainhat is a Martian," "Brainhat has accommodations," or "Colony Seven is on Mars." Propositions are usually if/then conditional statements that can infer relationships based upon context. You'll see them referred to as *inference templates* in A.I. jargon. It is easiest to define the facts before tackling the propositions, so we'll start there.

Defining Facts

Facts are statements that the FAQ engine is absolutely sure of. They are statements that give specific objects properties that can be used to build inferences within the propositions. The FAQ engine will have basic facts about itself and Mars Colony 7. The FAQ engine knows that it is being programmed and understands that any fact that refers to *you* is talking about itself, and any reference to a *speaker* is referring to the person who is talking to the engine.

Declarations of facts in a scenario must contain words that are defined within the Brainhat vocabulary files, either the default *words* file or a standalone file included within the data.in file. If a word is not recognized, Brainhat will try to respond but will use the word *something* in place of the requested item. If *mars* is not defined, a question like "Where is Mars?" will return an answer of "Where is something?" If a nonsensical statement is returned in response to a question, that usually means that the FAQ engine doesn't understand what is being asked. When "Where is Mars?" returns "the mars," the program isn't sure what you are asking for. Check your vocabulary file to verify that the word *mars* has been defined and that your list of facts contains a reference to the location of Mars.

Some facts about Brainhat have already been programmed into the basic scenario that was started in Listing 10.10. Brainhat knows its name, that it's green, and that it is a Martian. We have seen that the FAQ engine has two places to store scenarios. The brainhat.init file at the root level of the server directory contains the initial file of facts and propositions that will be loaded by default when the FAQ engine is started. There is also a scenarios directory that holds various scenarios for other types of dialog.

Listing 10.18 adds some facts to the scenario that was started earlier. Lines 8 and 9 are simple facts about the speaker, whereas lines 11 through 14 are a list of attributes Brainhat can expect to be questioned about from the caller. In this project, we will be handling the information about accommodations and put simple place-holder responses for the three other facts.

```
1. Brainhat is green.
2. Brainhat is a Martian.
3. Brainhat's name is Alisha.
4. Brainhat lives on Mars.
5. Brainhat is in Colony7.
6. Colony7 is on Mars.
7.
8.    The speaker lives on earth.
9.    The speaker is in New York.
10.
11. Brainhat has accommodations.
12. Brainhat has activities.
13. Brainhat has restaurants.
14. Brainhat has information.
```

Listing 10.18 Adding facts to the scenario.

After adding facts to the initial scenario, Listing 10.19 shows the responses elicited from the program. Confirmation of the additions to the updated scenario can be seen on lines 11 through 14, where Alisha is asked about activities. The caller then probes for what the program knows about him or her. In this case, the information is hard-coded for testing purposes, but in a real-world situation, the caller's phone number can be analyzed for a real-time response as to the caller's location.

```
1. >> greetings
2.  hello.
3.
4. >> do you have rooms
5.  yes. I have sleeping pod.
6.
7. >> where are you
8.  I am in colony seven.
9.
10. >> are there activities
11.  yes. I have activities.
12.
13. >> do you have information about activities
14.  maybe. I have information.
15.
16. >> where am i
17.  You are in new york.
18.
19. >> where do i live
20.  You do live on earth.
```

Listing 10.19 Confirming changes through the program output.

```
21.
22. >> where is mars colony 7
23.  mars. colony seven are on mars.
```

Listing 10.19 Confirming changes through the program output. *(continued)*

 Add information about yourself to the scenario. Probe the program and check the output to determine how accurate the responses are.

HANDS ON

Build Propositions

Propositions are conditions coded into the program as conditional statements: If something is true, the following condition is true. A series of propositions build a complex scenario, the propositions intertwining to form complex relationships and inferences. We'll start with a simple proposition, test how the program responds when asked questions in a variety of ways, and then continue adding more propositions.

Listing 10.20 shows the first proposition added to the brainhat.init file. Line 12 states that Brainhat has accommodations, which are interpreted as room, rooms, sleeping quarters, or anything else set as a synonym or reference link for accommodations within the vocabulary file.

Line 17 begins the proposition with an if statement. The condition checks to see if the program has been told it has a room. If a room exists, the room is considered available. The *words* file has the concept available as a default definition, so the program now understands that *available* and *have* are considered the same in this context.

```
1.  Brainhat is green.
2.  Brainhat is a Martian.
3.  Brainhat's name is Alisha.
4.  Brainhat is Alisha.
5.  Brainhat lives on Mars.
6.  Brainhat is in Colony 7.
7.  Colony 7 is on Mars.
8.
9.  The speaker lives on earth.
10. The speaker is in New York.
11.
12. Brainhat has accommodations.
13. Brainhat has activities.
14. Brainhat has restaurants.
15. Brainhat has information.
16.
17. If you have a room
18.     then a room is available.
```

Listing 10.20 Room availability proposition.

```
1. >> do you have rooms
2.  yes. I have sleeping pod. a sleeping pod is available.
3.
4. >> is a place to stay available
5.  yes. a sleeping pod is available.
6.
7. >> do you have a room
8.  yes. I have a available sleeping pod. a sleeping pod is available.
9.
10. >> do you have a place to sleep
11.  yes. I have a available sleeping pod. a sleeping pod is available.
12.
13. >> thank you
```

Listing 10.21   Testing the added line.

Output from testing the added line within the scenario is shown in Listing 10.21. The test proves that rooms, sleeping pods, and a place to sleep are all linked referentially to availability.

Add a proposition to the brainhat.init scenario. Check the output from Brainhat to confirm that the proposition is being interpreted correctly.

HANDS ON

Context-Sensitive Inferences

The FAQ engine understands what is being referred to by the context of a dialog. Each conversation with the FAQ engine builds new inferences dynamically within the conversation's context. Inferences to objects that are being spoken about are carried through the dialog. When talking about accommodations, *it* will refer to accommodations, rooms, a room, or any other synonym that has been defined in the vocabulary for that item. These are temporary relationships that will be terminated when the program exits.

Listing 10.22 checks to see if inferences regarding rooms are transferred through the dialog. Line 1 sets up the context that the discussion is about a room. Line 4 refers to the room as *it*, with the program responding properly on line 5 that *a sleeping pod* is available. Line 7 moves the discussion to a new context, asking the program's name. Line 10 checks to see what *it* now refers to, confusing the program because the context now refers to a name, which has nothing to do with availability. Line 13 moves the context of the dialog back to accommodations, and Brainhat once again understands that rooms are being discussed.

```
1. >>do you have a room
2.  yes. I have sleeping pod. a sleeping pod is available.
3.
4. >> is it available
5.  yes. a sleeping pod is available.
```

Listing 10.22   Checking dialog inferences.

```
6.
7. >> what is your name
8.  my name is alisha.
9.
10. >> is it available
11.  maybe. my name.
12.
13. >> do you have accommodatins
14.  yes. I have a available sleeping pod.
15.
16. >> is it available
17.  yes. a sleeping pod is available.
```

Listing 10.22   Checking dialog inferences. *(continued)*

Batch File Testing

A quick way to test for inferences is to set up a batch file and process a series of questions as a single dialog. Listing 10.23 shows a batch file that runs a list of questions against a scenario. Instead of using the run command, enter "brainhat -r filename" at the command line, where filename is the name of the file that contains the scenario and list of questions.

Batch file processing is an efficient way to test changes to a scenario before applying the changes to production code. When the batch file runs, the scenario at the top of the file is integrated into Brainhat's current working environment. The dialog at the bottom of the batch file is processed one line at a time, just as if the user were entering it at the keyboard. brainhat.log will contain the complete output of the transaction.

Listing 10.24 is the output from running the batch file in Listing 10.23. Lines 1 through 41 absorb the scenario into the environment. The list of questions with Brainhat's responses is output on lines 43 through 59.

```
1. Brainhat is green.
2. Brainhat is a Martian.
3. Brainhat's name is Alisha.
4. Brainhat is Alisha.
5. Brainhat lives on Mars.
6. Brainhat is in Colony 7.
7. Colony 7 is on Mars.
8.
9. The speaker lives on earth.
10. The speaker is in New York.
11.
12. Brainhat has accommodations.
13. Brainhat has activities.
14. Brainhat has restaurants.
```

Listing 10.23   Batch file with test questions. *(continues)*

```
15. Brainhat has information.
16.
17. If you have rooms
18.    then rooms are available.
19.
20. /* Test input for dialogue:
21. */
22. What is your name?
23. Where do you live?
24. Do you have rooms?
25. Are rooms available?
26. Do you have a room?
27. Is a room available?
```

Listing 10.23 Batch file with test questions. *(continued)*

```
1.  >> brainhat is green.
2.   I am green.
3.
4.  >> brainhat is a martian.
5.   I am a martian.
6.
7.  >> brainhat's name is alisha.
8.   my name is alisha.
9.
10. >> brainhat is alisha.
11.  I am alisha.
12.
13. >> brainhat lives on mars.
14.  I do live on mars.
15.
16. >> brainhat is in colony 7.
17.  I am in colony seven.
18.
19. >> colony 7 is on mars.
20.  colony seven are on mars.
21.
22. >> the speaker lives on earth.
23.  You do live on earth.
24.
25. >> the speaker is in new york.
26.  You are in new york.
27.
28. >> brainhat has accommodations.
```

Listing 10.24 Output from a batch file.

```
29.  I have sleeping pod.
30.
31.  >> brainhat has activities.
32.  I have activities.
33.
34.  >> brainhat has restaurants.
35.  I have restaurants.
36.
37.  >> brainhat has information.
38.  I have information.
39.
40.  >> if you have rooms then rooms are available.
41.  if I have rooms then rooms are available.
42.
43.  >> what is your name?
44.  my name is alisha.
45.
46.  >> where do you live?
47.  I do live on mars.
48.
49.  >> do you have rooms?
50.  yes. I have sleeping pod. rooms are available.
51.
52.  >> are rooms available?
53.  yes. rooms are available.
54.
55.  >> do you have a room?
56.  yes. I have sleeping pod. a sleeping pod is available.
57.
58.  >> is a room available?
59.  yes. a sleeping pod is available.
```

Listing 10.24   Output from a batch file. *(continued)*

Create a batch file that holds the current Mars Colony 7 scenario followed by a list of questions to test the scenario. Save the file as *batch-test* at the root level of the Brainhat directory. Run the file from the command line, using "brainhat -r batch-test" to activate the file.

HANDS ON

Intuitive Dialogs

The FAQ engine can continue a dialog by asking the user a question, by making a statement, or by waiting for more user response. In general, if the system is being used by experienced users, they will not need a lot of prompting to get the answers they need from your FAQ. They will ask specific questions or make declarative state-ments that jump to later parts of the dialog. Novice users need a little hand-holding and appreciate the verbal prompts.

As an example, experienced users upon entering the system would not ask if there were accommodations; they would immediately declare that they want a room: "I need a room." The FAQ engine would bypass any dialog having to do with explaining about rooms and get right to the heart of the matter, "Do you have a credit card?"

Listing 10.25 adds two more propositions to the Mars Colony 7 scenario. It relates the verbs *need* and *want*, linking them to a desire for a reservation. Lines 5 and 6 remind the caller that a room or reservation costs money. Listing 10.26 shows the output from the scenario. We will handle how much money in the next section.

```
1. If I need a room
2.    then I want a room.
3. If I want a room
4.    then I want a reservation.
5. If the speaker wants a reservation
6.    then tell the speaker a room costs money.
```

Listing 10.25 Adding propositions to a scenario.

```
1. >> i want a room
2.    You want a sleeping pod.
3.    You want a reservation.
4.    a sleeping pod costs money.
```

Listing 10.26 Output from a reservation request.

Handling Questions on Cost

The next extension to the scenario handles questions on cost. We need to create a proposition that will respond when a user asks about expense. Listing 10.27 has a proposition that will understand the question on cost and then ask if the user has a credit card.

The conditional statement on line 1 checks to see if the user is asking "How much is a room?" or "How much does a room cost?" The response is in mars-krugens, so we will have to define that term in the vocabulary file before we can go much farther.

A mars-krugen can be compared to a dollar when defining the term. Looking in the *words* file, we see that dollar is defined as a child-of things that are related to valuables. We define the mars-krugen in the extended-vocabulary.mpm file, relating a singular krugen to plurals krugens, which feeds up into a top-level of *things*.

```
define    krugen-1
   label          mars-krugen
   related        valuable-1
   child-of       krugens-1
define    krugens-1
   label          mars-krugens
   related        valuable-1
   child-of       things
```

As any good sales robot that has been trained properly will do, Alisha then asks if the caller would like a reservation. Handling of reservations is done in a future dialog. As Listing 10.27 shows, propositions can be joined into compound phrases using *and* as the join operator. Listing 10.28 shows the output from the question on cost.

```
1. If the speaker asks how much is a room
2.    then tell the speaker a room costs a mars-krugen
3.    and ask the speaker if the speaker wants a reservation.
```

Listing 10.27   Proposition on cost.

```
1. >> how much is a room
2.    an expensive sleeping pod costs a mars-krugen.
3.    do You want a reservation?
```

Listing 10.28   Output from dialog on cost.

Prepared Responses

Some questions deserve long, detailed answers. Brainhat can serve prepared responses to those types of questions. Listing 10.29, lines 7 and 8, shows a conditional statement that points to a file that contains the appropriate response when the caller wants a room or a reservation. This is more in line with what most people think of as an FAQ. For a simple FAQ engine, a developer might consider using the Brainhat engine to interpret a user's question and then serve up saved responses.

```
1. If you have rooms
2.    then rooms are available.
3. If I need a room
4.    then I want a room.
5. If I want a room
6.    then I want a reservation.
7. If the speaker wants a reservation
8.    then server reservation-info.txt
```

Listing 10.29   Serving an external response file.

```
1. >> I want a reservation
2. You can make reservations by calling 1-800-MARS-VII.
3. If you are on earth, approach the nearest vidphone, say
4. "Mars Colony 7" and you will be connected krugen free.
```

Listing 10.30   Output from external file.

The response is a simple text file saved on the server. It cannot be used for inference generation or extending a scenario. However, used properly, it adds a level of depth to responses that need more detail than a simple one-sentence output. Listing 10.30 shows the response when a caller wants a room.

HANDS ON

Create a text file that will handle the response when a user asks for activities at the colony. The response should be three to four sentences and saved as activities-response.txt within the data directory. Add a conditional statement in the scenario that will serve the file when the caller asks about activities on Mars Colony 7.

Final Scenario

Listing 10.31 shows a completed scenario for the Mars Colony 7 reservations line. It includes information that the program knows about itself, a set of facts that the program can use to answer specific questions, and a series of propositions to draw inferences from the facts. Listing 10.32 is the updated extended-vocabulary.txt file that defines the new terms in the scenario, and Listing 10.33 shows the content of the whereisc7.txt and whatisc7.txt files referred to on lines 18 and 19 of Listing 10.31.

```
 1. Brainhat is green.
 2. Brainhat is a Martian.
 3. Brainhat's name is Alisha.
 4. Brainhat is Alisha.
 5. Brainhat lives on Mars.
 6. Brainhat is in Colony 7.
 7. Colony 7 is on Mars.
 8.
 9. The speaker lives on earth.
10. The speaker is an earthling.
11. The speaker is in New York.
12.
13. Brainhat has accommodations.
14. Brainhat has activities.
15. Brainhat has restaurants.
```

Listing 10.31   Complete scenario.

```
16. Brainhat has information.
17.
18. If the speaker asks where is colony 7 then serve whereisc7.txt.
19. If the speaker asks what is colony 7 then serve whatisc7.txt.
20.
21. Mars is dry.
22. Brainhat likes mars because the weather is cold.
23.
24. If you have rooms
25.     then rooms are available.
26.
27. If the speaker ask how much is a room
28.     then tell the speaker a room costs a mars-krugen
29.     and ask the speaker if the speaker wants a reservation.
30.
31. If I need a room
32.     then I want a room.
33. If I want a room
34.     then I want a reservation.
35. If the speaker wants a reservation
36.     then ask the speaker does the speaker have a credit card.
37.
38. If the speaker has a creditcard
39.     then serve reservation-info.txt.
40.
41. If the speaker does not have a credit card
42.     then tell the speaker you do not have a room
43.     and ask the speaker if the speaker has a hovercraft.
44.
45. If the speaker has a hovercraft
46.     then tell the speaker you are happy.
```

Listing 10.31   Complete scenario. *(continued)*

```
1. define   greeting-informal
2.     label    hi
3.     label    whats up
4.     label    sup
5.     label    yo
6.     label    whats up homeboy
7.     child-of greeting
8.
9. define   goodbye-2
10.    label    q
11.    label    outta here
12.    label    later
```

Listing 10.32   Final extended-vocabulary.txt. *(continues)*

```
13.    child-of goodbye-1
14.
15. define    accommodations-1
16.    label     accommodations
17.    label     room
18.    label     place to stay
19.    label     place to sleep
20.    label     sleeping accommodations
21.    label     sleeping pod
22.    child-of rooms-1
23.
24. define    credit-card-1
25.    label     credit card
26.    label     creditcard
27.    child-of things
28.
29. define    krugen-1
30.    label       mars-krugen
31.    related     valuable-1
32.    child-of    krugens-1
33.
34. define    krugens-1
35.    label       mars-krugens
36.    related     valuable-1
37.    child-of    things
38.
39. define    vehicle-1
40.    label     hovercraft
41.    child-of things
42.
43. define    earthling-1
44.    label     earthling
45.    child-of human-1
```

Listing 10.32   Final extended-vocabulary.txt. *(continued)*

```
whereisc7.txt:
Colony 7 is located on the fourth planet of
the local solar system <break size="small"/>
third quadrant <break size="small"/>
northern section <break size="small"/>
parsec 7891<break size="small"/>
The main intersection is 12th Street and Vine.
```

Listing 10.33   Content of prepared text files.

```
whatisc7.txt:
Mars Colony 7 is a recreation dome for the other 6 colonies that are
doing the exploration and infrastruture expansion on the planet
surface! This now explains the numbering system of the
colonies, gives a reason for Mars Colony 7's existence, and assures
the colony of an ever changing population from Mars itself, not just
the quickie tourist from Earth.
```

Listing 10.33 Content of prepared text files. *(continued)*

Finish the Mars Colony 7 scenario. Update the extended-vocabulary.mpm file to define the new terms in the scenario. Add prepared text files for detailed explanations of complex items.

HANDS ON

Set Up the VoiceXML Entrance

Setting up the VoiceXML gateway to the Brainhat server is relatively simple once the scenario has been set up and tested. We will first set up a simple test script to confirm access to the Brainhat server and then create a short introduction that will be spoken when a user calls the server. Finally, a vocabulary must be created for the VoiceXML gateway that will be recognized by the speech-to-text translator and then passed to the Brainhat environment.

We will begin by starting the Brainhat server in VoiceXML Mode.

Start the Server in VoiceXML Mode

Execution of the Brainhat VoiceXML daemon mode takes place from a single directory. On a Linux machine, this will be /usr/local/etc/brainhat/vxml. On a Windows platform, the run-time directory will be wherever you start the daemon. For security, the daemon cannot access files in directories above the run-time directory.

There are a small handful of switches that apply to running Brainhat in VoiceXML mode. They allow choices as to what scenario will run, what grammar file should be served to the voice portal, what the initial greeting should be, plus a few other run-time parameters. A typical command line is shown in Listing 10.34. The complete command should be on one line; it is only wrapped for convenient reading. Table 10.3 is a complete list of command line options. You can also get the complete list of options by invoking the server with the -help option.

Table 10.3 Command Line Options for the Brainhat Server

SWITCH	EFFECT
-d	Sets text daemon mode
-h	Sets httpd/html daemon mode
-x	Sets httpd/voicexml daemon mode
-N	Enables n-Best processing for VXML
-g	Selects a grammar for voicexml mode (default is brainhat.gram)
-i	Chooses an init file (default is brainhat.init)
-I	Chooses an introduction for Brainhat to voice (default is brainhat.intro)
-R	Chooses a restart file
-p	Sets an apparent source address for subsequent http gets; may be necessary if operating through an address translating gateway or firewall
-t	Outputs a pattern trace
-e	Outputs inference tests
-E	Turns on echo for input files
-r	Runs input file and stops for testing
-j	Turns on java CC graph output in dynamic HTML
-S	Run as a stateful http daemon

The command line in Listing 10.34 instructs Brainhat to run in VoiceXML mode, via the -x flag. The -N 3 option tells Brainhat to ask the voice portal for its three best guesses of what the user might have said each time there is a response. Brainhat will choose from among them. The -I flag chooses a file that contains an initial greeting. In the example, the initial greeting will be "This is the Colony Seven frequently asked questions server. How can I help you?"; it is stored in the brainhat.intro file, which is the default greeting file.

The -i option chooses a scenario. The default is brainhat.init. The -g option tells Brainhat what file to forward to the voice portal to use as the VoiceXML grammar. If you are running behind an Internet firewall, you may need to use the -p flag as well. Again, review the options from the command line -help flag.

The last item on the command line, data, is the path to the precompiled words and patterns that we discussed earlier in this project. Note that the run script causes precompilation of the words and patterns to occur. The preceding command line assumes that the precompilation has already taken place. This means that if you make a change to the vocabulary, you will want to have used the run command before you start Brainhat in VoiceXML mode so that your changes will be incorporated.

```
1. brainhat -x -N 3
2.    -I brainhat.intro
3.    -i brainhat.init
4.    -g brainhat.gram
5.       ./data/data
```

Listing 10.34   Starting the Brainhat server in VoiceXML mode.

The VoiceXML server in Brainhat does not precompile the data files as it does when using interactive mode on the command line. You must run the program from the command line first before starting the VoiceXML server.

NOTE

Create Simple Access Script

Other projects we have worked on have pointed to Web servers to retrieve dynamically generated data. In this project, the Brainhat engine will act as the Web server, processing a caller's request and outputting VoiceXML documents on the fly. It will respond differently, however, to a few special URLs. This is the key to use the program as an FAQ server.

Once the daemon is running, you may access Brainhat from your BeVocal account by using a URL of the form: http://yourserver:8080/index.xml. (See Figure 10.3.) Testing your URL should return no errors. If you wish to make a more primitive test, you may telnet to your server on port 8080 and pull the initial page by hand: telnet yourserver 8080 get/index.xml HTTP/1.0

The Colony 7 server at Brainhat, pointed to as a test environment in the next set of scripts, is available to developers to use for proof of concept. To download the latest scenario and vocabulary files running on the Colony 7 test server, go to colony7.brainhat.com/faq-files.

NOTE

The first reference to the Brainhat server, /index.xml, as shown in Listing 10.35, returns a dynamically generated VoiceXML page with the initial greeting. It also contains a reference to a VoiceXML grammar that the voice portal will need to interpret the caller's response. Subsequent accesses will be to pages with URLs of the form /dialogXXXX.xml (perhaps served on a different port), which are generated dynamically by the server, where the XXX represents any random number created to discourage caching of documents by the voice portal.

The <submit> element allows VoiceXML scripts to point to external sources for their data. Listing 10.35 is a script that points to the Brainhat test environment. Once you have pulled the initial page successfully, you may begin expanding and testing your application.

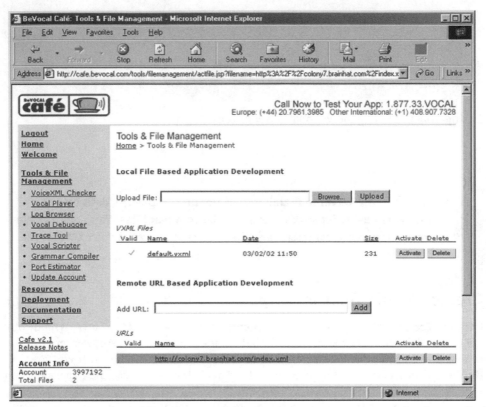

Figure 10.3 Use the "Add URL" form on the File Management page to upload a URL and activate it as your default application.

Caching Documents and Grammars

The voice portal will want to cache the dynamically generated pages. If you make a change in the grammar, you may wish to change the grammar name and slightly modify the name of the initial page that you give to the voice portal. This will force the voice portal to pull a fresh copy of the page or grammar. You can reference the first page with a modified name; Brainhat doesn't care if you ask for index.xmlx or index.xmlz or any other combination of trailing characters.

WARNING The voice portal will try to cache dynamic pages, freezing an application's grammar. If changes to a grammar are made when updating an application, rename the grammar file, adjust your application to point to the new file, and rename the entrance file's extension.

```
1.  <?xml version="1.0"?>
2.
3.  <vxml version="2.0">
4.   <form>
5.    <block>
6.     <submit next=http://maddie.brainhat.com:8080/index.xml
7.             method="get"/>
8.    </block>
9.   </form>
10. </vxml>
```

Listing 10.35 Accessing the Brainhat server.

Create a VoiceXML Grammar

Aside from starting Brainhat in a different mode, the only other thing we have to do is craft a grammar for the voice portal. You already know how grammars are made from your work in previous chapters. This grammar will be slightly different in that it will try to capture dynamic dialog.

Listing 10.36 is a grammar to support the Mars Colony 7 FAQ server. The grammar includes templates for the questions and statements the program may need to handle, plus the individual adjectives, nouns, verbs, and so forth, to support the dialog. The grammar is saved in the file brainhat.gram. As you continue to develop the application, add more terms to the grammar file to extend the recognition of phrases.

As a grammar becomes more complicated, it offers opportunities for misrecognition. The best results come when you constrain the grammar to the dialog expected. Large grammars can also be precompiled as binary files for more efficient access. Check the documentation on your platform for techniques for precompiling grammars.

HANDS ON

Create the grammar file from Listing 10.36 and store it at the root level of the Brainhat server. Save it as brainhat.gram.

```
1. Dialog        [([YES NO] ?CSENT) CSENT]
2.
3. YES           [yes correct right okay] { <Stmt $string> }
4.
5. NO            [no nope]
6.
7. CSENT         [SENT QUESTION GREETING]
8.
9. QUESTION      [(how ?much TOBE SUBOBJ)
10.                (TOBE SUBOBJ ATTRIBUTE)
11.                (do you ACTIONS SUBOBJ)
12.                (what TOBE SUBOBJ)
13.                (can [i you] ACTIONS SUBOBJ)
14.                (what SUBOBJ do SUBOBJ ACTIONS)
15.                (where TOBE SUBOBJ)
16.                why]
17.
18. SENT         [(i ?[(do not) don't] ACTIONS SUBOBJ)
19.                 (SUBOBJ TOBE ATTRIBUTE)
20.                  ATTRIBUTE]
21.
22. SUBOBJ       [i you (?ARTICLE ?ATTRIBUTE THINGS)]
23.
24. GREETING     [hello hi goodbye bye]
25.
26. TOBE         [am are isn't aren't]
27.
28. THINGS       [name martian mars (colony seven)
29.                 (brain hat) restaurant accommodations
30.                  information room mars-krugen reservation
31.                  (credit card) hovercraft weather]
32.
33. ARTICLE      [a an the any]
34.
35. ATTRIBUTE    [green red blue yellow hot cold dry fun happy sad color]
36.
37. ACTIONS      [want say have get like need live cost]
```

Listing 10.36   VoiceXML grammar file.

Processing Input

The final setup on the server is the VoiceXML script that handles the processing of the input. Listing 10.37 is the complete file for accepting the input; it checks for grammar recognition and outputs the response from the Brainhat server.

Line 33 of Listing 10.37 takes the return value from the function *catresults* that is defined on lines 11 through 21 and sends the concatenated results as the input string to the Brainhat server. The server responds with output, just as it has from the interactive command line, only formatting the return as a VoiceXML file.

```
1.  <?xml version="1.0"?>
2.  <!DOCTYPE vxml
3.    PUBLIC "-//BeVocal Inc//VoiceXML 2.0//EN"
4.   "http://cafe.bevocal.com/libraries/dtd/vxml2-0-bevocal.dtd">
5.  <vxml version="2.0">
6.  <form id="Dialog">
7.
8.  <var name="results"/>
9.  <var name="best"/>
10.
11. <script>
12. <![CDATA[
13.    function catresults(allResults) {
14.    var cat = "|";
15.       for (i = 0; i < allResults.length; i++) {
16.          cat = cat + allResults[i].utterance + "| ";
17.       }
18.    return cat;
19. }
20. ]]>
21. </script>
22.
23. <field name="Stmt">
24. <property name="maxnbest" value="3"/>
25. <property name="bevocal.maximuminterpretations" value="1"/>
26.    <property name="confidencelevel" value=".2"/>
27.    <grammar src="brainhat.gram#Dialog" type="application/x-gsl"/>
28.   <filled>
29.    <if cond="application.lastresult$.length &gt; 1">
30.       <assign name="results" expr="application.lastresult$"/>
31.       <assign name="best" expr="catresults(results)"/>
32.    <else/>
33.      <assign name="best" expr="application.lastresult$.utterance"/>
34.    </if>
35.    <submit next="http://208.253.38.98:24011/index.xml"
36.            method="get"
37.            namelist="best"/>
38.    </filled>
39. </field>
40. </form>
41. </vxml>
```

Listing 10.37   Script to process and respond to input.

Final Thoughts

This project was the most fun because responses did not have to be hard-coded as in previous projects. Personal assistants, kiosks, switchboards, and help desk applications can be built using the technology that was developed here. With a little more work, the Brainhat FAQ engine can be extended to act as a natural computer interface for a robot or other program.

I would like to see a group of developers hook up a peer-to-peer network that allows access to each other's vocabularies and scenarios on the fly. Fifty people could be working on the same scenario and the information could be concatenated into one, gigantic knowledge base about the subject. It would be a great way to extend a vocabulary.

The listings for this project can be downloaded from the BeVocal Web site at cafe.bevocal.com/wiley/10projects. They are saved as text files, useful as templates for creating your own VoiceXML scripts. Join us in the online discussion board for this project and tell us how you will be using the project. If you create a form that would make this project work better, it might be incorporated into the project code online so that others can use it.

Glossary

ABNF Augmented Backus-Naur Form

ASP Application Service Provider

ASR Automatic Speech Recognition

attribute A characteristic of an element.

bargein The ability of a user to interrupt a prompt.

browser Software for accessing information on a network.

character entity An alias for XML reserved characters.

client The requesting end of a client/server relationship.

Cold Fusion Web application development tool for dynamically generating content.

confidence level A measurement of the speech recognition engine's ability to recognize an utterance.

content model   Description within a DTD that describes what an element or attribute may contain.

dialog   Section within a VoiceXML application that generates input from a user, including <form>, <menu>, and <link> elements.

DTD   Document Type Definition

DTMF   Dual Tone Multi-Frequency

element   The base unit within an XML document.

FIA   Form Interpretation Algorithm

field level element   Elements contained within a form that are at the sibling level of a <field> element, such as <block>, <initial>, <subdialog>, <object>, <record>, and <transfer>.

flatfile   Text file holding ASCII text.

form-level element   Elements within a VoiceXML document contained at the same level as a <form> element, such as a <link> or <menu>.

full duplex   Ability of a platform to allow transfer of information in two directions.

grammar   Element holding tokens that will be recognized as valid utterances from a user.

half duplex   Ability of platform to allow transfer of information in a single direction.

HTML   Hypertext Markup Language

interface   What a user interacts with when accessing data.

ISP   Internet Service Provider

IVR   Interactive Voice Recognition

JSP   Java Server Pages

mixed initiative form   A form that allows a single utterance to fill multiple fields.

PDF   Portable Document Format

Perl   Programming language for creating dynamic content from a Web site.

root element   Top-level element of an XML document.

schema   Definition of rules for the content models of elements and attributes.

server   Software that allows access to a computer providing services or information to other computers.

speech recognition   Ability of a platform to understand user input through speech.

STT   Speech-to-Text; user speech input translated to text.

stylesheet   Formatting instructions for output of data.

tag   Synonymous with element.

TTS   Text-to-Speech; translation of text-based output to speech.

URI   Uniform Resource Identifier; a unique string of characters identifying a specific resource.

URL   Uniform Resource Locator; a unique string of characters identifying a specific online resource.

utterance   User input over a telephone.

voice gateway   Combination of hardware and software that handles the telephony exchange in a VoiceXML application.

voice portal   Company hosting services providing a voice gateway.

voice recognition   Ability to distinguish different voices as unique items.

VoiceXML   Voice eXtensible Markup Language

VoiceXML Forum   Industry organization promoting VoiceXML specification as a standard way to make Internet content available over a telephone.

W3C   World Wide Web Consortium

Web server   Software providing access to network information.

Web site   Files stored on a Web server that are accessible over a network.

XML   eXtensible Markup Language

XSLT   eXtensible Stylesheet Language: Transformation

Index

SYMBOLS

" (double quote) character
  literal content, 102–103
  XML tag attribute values, 9
(number sign) character, fragment
  identifier, 48
* (asterisk) character, zero or more
  quantifier, 11
/ (slash) character, XML closing tag, 9
; (semicolon) character, including
  comments in grammars, 220
? (question mark) character
  optional element definition, 11
  optional tokens, 185
[and] (square brackets) characters, or
  disjunction, 179
' (single quote) character
  literal content, 102–103
  XML tag attribute values, 9
| | (double pipes) characters, short circuit
  operators, 130–131
+ (plus sign) character, one or more
  quantifier, 11
= (equal sign) character, assignment
  statement, 51
== (double equal sign) characters,
  comparison, 51

A

about-marscolony7 scenarios, 330–331
absolute references, external VoiceXML
  document, 48
accept attribute, 83
accessAttempts variable, 210
accesscode value, name attribute, 50
accounts, BeVocal Cafe setup, 22–34
address template, Common Components
  project, 163–164
<answer> element, 263, 283
<answers> element, 283
answers template, XSLT, 283
answer template, XSLT, 283
application attribute, 73, 74, 158
application layer, XML architecture, 5–6
application root document,
  links project, 73–75
applications
  activating in BeVocal Cafe, 32–34
  Hello World, 42–46
  showcasing in BeVocal Cafe, 32
Application Service Provider (ASP)
  account setup, 22–34
  Bevocal.com, 21
  free and for-fee services, 20
  HeyAnita.com, 21